# The Memoirs of an Opera Bug

## by Beaumont Glass

LEYERLE

PUBLICATIONS

# The Memoirs of an Opera Bug
## By Beaumont Glass

Copyright © Leyerle Publications 2006
ISBN 1-878617-69-9

**LEYERLE PUBLICATIONS**
**Executive Offices**
**28 Stanley Street**
**Mt. Morris, New York 14510**

*This book can be ordered directly from*

**LEYERLE**
**PUBLICATIONS**

**Box 384**
**Geneseo, New York 14454**

## Dedication

To my lovable little grandson Alexander Talcott,
who at two-and-a-half has just discovered opera,
and to my daughter and son-in-law, Melody and Michael Talcott

## Acknowledgements

I am deeply indebted to John Pennino of the Metropolitan Opera Archives for the beautiful, clear photos of Martina Arroyo as Madame Butterfly, Hilda Burke as Micaëla, Roberta Peters as Lucia, Rosa Ponselle as Carmen, Cesare Siepi as Don Giovanni, and Eleanor Steber as Sophie.

My son-in-law Michael Talcott gave me indispensable help with all computer problems and spent many hours scanning all the photos and integrating over a hundred of them into the text.

And I wish to thank William Leyerle for his encouragement and support.

*Happy Birthday 2009*

*Ruth & Henred*

**The Memoirs of an Opera Bug**
By Beaumont Glass

Table of Contents

# THE MEMOIRS OF AN OPERA BUG

Some Random Vignettes:

## The Night My Hair Turned Gray

It was my second production for the Northwest Grand Opera Company, home-based in Seattle. The first, *La traviata*, with Met star Dorothy Kirsten, had been a big success with a couple of excellent reviews for my work, that got my new career started in a positive way. So I was invited back for a second season. This time three operas were planned, *Faust*, *Lucia di Lammermoor*, and *Carmen*. But there was one huge problem: no money. Big backers had withdrawn their support. Rehearsals had been going well, the locally-cast secondary roles were in good hands, the chorus was young and attractive, new scenery was being built, mostly on schedule. The three stars duly arrived from New York. The dress rehearsal would be in Seattle, the first performance in Portland, Oregon (the opera company toured to a number of cities in the Northwest, including Vancouver and Victoria in British Columbia).

I was nervous about the many as yet untested magic effects that are called for in *Faust*—a flash of light and a puff of smoke for Mephistopheles' arrival from the netherworld, the ethereal vision of Marguerite at her spinning wheel, a shimmering stream of magic wine, the flowers that glow with a mysterious light when Mephisto invokes their seductive charms, the radiant apotheosis at the end. Imagine my outrage when I learned that there would be absolutely no electric equipment other than house lights and work lights for that all-important, one-and-only tech rehearsal!! No chance even to light the scenery, let alone try for any magic! The Northwest Grand Opera had run out of credit. No cash, no light board. At least Nadine Conner, Metropolitan Opera soprano, was a good sport and climbed the rickety ladder up to the tiny platform where the vision would

Nadine Conner as Marguerite, inscribed
*"To Beau Glass, a gifted and talented artist."*

have been visible behind a scrim if we had had some lighting.

Off by train for Portland. As soon as the scenery was moved into the theater, I started lighting the sets, beginning with the last scene and working our way backwards to the first. Then a quick bite to eat and backstage for last-minute notes for the cast. The overture sounded fine, the applause was encouraging; then came the opening music of the first scene. I gave the cue for the curtain. It rose exactly when it should. But what's this? Where's the audience? I saw only blackness, no conductor, no exit lights, nothing! Suddenly it dawned on me: the asbestos curtain was down! Nobody had told me. I hadn't ordered it—but there it was! And the only controls were up in the flies. Frantically, on the squawk box, I tried to wake up the lone stagehand who had fallen

asleep up there. Five seconds before the tenor's first notes the fire curtain was on its way up, just enough to let the audience see Faust's face as he drew a breath to sing. Meanwhile someone sent me a message from Mephistopheles in his hiding place under the stage: he had split the backside of his tights. I sent the wardrobe mistress to the rescue. Armed with a needle and thread she crawled under the scenery to the spot where he was squatting and sewed up the split,

William Wildermann as Mephisto

both of them in the most undignified position imaginable. At least his *public* modesty was restored.

Scene 1 finished without further disaster. Then came the scene with the magic wine that is supposed to come pouring out of a tavern sign, a painted Bacchus astride a keg. An open barrel was there to catch it and keep it from flooding the floor. Magic wine being unavailable, back in Seattle we had tried out various substitutes, including purple glitter. None had flowed through the hidden pipe fast enough. So we settled on raspberry pop. Mephistopheles was supposed to catch some in a metal goblet and propose a toast to Marguerite. But there was an unforeseen problem: in the heat of the moment Mephisto grabbed the wrong prop. Instead of the goblet, he snatched up one of the beer mugs meant for the chorus. Now those beer mugs were actually flour sifters from Woolworth's Five and Ten, painted to look like picturesque German beer steins and fitted with cardboard bottoms, so that the audience wouldn't see the faces of the chorus men through the lower end of the flour sifters when the roistering "students" were pretending to drink their imaginary beer. Well, a stagehand poured the raspberry pop through the pipe and Mephisto caught it in his upheld flour sifter. Suddenly he became aware of something wet and sticky trickling down the sleeve of his costume. The raspberry pop had quickly soaked through the cardboard. "*À Marguerite!*" sings our basso. Suddenly the cardboard disk gave way totally and with a large plop the raspberry pop splattered all over the stage.

But the Fates had worse in store. Somehow the garden scene came and went without a hitch. The black light on the flowers made a stunning effect during Mephisto's invocation. Then came the scene in the church…

Everything seemed to be ready. The choristers were grouped around the electric organ in the wings. The organ prelude began and Miss Conner knelt down on stage to prepare to pray. The orchestra, in the pit, had nothing to play for a while. Then came a gigantic, hideous downward slide on the organ, followed by a deathly silence. Miss Conner looked at the conductor. He gestured to the percussionist to make a rumble on the kettle drums. Suddenly a loud voice came over the loudspeaker and reverberated through the whole house: "Jesus Christ, where the hell's the plug?" Clearly, some chorus member in the backstage darkness had unintentionally kicked out the cord for the electric organ; but the *mike* was still plugged in. The drum roll resumed. It seemed interminable. Miss Conner mimed a silent prayer for all she was worth. She was probably *really* praying. Then the outlet was found. The organ started up with a long upward slide. The opera could continue. Marguerite prayed her heart out. The devil tormented her, the chorus thundered out its warning of Judgment Day, the day of wrath. Marguerite's voice began to soar thrillingly above the chorus in a last, desperate prayer. Just before the glorious climax—you guessed it! Darned if the organ didn't drop out all over again. Sheer chaos!

Could anything else go wrong? What do *you* think? At the very end of the opera, after Marguerite dies, the prison gates were supposed to be opened by unseen, presumably angelic hands, to show dawn in the sky and a ray of heavenly light to symbolize Marguerite's redemption. The only trouble is that one of the gates got stuck, and the less-than-angelic stagehand who was tugging at the hidden wire kept jerking at it, shaking the entire set, till it suddenly broke loose and flew open with a loud crash. Some apotheosis!

The curtain came down. The cast took their bows to well-earned applause. I felt totally drained, totally humiliated. I wished I could drop through a hole in the earth and quietly disappear. Instead, I had to be in charge of striking the set and supervise the loading of the truck. We had three more performances to give, each in a different city. Before hitting my bunk on the train I happened to look in a mirror. My temples were completely gray.

## Camouflaging the Pyramids

When we arrived in New York my wife and I first looked for an apartment, then for a copy of *Variety*, the performers' indispensable guide to opportunities. And there, lo and behold! auditions were announced for *Cavalleria rusticana* and the performance date would be my birthday. What an omen! Santuzza had been one of Evangeline's

Evangeline and Armand Tokatyan rehearsing *Cavalleria*

parts at the Music Academy of the West. In Lotte Lehmann's absence, she had been directed by Armand Tokatyan, who had often sung the role of Turiddu at the Met. So I called up to ask for an audition appointment for my wife.

The lady who answered, a Miss Marguerite Moore, informed me in an imposing singing tone that her Broadway Grand Opera Association was "New York's second opera company, and the only one with international press coverage" (that turned out to be the *Italo-Americano*—she knew their music critic). I let the relative ranking pass, though that very afternoon I had been hired as a coach by the New York City Opera. Miss Moore raved about her scenery, borrowed from the San Carlo Company, and the splendid and original lighting effects we could expect.

Evangeline Noël

Evangeline—now Eva Noël—sang the audition and got the part. Rehearsals took place in Miss Moore's rented studio at the old Metropolitan Opera House. The seat of the couch was an ironing board covered with chintz. If two people sat down at the same time it served its purpose; if one happened to get up suddenly, it became a see-saw. The other sitter would end up on the floor. The room was decorated with photos of our hostess in all the leading soprano roles she could improvise costumes for.

The tenor and baritone were fine. So was the conductor. What young singers wouldn't do in those days for a chance to sing opera! But the elderly lady with missing front teeth who was to sing Mamma Lucia didn't seem to have a clue. I was concerned, since Evangeline's first scene was a crucial confrontation with that character. So I invited the mezzo to our apartment for an extra rehearsal. I went into a detailed analysis of the scene, of the strained relationship between the two participants, of her feelings for the woman who had seduced her son and disgraced herself in the community. Our Mamma Lucia stared at me in blank amazement. "You mean to say I'm thinking all that stuff? You want me to think and sing at the same time??"

The Broadway Grand Opera Association did not believe in dress rehearsals. Or couldn't afford the extra hall rental. But Miss Moore kept reassuring us that the scenery and lighting would be magnificent and that the theater had everything ready for her show.

Well, the performance date duly arrived. I had invited two important guests. There was the orchestra, tuning up. Some scratchy sounds, but the conductor would surely get them at least to play together. And there was the large bare stage. On the floor was an enormous canvas backdrop, evidently once used for a road-company *Aida*. Three or four people with pots of green paint were busy on their hands and knees painting Sicilian pine trees over the camels and pyramids. With a sinking feeling, I asked Miss Moore: "Where is the church, where is the tavern?" Well, as we had rehearsed, the church was stage left. "How does the audience know that?" Her solution was ingeniously simple: she cut out a cardboard cross and calmly pinned it to the stage-left drapery. I thought about our soon-to-arrive influential guests and felt sick in the pit of my stomach. Thank God that at least one of them didn't show up!

Miss Moore had an innovation up her lacy sleeve: the tenor's opening solo, a serenade to another man's wife, would be sung on the open stage, not behind the curtain, as called for in the score. He would enter during a blackout, the prelude would begin, and then we would be treated to an awesome sunrise effect. Well, it was awesome in its way. There were no dimmers; so each successive color came on boldly without warning. First all was black; then—bang! purple; then—wow! bright red; then—ye gods! orange, then yellow, and so on until full daylight was achieved. The evening was ruined before the overture was over. The last straw: Mamma Lucia was so concerned that Santuzza wouldn't enter on time for the end of the opera that she started to flag her down several bars before the cue and forgot to sing her own last line.

Needless to say, our honored guest was not impressed. It was Constance Hope, publicity agent for some of the biggest names in the music business and consummate professional. Her list of clients included Lily Pons, Lotte Lehmann, Grace Moore, Ezio Pinza, and Lauritz Melchior. Jascha Heifetz and Artur Rubinstein played at her wedding. I knew her through my mother, who had studied her lieder repertoire with Miss Hope's father, Eugene Bernstein, an eminent vocal coach. Sometimes I had been invited to escort her mother to performances at the Met. A beautiful relationship was in danger of ending.

My mother studying with Mr. Bernstein

The guest who *didn't* show up was John Gutman, Rudolf Bing's second-in-command at the Metropolitan Opera. His very complimentary remarks, after I had accompanied the Met's regional auditions at Santa Barbara a few months before, had encouraged me to move to New York in the first place, lock, stock, and new-born baby. He had specifically told me: "We could use people like you at the Met." That was the California version. Naïvely, I took him seriously. Shortly after my arrival, he graciously gave me an interview in his office and introduced me to Mr. Bing. But I shall never forget his words, the *New York* variant: "Mr. Glass, I hate to *disabuse* you, but the Met already has a full staff of coaches, so there would be nothing for you here."

Nevertheless, I had hoped that he would hear my wife. With *Die Walküre* coming up, perhaps they'd be interested in a potential valkyrie with a great high C (eventually she did sing Gerhilde, at the San Carlo in Naples). Though Evangeline kept her head and sang beautifully in the midst of chaos, It's just as well that Mr. Gutman had something better to do that ludicrous night of October 25, 1959.

**World's Phenomenal Baritone**

New in New York, with wife and baby, I wasn't turning down any engagements—not with a New York apartment to pay for. One day a man called in answer to my ad in *Musical America*. He said he had just sung a recital "at Carnegie Hall" and wanted to rehearse with a pianist five hours a week. I named my modest fee and we made an appointment. When he arrived, he presented his card, a 3x5 lined file card on which he had stamped his name and "world's phenomenal baritone." He insisted on showing me his reviews, mounted in a scrapbook. In every sentence a word had been deleted with black magic marker. A typical review went something like this: "Yesterday evening at Carnegie Recital Hall an audacious **blank** gave one of the most unbelievably **blank blank blank** programs this reviewer has ever had the **blank** luck to hear." My guest seemed pleased with it. He handed me an old book of miscellaneous songs by composers I had never heard of. His warm-up piece was a gem called *"Dal profondo dell' abisso."*

I shall never forget it. He would bend forward, drop his jaw, and start revving up with that opening syllable: "Daw...daw... daw...daw daw daw  dawl profundo, daw daw dawl profundo d-d-d-dell' abisso..." He sounded *exactly* like Mortimer Snerd. When I attempted to correct his Italian pronunciation, he snarled: "No coaching; just play the piano part; I know what I'm doing." Every session started out with the same ghastly piece. I got so bored I could hardly stay awake. To help me survive, our by then two-year-old daughter would peek through the door when his back was turned and amuse me with funny faces. That helped to keep me relatively sane.

One day he felt himself ready for his next recital. He had hired a hall in Rittenhouse Square, Philadelphia, and I was to accompany him. I wondered if I ought to invest in a false beard. I needn't have worried: only five people actually showed up. For his opening number he had chosen "*Eri tu*" from *Un ballo in maschera*. In his old aria book the piece was printed without an opening chord. I told him I would gladly supply one.
—"Oh no! I want to wow the audience with my perfect pitch. I always get that note."
—"But you just might be a bit nervous before your first number; I can give you the pitch in the green room."
—"NO! I always find that note. I have absolute pitch."
Well, out we stepped onto the stage. I sat down at the concert grand. He cleared his throat, moistened his lips, and let out the highest, loudest sound I had ever heard him make. It was much higher than the opening Verdi had had in mind. After a phrase or two I had some accompaniment to play; the only problem was that—whether or not *he* had "perfect pitch"—I did *not*; so I had no idea what key he was in and could only play what was printed in front of me. The aria stayed bi-tonal to the bitter end, he in his key, I in mine. Verdi had never sounded so up-to-the-minute contemporary!

## Sell-less-tea, Ayida

A long distance call from Harrisburg, Pennsylvania: a tenor had an audition date at the Metropolitan Opera; would I accompany him? What arias had he prepared? "Sell-less-tea, Ayida" and "Vesti la Juber." As discreetly as I could, I suggested that he should first find a native Italian speaker—surely there would be *someone* in Harrisburg—and check out his pronunciation, since the Met was known to put great stress on authentic diction and style. "That won't be necessary," he assured me; "my singing teacher *is* Eye-talian."

As I said before, I did not generally turn down paying gigs. I assumed that there must at least be a promising *voice* there. The Met doesn't give an audition date to just anyone who walks in off the street. So I finally agreed to accompany him if he would first come to me for a few serious coaching sessions. That would be no problem: he had a friend in New York he could stay with. So he duly showed up at my door. He placed his dog-eared sheet music on my piano. "Celestial Aida" in D major, transposed down a minor third, the highest note a G natural instead of that notoriously difficult B flat! I tried him out in the proper key. Hopeless. The poor wretch couldn't sing above a G anyway. Criminally, the publisher had given no hint on the title page that this was a transposition. I had the unpleasant duty to convince that not-quite tenor that a Met audition would not be in his best interest at this time. Maybe someday as a first bass for the chorus, if not at the Met then maybe in Harrisburg. His trip was not in vain: at least he learned how to pronounce a few words in Italian.

## The Diva of La Puma

One evening the phone rang. The caller asked me if I would play piano in the pit for a performance of *Norma* the following evening at the La Puma Opera. He would be the conductor. I got my score and he dictated all the many cuts. After he hung up, I spent the rest of the evening playing through the entire opera.

The next morning he called again. Someone was indisposed, so the opera would be changed. Instead of *Norma* it would be *La forza del destino*. Same prima donna, but a different mezzo. Once again I got out my score and wrote in the cuts. Then came a strange request: since most of the orchestra had jobs during the day and came from varying distances, I should not be alarmed if there were only a few other musicians in the pit at performance time. I should simply start by playing everything in the piano reduction; then when an oboe arrived, for instance, I could leave out the oboe's melodies; and as the pit kept filling up, I would gradually have to play less and less of the score.

Well, at least I was forewarned. As I recall, I was alone in the pit except for a cellist and maybe a flute. The conductor entered to scattered applause. I looked up at him, my hands poised to play the opening notes. He looked down at me. The pause seemed endless. Finally it occurred to me that he was waiting to get the tempo from *me*! So I plunged into the "Force of Destiny"; and, sure enough, he began to follow me and beat the time I had established. Unfortunately, at that early stage in my life I was not as familiar with Verdi's score as I later became. I'm afraid my *tempi* may have been rather untraditional (except for the big arias that I knew well even then). By the end of the overture there may have been ten men in the pit, by the end of Act I maybe twenty.

Meanwhile the prima donna had made her entrance, to tumultuous applause. It was Olive Middleton, once—aeons earlier—a respected soprano in her native England, now a cult idol with a huge, loyal following. I had heard of her, of course. In those days everyone had. But I was still unprepared for the startling tones that issued from her throat. I *had* to take a look at her, temporarily taking my eyes off score and conductor. She must have been in her eighties. Her legs were badly bowed, so she had to walk on the outer sides of her shoes. The higher she sang, the greater the distance between *her* pitch and that of the note Verdi actually composed. But she knew the role, all right. She had a huge repertoire and was ready to sing any part of it at a moment's notice. One had to respect such a memory.

Her fans adored her. And she served a benevolent purpose: all the other roles in La Puma productions were sung by talented young singers who were grateful for the opportunity to get some stage experience. Leading soprano roles were pre-empted, of course; but mezzos, tenors, baritones, and basses got a precious chance to try out their roles in public. The *later* their big scene, the better their chance of an orchestral accompaniment.

Some weeks after that memorable night, I received another call from the same conductor. This time for *Tosca*, no cuts, same star. I asked only for a complimentary ticket for my wife. She mustn't miss the experience. After the performance, she described the most dramatic moment. When Scarpia, with a lascivious leer, moved in to kiss Tosca's bare shoulder, he suddenly froze and backed away with a horror-stricken look on his face and an audible gasp. Tosca's shoulder was adorned with an outcropping of wobbling warts. The more Tosca trembled, the more they bobbled. Scarpia totally lost his lustful appetite. He played the rest of the seduction scene from a cautious distance.

## The Stivanello Touch

My wife, who had already sung Nedda in a well-conducted and decently staged production of *Pagliacci*, was engaged to sing the role again in an outdoor performance on Randall's Island. The conductor was Maestro Anton Guadagno, who went on to make a distinguished international career. All the singers were excellent young artists. The musical run-through had gone extremely well. Then came the one and only blocking rehearsal with Mr. Anthony Stivanello, a busy fellow who in those days served as the stage director of numerous regional opera productions, as well as the provider of rented scenery and costumes. He blocked the first act in time-honored, "instant opera" fashion. Then he gave the cast a breezy goodbye and took off for Miami, or somewhere equally far away. "When do we rehearse the second act?"—"Sorry, I've a train to catch." Of all the scenes in *Pagliacci*, the one most in need of some detailed blocking is the little play within a play known as the "*commedia*." It was unthinkable that the cast would be expected to improvise the complicated action on the spur of the moment on opening night! So *I* staged Act II, in what was left of our scheduled rehearsal time. The performance took place on a lovely moonlit night. The audience had a good time. The singers breathed easy, once it was over. That was my unpublicized, uncredited New York debut as a stage director of opera—at least of half a one.

## How I Caught the Opera Bug

When I was nine years old I was taken to see a production of *Faust* by Tony Sarg's touring marionette theater. Magic, skeletons, a witty devil, a witch, a swordfight! I loved it! Back home after the puppet show, my mother told me that *Faust* was a famous opera. She showed me the old Victrola Book of the Opera, vintage World War I, with fascinating photos of settings and performers in costume, as well as full-page reproductions of an artist's conception of several scenes from *Faust*. Then my mother played me a 78-rpm recording of the thrilling Prison Scene Trio, sung by Geraldine Farrar, Caruso, and Marcel Journet. That did it. I was completely carried away! I soon devoured the opera book. All those exciting stories! *Tosca*, torture chamber and firing squad. *Tannhäuser*, magic grotto

and medieval knights. *Aida*, Egyptian temples and tombs. *Lohengrin*, a mysterious stranger, a swan boat, and a forbidden question. *Pagliacci*, clowns and a double murder. *The Ring of the Nibelung*, dwarfs, giants, a castle on a mountain top, a rainbow bridge, a dragon, and those three naked Rhine-maidens. I couldn't wait to *see* an opera, and kept pestering my mother to take me to one. Meanwhile, I listened to all her old phonograph records and played through the score of *Faust* when I should have been practicing what my piano teacher actually assigned to me.

I decided to produce the opera myself, in a barn. My sister would play Marguerite, in a totally inappropriate but beautiful beaded dress from the '20s that we found in an old trunk in the attic. My cousin Jack, who knew how to fence, would be Mephistopheles, my cousin Peter would be Valentine, and—of course!—*I* would be Faust. Grandma made me a plumed hat and a dashing red and gold cape; Jack already owned a devil costume. There exists a ludicrous snapshot of us rehearsing the duel, my bare legs and anachronistic short socks sticking out from beneath the hem of that swashbuckling cape. The show we planned never got much farther than that. But I did actually read Goethe's play—an English translation, of course. I understood just enough to love it even then, and I have revered the original all my life.

Though actually *producing* our version of *Faust* was not as easy as dreaming about it, I did tell the story of the opera to my fourth grade class and show them pictures I had drawn of the settings. I'll never forget how the teacher giggled when I tried to explain what

Marguerite was doing in that prison. It wasn't until a few months later that I learned the facts of life from my cousin Peter (who was two years older than I and had a rather garbled version to pass on).

When I was ten, I finally saw my first opera. A friend of the family had a subscription to the Metropolitan. She let us have her two tickets for a Monday evening *Rigoletto*. In preparation, I read the story and listened to the Quartet and Nellie Melba's "*Caro nome*" (what a beautiful trill!). Those were the only two records we happened to have from that opera. We took the train to New York. The inside of the old Met made a deep impression on me. What a thrill when the curtain rose on that glamorous opening scene, all

What I saw when the curtain went up, *Rigoletto*, Act I, 1936

pink and blue light and gorgeous rich costumes. I practically fell in love with Countess Ceprano in that golden blond wig. Rigoletto was John Charles Thomas (later one of my wife's singing teachers). My memories of that performance are still vivid. My two biggest thrills were "*La donna è mobile*"—the orchestral introduction sent chills down my spine!—and the storm scene, with marvelously realistic lightning, scudding clouds, and the humming chorus backstage that really sounded like the wind. I also remember that Bruna Castagna seemed to me to be too fat to play Maddalena (later I thought her a fabulous Amneris). One strange thing about that performance was the omission of the touching final duet between father and daughter, as she dies in his arms to exquisitely ethereal music. To this day I wonder why. I do have a theory. Although Josephine Antoine was the Gilda that night, the star coloratura of the Met was Lily Pons. Maybe she didn't like being shut up in that burlap bag, breathing dust into her million-dollar windpipe; maybe the cut was for *her* sake and just stayed marked in the parts when the second cast took over.

A year later the same benevolent subscriber gave us tickets to *Carmen*, with Rosa Ponselle. What a night! The overture thrilled me with its crashing cymbals and irresistible energy. Micaëla was lovely Hilda Burke. *Her* blond wig was even prettier than the one

Hilda Burke as Micaëla

with which Countess Ceprano had seduced me the year before. But Carmen herself was the most fascinating female I had ever seen or heard. Every move she made, every inflection of her darkly rich voice, kept me at the edge of my seat. I loved her vivacity, her grace, her sense of humor, as in the delightfully brazen way she puffed cigarette smoke into the face of Captain Zuniga while he was interrogating her after the cat-fight in the factory. My memories of that 1937 performance are still vibrant sixty-eight years later. Best of all, I met Rosa Ponselle herself after the show. My mother, who had been introduced to her once by a mutual friend, took me by the hand, headed backstage, and barged through a door clearly marked "Positively No Entrance." There in the hallway outside her dressing room stood the diva, in the stunning, notoriously untraditional female version of a bull-fighter's costume that she wore in the last act. What struck me most was the thickly

18

caked stage makeup, full of cracks, on her face. It was the color of terra cotta. She reminded me of a cigar-store Indian. From out front she had looked utterly beautiful. Close up, she looked a mess. But a very gracious, very charming mess.

In those days, the hot tickets at the Met were those for any performance that featured Kirsten Flagstad and Lauritz Melchior, especially when they sang together in *Tristan und Isolde*, which always sold out and was presented more times each season than any other opera. They say that

Rosa Ponselle as Carmen, Act IV

those Wagner nights saved the Met during the lean years of the Great Depression. My craze for opera had already infected my cousin Jack, who was four years older than I. My mother took him to *Tristan* when I was too sick to use my ticket. We both listened to all the Saturday broadcasts and fell under the spell of Wagner's incomparable music. We became Wagner fanatics, started

Flagstad and Melchior, *Tristan* Act II

collecting records, sharing our piano-vocal scores. You might even say that we became Wagner *snobs*. For three years we went exclusively to Wagner's operas, made stupid fun of Verdi's oom-pah-pah accompaniments (although I had previously been deeply moved by Eidé Norena and Lawrence Tibbett in *La traviata*), and looked down our adolescent noses at most of the repertory that had seemed so attractive before.

In 1938 we saw the *"Ring"* at the Met, with bonus performances of *Tannhäuser* and *Die Meistersinger* included with the cycle that year. Our tickets were in the next-to-the-top row of the Family Circle, the stratosphere. Flagstad, Melchior, and Friedrich Schorr were the stars. We were too high up to see the rainbow bridge or Valhalla in flames, but what we did see through our powerful binoculars was fascinating enough. After each opera—or even *during* a performance, scribbling in the dark on our programs—we would draw details of the scenery for future reference. For to-gether we had formed a grandiose plan.

We decided to present Wagner's *"Ring"* in Grandma's cellar, starring the recorded voices of all the great Wagnerian singers, visually represented by marionettes on strings. Jack, who knew carpentry, designed a revolving stage made of plywood, with a circumference of twenty-five feet, that turned quietly on padded rollers mounted on a wooden platform. Above the stage we suspended two rather rickety structures, on which a helper and I would lie on our stomachs while we operated the marionettes. Jack was needed down below to work the lights and change records. We had two phonographs. One played everything a quarter tone higher than the other. Each side of a 78-rpm shellac took between three and four minutes, so there was a constant need to transfer from one record-player to the other. Whenever possi-ble, an extended musical excerpt would start at the lower pitch, then shift excitingly to the higher (rather than the other way around). As for the marionettes, some we made, some we bought. There were smaller duplicates for when the characters appeared in the distance.

The dragon was our pride and joy. The morning before the *Siegfried* matinee at the Met, my mother had had some shopping to do at Macy's. There, in the toy department, I found just what we had dreamed of: a gorgeous dragon with bat wings, a ferocious tail, long claws, a movable jaw, and fierce red eyes that lighted up from within. After much pestering, my mother bought it for me and had it wrapped. We got to the performance just in time, but too late to show my cousin my surprise. So in the first intermission I unwrapped the dragon, and we both exulted our hearts out. But then the music of the second act started to sound. Every time I made the slightest movement the stiff brown wrapping paper and the crinkled tissue paper would provide a loud obbligato. Everyone in front of me and behind me shushed me and hissed at me. So I spent the entire, long second act of *Siegfried* with my hands clutching my shoulders and my aching elbows held up high, so as not to activate the percussion section on my lap.

Fortunately, my female cousin Cozy, who was older than either of us, was then a smoker. She was enlisted as the dragon's breath. Whenever he opened his jaws, she would exhale a puff of smoke through a tube that ran through his body.

Dark curtains hung from the cellar ceiling to divide the audience from the backstage area. The proscenium arch was a large, baroquely ornate, gilded picture frame. Footlights were ranks of Christmas tree lights, each color on a separate dimmer. There were trapdoors so that Wotan and Loge could start their journey to Nibelheim and the Norns could sink down to Mother Erda. Magic fire was jagged strips of flame-red silk over a hidden electric fan. The depths of the Rhine were viewed through green florist's paper under blue light. The Gibichungs' hall came in two versions, one before and one after the conflagration. There were cloud curtains, mist curtains, and a translucent window shade painted with strata of rocks, veins of ore, and streaks of lava. When we pulled it upwards, lighted effectively from behind, you could imagine a descent into the bowels of the earth; for the return trip we only had to change the direction. The graphic music did the rest.

After two summers of preparation and experimentation, our mini-Bayreuth finally held its grand festival. That *Ring* was such a success with friends, family, and visiting theater people, that we decided to expand our repertoire. We began to build scenery for *Tristan, Meistersinger*, and *Parsifal*. The ship for Act I of *Tristan* was Jack's masterpiece, a miniature replica of Joseph Urban's much-admired setting. It was in place for our first rehearsal. My helper and I climbed up to our scaffolding above the stage. Suddenly there was a tremendously loud cracking sound and we both crashed down onto the stage in a shower of splinters, smashing not only King Mark's gallant ship but the entire revolving stage as well. When Jack and I built that aerie, we didn't stop to think that we were growing boys and would soon weigh more than a couple of two-by-fours could reasonably be expected to support. That was the end of our Little Bayreuth. Besides, we had both discovered girls by then. We began to spend our summers outside of the cellar.

When I reached high-school age, I was allowed to go to New York by myself. That meant a two-hour trip by train from Spring Lake, New Jersey. I often skipped gym to sneak off to the opera. As soon as the train got to Pennsylvania Station, I would run all the way to

My home in Spring Lake, 15 Madison Avenue

39th Street, to the end of the standing room line. On Saturdays I sometimes would stand through two operas, running around the corner to join the line for the second one as soon as the first was over. That way I saw Eleanor Steber's Met debut as Sophie, opposite Risë Stevens' wonderful, definitive Octavian, in *Der Rosenkavalier* in the evening, after a delightful matinee of *The Marriage of Figaro* with Ezio Pinza, Elisabeth Rethberg, Licia

Eleanor Steber as Sophie

Albanese, Jarmila Novotná, and Salvatore Baccaloni. After the operas, I would sneak backstage for autographs of the stars, then dash to the station to catch the "Night Owl." If I missed that, it would be the milk train, and I'd get home around four in the

Risë Stevens as Octavian

morning. Two or three times I fell asleep on the train and woke up at the end of the line, with a fourteen-mile hike ahead of me to get home. For fear the squeaking stairs would wake my father, I used to climb up a bookcase to the indoor balcony outside my room, or up a wisteria vine to my window.

I used the bookshelves as a ladder to my room beyond the balcony

My father was a fine musician. He had played violin in the Philadelphia Orchestra under Leopold Stokowski. Dad founded and conducted our local Spring Lake Sinfonietta. Those concerts,

Dad conducting his Sinfonietta at the Spring Lake Community House

season after season, made a huge contribution to the cultural life of the New Jersey shore. Dad's string quartet met every Friday evening at our home, or at one of the other member's houses, and explored the entire chamber repertoire before an appreciative audience. Beside the violin, Dad also played the viola, the flute, and the piano.

My mother, father, sister, and me in the "woods" behind our home

But he didn't approve of opera. He was far from happy about my obsession. So while he was listening to the Saturday baseball game on the living room radio, I would be out in his parked car, running down the battery with *Tristan und Isolde*.

Once Dad was asked to play a violin solo at the local Methodist church. After performing, he had to sit up near the pulpit in full sight of the congregation. The rest of us were amused and embarrassed to watch him squirm through the sermon, especially when the pastor asked his flock: "Why do you come to church? It's certainly not for the music: you can hear better music on the radio."

Fortunately for me, my mother didn't share Dad's prejudice against opera. She had a lovely mezzo-soprano voice and had dreamed of a singing career. Giuseppe de Luca heard her sing and said she had "*una voce per il teatro*"; but three children and the depression intervened. During the early 1930s Mother sang a weekly program over radio station WOR in Newark, one of the big four. She kept the fan mail; and when I read it after she died, I was deeply moved to realize how many hearts she had touched through her voice.

When I was very young, Gina Ciaparelli Viafora, a former Met soprano, was my mother's singing teacher and our more-or-less permanent guest, together with her husband, a brilliant caricaturist. Madame Viafora had often sung with Caruso, and told my parents how he would threaten her in the last act of *La bohème* as she lay on the squeaky bed: "Gina, spaghetti tonight or I tickle." Later other, more recent Met singers also stayed at our home. Hilda Burke, whom I had heard as Micaëla and Freia, tried out her program in Spring Lake before facing the New York critics. The night before her recital, she regaled my parents with titillating opera gossip. I was supposed to be doing my homework, but I couldn't resist sneaking out onto the balcony over our living room, where I could hide unseen behind a Persian rug that was draped over the

Dad, as seen by Signor Viafora

railing. She described with relish how big Rosa Ponselle's backside had been before she dieted to sing Carmen. She said that you could only get a good review from one of the Herald Tribune's critics if you ordered your concert gowns from his boy friend.

Miss Burke's recital was a smashing success. Her singing was lovely, but she made the greatest impression on our local audience with her elaborate curtsy. After arias from *Madame Butterfly* and *La bohème*, she spread out her wide accordion-pleated skirt and sank all the way down to the floor. It made quite a picture, and the crowd loved her for it. The next day she posed with the local girl scout troupe for *The Spring Lake Gazette*, one of those papers where every sentence is written in the passive voice, e.g.: a reception was held, tea was served, songs were rendered, cake was enjoyed, and the minutes were read by the secretary.

Hilda Burke with the Girl Scouts and other music lovers
(brother Charlie looking up at Miss Burke, sister Gini second from right)

One of our fascinating guests—thanks to Hitler's purges—was the composer-pianist Hermann-Hans Wetzler. As a young man, he had studied with Clara Schumann! He told us that if, when he arrived at her house, Brahms' overcoat was hanging on the hall tree, he would understand that his lesson had been postponed and would discreetly go home. His piano technique was stupendous.

He sat down at our baby grand and played Beethoven, Schubert, and Chopin like a god. He had composed an opera, *The Basque Venus*, which was finally performed at some venue in New York many years later. The first time he came to dinner we happened to be serving corn on the cob. It was a novelty for him. He claimed to find it delicious and wondered why it was considered pig feed in Europe in those days. From then on, every visit from Herr Wetzler meant corn on the cob. I hope that he wasn't just being polite.

By this time Mother was mainly singing in church, though sometimes we would do programs together for the women's club or some such organization. Dad joined us in the Brahms songs for alto, viola, and piano. On other occasions I would tell the story of *Carmen* or *Samson and Delilah* and Mother would sing the arias.

And of course I was always trying to get to the Met. I fell in love with Risë Stevens midway through *Samson et Dalila*. What a velvety voice and what a beautiful woman! Those dulcet tones and that diaphanous second-act costume seduced me even sooner than they did Samson!

Later that same season I heard Flagstad in *Fidelio* (with Bruno Walter conducting), then as Kundry, and twice as Isolde, including her very last performance before she left to join her husband in wartime Norway. She had given her absolute best; then she came out in

Risë Stevens as Dalila, Act I

Flagstad and Melchior at the curtain call

front of the curtain and announced her decision. The audience was stunned. There were cries of "No! No! Don't go! Flagstad! Flagstad!" People were weeping. After a sublime performance, it was an outpouring of overwhelming emotion, stirred also by memories of so many other glorious evenings at the opera.

One of my father's cousins treated me to membership in the Metropolitan Opera Guild, so once each season I was able to attend a dress rehearsal. That first year it was *Alceste*, with Marjorie Lawrence. Shortly afterwards, she contracted polio and lost the use of her legs. She had been one of the most athletic of prima donnas, famous for leaping onto her horse and galloping into Siegfried's funeral pyre in *Götterdämmerung*, as well as for doing her own dance of the seven veils in *Salome* (in a costume designed for her in Paris by the man who dreamed up little nothings for the *Folies Bergère*). Two seasons later I had the happy fortune to see her sensational come-back as Venus in *Tannhäuser*, a role

Marjorie Lawrence as Salome

she could sing from a reclining position. After that, I saw her as Isolde. She sat on the couch throughout the first act, on the garden bench in Act II, and was carried onstage by Kurwenal for her last entrance, logically enough, since the stage was strewn with huge boulders. In spite of her handicap, she was a thrilling Isolde.

I had a brainstorm: I suggested a trip to the opera for my high school music appreciation class. The kids were enthusiastic, and so was the teacher. She asked *me* to make the arrangements. I wrote a special-delivery letter to the ticket service of the Metropolitan Opera Guild and naïvely asked them to reserve twenty seats in the balcony for a matinee performance of *Tannhäuser*. Meanwhile I told the class the story, showed them pictures, and played recordings of the Overture, the Entrance of the Guests into the Wartburg, and the Evening Star. The days went by with no word from the Opera Guild. Finally, desperate, I took a train to New York and went to their office. They more or less laughed in my face. Of course the performance would be sold out. Of course one can never expect to get such a big block of tickets for any of the operas. They could at least have answered my letter. Imagine what a failure I felt when I had to go back and tell my classmates!

The next season, I again skipped a class at high school and ran off to New York in my school clothes, having no time to change. While I was standing through the first scene of *Don Giovanni* I spotted an empty seat in the front row of the orchestra section. The house lights were still dim for the brief scene change. I snuck down the nearest aisle and slipped into that empty seat. I was rather conspicuous in a lumberjack's plaid shirt and sneakers, among all those formal evening clothes. For the rest of the opera I fully expected to be thrown out at any moment. But I'll never forget Zinka Milanov's ethereal high B flat at the end of the Maskers' Trio or the inspired clowning of Pinza and Baccaloni. The Ottavio was Tito Schipa. That night he seemed to be merely walking through his role. Later I came to prize his recordings; but the two times I heard him "live" I was rather disappointed.

When the Met presented *The Magic Flute* in English, I managed to get hold of the new translation. I played and sang many of the scenes for my kid brother Charlie, who was then eight years old. He lapped it up. So we decided to take him to see his first opera. We would spend two nights in New York with our cousins. My uncle thought our mother had taken leave of her senses: what a waste of money! What would a little kid like that know about a Mozart opera? I said: "Tell him, Charlie!" And my brother sang by heart at least a third of the opera. That settled that argument!

Jarmila Novotná in *La traviata*

Charlie was fascinated by every detail of the performance. Afterwards, we went backstage. Charles Kullman, the Tamino, cordially signed his program and John Brownlee told us about his own little boys and even gave Charlie a feather from his Papageno costume. Then we dashed over to the women's side of the house. By then it was too late to catch the ladies still in their dressing rooms, but there was lovely Jarmila Novotná, the radiant Pamina, just settling into her taxi. Before I could stop him, Charlie leaped into her lap and gave her a big kiss on the cheek.

Then in December 1942, as a Christmas present, my mother gave me $100 and told me I could spend a week by myself in New York. I got a decent room at the Henry Hudson Hotel for four dollars a night, ate at the "automat" (when I remembered to eat at all), and went to the opera NINE times!!! *The Magic Flute, Aida, Traviata, Tosca, Lohengrin, The Daughter of the Regiment, Salome, Boris Godunov,* and the Gala Evening that featured the return of Marjorie Lawrence, already mentioned, along with staged scenes from *Traviata* and *Manon* and arias by Lily Pons and Ezio Pinza. On days when there was no opera matinee, I took in several plays. All that for a hundred dollars!

Constance Hope, the public-relations wonder-woman, noticed that I was a loud clapper and could yell *"bravo"* as stentoriously as anyone. So she gave me a pricey orchestra seat for *Tristan und Isolde* with the request that I display plenty of resonant enthusiasm for Erich Leinsdorf and call out his name at every appropriate opportunity. That night I was his one-man claque. I got to see Helen Traubel's Isolde. I remember the trouble she had maneuvering over all those rocks in the last act. Flagstad had always entered running, her long gray veil floating behind her. It made a memorable picture. What a contrast to see Miss Traubel holding up her skirt with both hands and looking down at her feet as she cautiously and ponderously approached her dying lover! At least she managed to get to his side in time to respond to his last gasp—but only just!

For my last year of high school I had the great privilege of attending Phillips Exeter Academy. There the realm of great literature was opened up to me by a teacher, Hamilton Bissell, to whom I shall always be grateful. Reading *Macbeth* under his guidance was a life-altering experience. The study of Shakespeare that began there at Exeter served me well when I later became a stage director of opera. Meanwhile, when I had a free hour, I would haunt the basement of the chapel, hunting for an unoccupied practice cubicle with a piano, and play through the score of *Der Rosenkavalier*. On Sundays I sang in the choir. I enjoyed it so much, that I decided to ask the director for singing lessons. He listened to my struggle with the top note in *"O del mio dolce ardor"* and threw up his hands. "How can I make a silk purse out of a sow's ear?" That was his only comment. That was my first and last voice lesson.

More successful was my study of the organ, shortly before I went to Exeter. I was asked to play the prelude, the offertory, and the postlude at a service in a huge church at Ocean Grove, New

Jersey. It was a very hot summer, so one scorching day, thinking I was alone in the church, I took off all my clothes down to my underpants while I was practicing for the big event. All of a sudden some ladies from the altar guild materialized out of nowhere in the organ loft with armfuls of gladiolas. I don't know who shocked whom the most! Footnote: on the day of "my" service, those same good ladies, presumably, had filled the church with about a hundred live canary birds, in cages hanging between garlands of flowers. They completely drowned out my playing. We weren't even in the same key. But those birds stole the show every time the organ sounded. (They could have picked on the preacher.)

## Training for Opera in the U.S. Navy

I as a sailor, standing on the left

I became eighteen a year and a half before the end of World War II. So, having a choice of service, I chose the Navy. At boot camp in Bainbridge, Maryland, my company commander recommended me for the U.S. Naval Academy. I and 199 other men from the fleet were assigned to a special preparatory program. While waiting for it to start, we were given every imaginable odd job. At a mushroom farm, I shoveled manure for the admiral's lawn. I rode around on a garbage truck emptying huge containers full of rancid ice cream cartons. I cleaned urinals with steel wool and a tooth brush. Mountains of raw hamburger meat were dumped onto the metal floor of the mess hall; my job was to roll up my sleeves, plunge my hands in, grab a hunk, and slap it into shape, then repeat the operation about a thousand times. Salads were made in a monster vat; the chef had to jump in, Band-Aids and all, and mix it up from the inside. Some of my mates lost their appetites after that day in the galley. But only temporarily. At any rate, I've been a vegetarian for the last forty-seven years. Maybe those meatballs planted the seed.

One day several barracks were emptied at random and their inmates were ordered to attend a concert in a huge auditorium on the base. "Dancing girls!" we were told. Well, it turned out to be a joint recital by Martha Lipton, mezzo-soprano of the Metropolitan Opera, and Charles Kullman. Not a dancing girl in sight. They opened with the duet between Amneris and Rhadamès from *Aida*, Act IV. You should have heard the tempest of groans, catcalls, and snores. I felt devastated for the well-meaning artists. There were navy men at that base who would have appreciated their efforts, probably enough to have filled one of the chapels, for instance. But the audience was recruited by fiat, with false inducements. Those of us who would have enjoyed the program were humiliated instead.

In due time I was sworn in as a midshipman at the U.S. Naval Academy. At the end of our first year there, we were finally allowed to leave the "yard" and freely visit the town of Annapolis. Naturally, I made a bee-line for the local record shop and would continue to spend most of my meager pocket money there. One day I found the last two 78rpm sides from the complete recording of *La bohème*, with Licia Albanese and Beniamino Gigli. That evening I put it on my record player after I

Midshipman Glass with a gorgeous date

had finished my homework. My roommate was still struggling with a navigation problem. He didn't seem to be listening. Suddenly, near the end of the last record, he astonished me by bursting into sobs. "What *is* that moving music?" he asked. That young American navy man had never been exposed to opera before. He knew not a word of Italian, nothing of the story, nor of the situation expressed in that scene. Yet Puccini's music, as sung by that cast, had gone straight to his heart.

On leave from the Naval Academy, I went to New York to hear *Der Rosenkavalier* at the Met. Before the performance, some friends invited me to their apartment for cocktails. They were serving "stingers," a drink that was new to me and so delicious that I was easily persuaded to down three of them. After our cozy little party I went to the opera. Lucky that it happened to be a comedy! Thanks to the stingers, I couldn't stop laughing all evening. The well-bred subscribers on either side of me looked askance at such rude irreverence in a hallowed temple of high art.

My last summer cruise as a midshipman took me to Italy. We docked at Genoa. As usual, I headed for a record store. Two young Italians were trying to find an aria and sang a phrase to the clerk, because they couldn't remember the title. I stepped forward and identified the fragment as the last part of *"Eri tu"* from *Un ballo in maschera*. That started a pleasant friendship. They were both "football" players (soccer to us), and they both liked opera. Most Italians did back in 1948. I heard people whistling or singing snatches of operatic melody wherever I went. That is, sadly, no longer the case. Not since rock and roll took over. But those two knew many of the popular Italian arias by heart. And they sang one or two with me at a restaurant table that evening, until the other diners took up a collection of the lousiest, dirtiest, smallest bits of paper money they could dig out of their pockets and got the waiter to dump them on our table. That shut us up, as it was meant to do. My new friends also loved American movies. They especially admired an actor they called *Spen*-et-chair *Trah*-chee. That translates as Spencer Tracy. Rita *Eye*-vort was their favorite actress.

Most young American males would have voted for her too.

A group of us midshipmen took a tour to Rome, where we had the privilege of an audience with Pope Pius XII. His Holiness was very gracious and had a few words of blessing for each of us. Everyone was deeply impressed with a quality of spiritual radiance that seemed to emanate from him. Then some well-meaning idiot proposed a football cheer, as our way of expressing our thanks. What to do? A half-hearted shout would be even more embarrassing. So we gave it all we had. The old walls of the Vatican must have groaned at the gaffe. "O.K., boys, how about 'Sunshine Pope'? Ray! Ray! Rah!—Pope! Pope! Pope!" The Holy Father smiled indulgently. But I still shudder at the memory!

On that same trip to Rome I saw Maria Callas as Turandot and Tito Gobbi as Renato, on starry nights in the ruins of the Baths of Caracalla. I also began to learn conversational Italian. I already had a good head start, thanks to all the opera arias I knew by heart.

Some years later my brother made his way through Italy speaking *Traviata* and *Trovatore* instead of standard Italian. Quaint, but better than nothing. You can't order an oil change. But at least it breaks the ice. In Austria he got by on *Rosenkavalier*.

After my graduation from Annapolis, my first assignment was as Education and Training Officer on an aircraft carrier of the then-largest class, the U.S.S. Midway. Believe it or not, I actually had a piano in my office! There were two others on board, one in the officers' wardroom and one in the library. I ran into an outstanding musician who played the flute in the ship's band, a very gifted classical pianist named Eugene Kass-

My graduation photo, 1949

man. The prescribed barrier between officers and enlisted men did not keep us from becoming good friends. Gene introduced me to the pleasures of piano duets, Schubert's F sharp minor Fantasia, Brahms' Hungarian Dances, various works by Mozart and Johann Christian Bach. We were doing so well together that we began to nourish grandiose ideas. We dreamed of performing Mozart's two-piano concerto with the Norfolk Symphony Orchestra. We managed to move my office spinet into the ship's library, so we could have two pianos side by side. We rehearsed our concerto with diligence and enthusiasm. Then our ship ran into a violent storm in the Caribbean. Both pianos fell forward onto their protruding keyboards. When we hauled them upright, they had buck teeth. Both had become unplayable. Our dream of glory ended somewhere off the coast of Puerto Rico.

The Midway spent most of 1950 in the Mediterranean. While there I made it my business to learn French and improve my Italian. I had pretty good fluency in German already, having spoken it as a child with my grandmother and my German nurse at home, then studied it through high school and at the Naval Academy. On the way across the Atlantic I had memorized Italian grammar and vocabulary whenever I had a free moment. One of our first ports was Augusta, Sicily. I began speaking to everyone I met. They laughed at my often ludicrous mistakes, but were kind enough to correct them. So I learned. But in Naples I discovered that the most efficient way a man can learn a language is to get himself a girl friend who speaks it. A pretty blond singer named Laura Tomassoni was my unofficial instructor. She followed me to whatever port my ship chose to visit. Once, in Palermo, we stayed at the "Grand' Albergo delle Palme" where Wagner had completed the composition of *Parsifal*. When the Midway came to Livorno, so did Laura. The officers and crew were on a three-day rotating schedule: one day of duty, one day ashore, one day of rest. The port was not big enough—or had too few bars—to accommodate the combined crews of a huge aircraft carrier and its escort of destroyers all on the same day. Well, Saturday was my day ashore. Sunday would have been my day of rest. I felt certain that there would be no roll call for the officers on a Sunday. So I decided to go to Florence with my girl friend, spend the night and most of Sunday there, and mingle with the returning crowd at the dock Sunday evening, to slip back aboard unnoticed. Laura and I visited Pisa and its Leaning Tower on the way. She had cousins in Florence. We had fun with them at a night club. On Sunday we paid our respects to Giotto and Brunelleschi, then rented a boat and rowed about on the Arno. It was a glorious day, at least in Florence. When we got back to Livorno, I began to wonder where all the sailors might be. I took a taxi to the dock. Where was my ship? Where was *any* ship? While I stood there, flabbergasted, two shore patrol men approached me. "Are you Ensign Glass? We've been searching for you all day among the ruins!" *What* ruins?! Wouldn't you know, there *had* to be a devastating earthquake in Livorno the very day I had chosen to go AWOL! So they radioed the ship, already far at sea, and ordered a helicopter to pick me up and bring me back in solitary, ignominious disgrace. At least half the crew was on deck to witness my undignified return. As punishment I was relieved of all duties for two weeks. So I divided my time between my stateroom and the officers' wardroom and took advantage of my enforced leisure to study French. The next stop was at Malta. The other officers were invited to a reception where they were presented to Princess Elizabeth and the Duke of Edinburgh, now the queen of England and her consort. I regretted missing that. But my executive officer gave me an indulgent fitness report. He had to mention my grave transgression, of course, but he added the opinion that every ensign is allowed one chance to make a complete ass of himself. I suspect he felt it had been in a good cause.

My progress in French turned out to be immediately useful. The Midway anchored off Cannes, where I met two charming French girls on vacation. Later, one of them invited me to Paris, where she and I saw *Faust* at the Opéra and Louis Jouvet in *Tartuffe*. I later ran into the other when the Midway paid a visit to Algiers. There a strange thing happened. The shore patrol raided the famous local brothel called "*Le Sphinx*," looking for straying sailors. They burst in on one poor fellow at a most inopportune moment. He scolded them in French. Somehow the rumor got around the ship that *I* was that man, presumably because I was the only person on board who spoke French. How outrageously embarrassing—both for the interrupted Frenchman and for me!

A bit of *dolce vita* on the French Riviera

Our admiral made friends with the Aga Khan, the grandfather of the present holder of that title. One day he decided to visit our ship, together with his son, Ali Khan, and—to our immense delight—his glamorous daughter-in-law, Rita Hayworth. The visit was quite a production. The Aga Khan was enormously fat. Each year on his birthday he received his weight in gold; when he was seventy-five, diamonds took the place of gold. So it behooved him not ever to diet. But there was a problem when he arrived at our ship in his yacht. He was too portly to climb the "accommodation ladder," as the flight of steps was called. So his entire yacht was hoisted up to the flight deck by a huge crane. Then a broad chair with lots of pillows was raised up to the level of *his* deck by a movable lift. Several people helped our distinguished guest to get into the chair. The rest was a snap. Meanwhile all of us who were not officially otherwise involved had found ourselves some strategically advantageous spot from which we could feast our eyes on the visiting movie star without being too obvious about it. My first impression was disappointing: she looked just like any other attractive American girl. She was wearing something tweedy, a bandana, and sensible low-heeled shoes. Not a smidgen of the expected allure. She could have been the admiral's niece. But what a change the next evening at the ship's dance! She came back in full makeup and a glamorous ball gown, her red hair cascading over her shoulders. And she graciously danced every single number, letting the sailors "cut in" at will. Every one of them could tell his friends back home that he had danced with the Hollywood love goddess of that era. I was impressed with her exceptional kindness, and with her stamina.

In Naples I heard *Adriana Lecouvreur* for the first time. Maria Caniglia sang the title role and the composer, Francesco Cilea, sat in a stage box. Both received ovations. I was enchanted by the music, mystified by the plot. Cilea died just a short time later.

At Athens I heard *Lucia di Lammermoor* in Greek. I'll never forget my first glimpse of the Acropolis from the sea, by the first light of dawn, as we headed for the harbor.

Ours was the first American warship to visit Istanbul. The city gave us an exceptionally hospitable welcome. They set up a "USO" where we could meet people who spoke at least a little English. We were provided with free transportation throughout the city. After a fabulous day ashore, I walked to the beautiful white palace where a boat was to pick us up for our return to our ship. Over the palace gate some insensitive clod had put up a large sign: "U.S. Navy Prophylactic Station." Any sailor who had forgotten to pick up a supply of condoms on his way to town could get a free tube of curative ointment before his return to the ship. It was not a great moment in the history of U.S diplomacy.

A scene from our show

On the way back from Europe, I wrote a musical comedy about our experiences in the Mediterranean. One of the men in the ship's band made a great arrangement of the music I had composed. When the Midway went into dry dock at Portsmouth, Virginia, we put on our show at the local USO. It was a big hit. That was my first experience as a producer and stage director. My greenness showed in my underestimation of the time it would take to build the scenery. The night before the first performance we were all up until 2:00 a.m., painting. On stage, far too few hours later, I was a bit hoarse for a high note or two, but the audience liked us. We were invited to repeat our show in Norfolk.

Recently, fifty-one years later, I pushed the button on my telephone answering machine and was flabbergasted to hear the opening number of my nautical musical, sung by Joe Pugliese, a shipmate whom I had not seen since we were fellow officers on that ship, all those many years ago! He remembered the lyrics better than I do, even though I wrote them.

After my two-year tour of duty aboard the Midway, the Navy informed me officially that I was to be stationed in Naples, Italy. I was jubilant. The land of sunshine, opera, art, pasta, pizza, and romance! About two weeks later my orders were changed. My shore duty was transferred to London. Fog instead of sunshine. Rationing. Belt-tightening. Jugged hare and kippered herring for breakfast. Stiff upper lips. I wrote the Bureau of Personnel and asked if they wouldn't like to reconsider. They ignored my request.

I arrived at the airport on a dark evening. Rain was pouring down. On the bus, halfway to the downtown terminal, I was suddenly overcome with euphoria. All of a sudden I sensed that I was embarking on a wonderful adventure. From that moment on, I never regretted the loss of a post at Naples. I felt totally at home in London.

Fortunately, I had two valuable connections. My "kissing cousin" Fay Gildersleeve (now Stetzer) had been living there for several years and had lots of interesting friends. One of them owned a mews house of unusual, quirky charm, at 4 Kinnerton Street. It was available for rent, and I snatched it up as soon as I saw it. The other invaluable contact came through one of my best friends since childhood, Howard McKinley, who had spent a year at Oxford as a Rhodes Scholar. Apparently he was still a sort of legend around the university. One of his awed admirers invited me to a banquet of the Shakespeare Society. As my host was showing me about town, every nook and cranny seemed to evoke one of Howard's escapades. Very soon slews of Oxonians were camping out in my living room on weekends. Fay graciously loaned me her capable cook. Since I had access to the navy store and everyone else was scraping by on rationing coupons, I became quite popular.

One day I picked up some bottles of milk at the dairy on my way home from work. As I passed by number 24 Kinnerton Street, just a few doors from my new home, I distinctly heard the voice of Kirsten Flagstad coming from what appeared to be a basement window. She was rehearsing *Frauenliebe und –leben*. I had noticed the posters announcing her upcoming recital. Hugging the milk bottles to my chest, I stood there transfixed, bent almost double so that my ear might stay close to that sunken window. The posture was awkward, not to say undignified for a naval officer in uniform; but I couldn't tear myself away from such a treat until the last song had been sung. A few days later, as I was again passing the house, its owner happened to come out. It was the well- known accompanist Ivor Newton, whom I recognized from his recitals. I told him how much I had enjoyed eavesdropping on his rehearsal. He responded by inviting me to a party, where I had the pleasure of meeting Maggie Teyte, whose recordings were treasured gems in my collection.

Before long I became one of Miss Teyte's studio accompanists (she was not yet Dame Maggie, back then). I also accompanied some recitals that featured her current students.

Though always wise and consistent in matters of purely vocal technique, she was nevertheless a rather unpredictable and eratic teacher. One of her new students was a baritone. She changed his assignments and his voice-category every week. He absolutely *must* learn Tristan! I coached him in several of the extended solos.

Maggie Teyte, inscribed:
*To Beau, souvenir of Mélisande from Meg*

Miss Teyte never heard a note of any of them. At his next lesson he had to become a light lyric tenor....

One night she came to my house for dinner and took me through some *mélodies* by Fauré. She told me that she had just been to Vienna to work with Joseph Marx on his songs. They had a problem communicating. He spoke neither English nor French. Her German was sub-rudimentary.

I loved to hear her reminisce about Claude Debussy, usually over gin and grapefruit juice. Sometimes her lessons included scenes from *Pelléas et Mélisande*, an opera she had studied with the composer himself. Naturally I took mental note of every nuance. She taught her pupils the vocalises she had learned from her own teacher, the great Jean de Reszke, exercises on the vowel "oo" that stressed "high palate" and helped to develop lovely floating head tones. Her own singing was still exquisite, though she was well into her sixties. Her ambition was to sing a public recital on the fiftieth anniversary of her debut. She missed it by one year only. But that was some time after I had left London.

At another party, Ivor introduced me to Marguerite d'Alvarez, a grand diva of classic proportions who had once charmed Oscar Hammerstein the First into plastering her portrait all over a theater he was building for her. In her autobiography, *Forbidden Altars*, she claimed that her mother had been a Peruvian princess. Ivor told me she came from Liverpool. Be that as it may, she had once been a famous Delilah, Favorita, and Carmen. My mother had some of her records.

Kinnerton Street was famous for some of London's most popular pubs. My neighbors included several theater people. One of the most amusing was comedienne Hermione Gingold, who became a good friend. At another party there, I met lovely Moira Shearer, the ballerina who starred in *The Red Shoes*. She was even more beautiful in real life than on the screen. My head

Marguerite D'Alvarez in a characteristic pose

was soon spinning. Maurice Evans, the distinguished Shakespearean actor, was my dinner guest once. Muriel Smith, the original Carmen Jones, who was playing in *South Pacific* at the time, came to my birthday party. I met John Gielgud at another shindig. And Hildegarde, the famous "*chanteuse*," at still another. And Douglas Fairbanks Jr., who had served in the Navy during the war, came over to say hello when he saw me in my uniform at Noël Coward's opening night at the Café de Paris. As you see, I became an insufferable name-dropper.

Lest the reader get the impression that my chief duty as a naval officer in London was to attend as many parties as possible, let me set the record straight. I worked eight-hour shifts, six days a week, encoding and decoding top secret dispatches at the Navy's office in Grosvenor Square. The job sounded quite exciting, at first. Cloaks and daggers! Spies reporting from exotic ports! After a few weeks the glamour wore rather thin. Most of the messages were stultifyingly boring. At Vladivostok so and so many containers and so and so many cartons were loaded onto such and such a vessel. My main problem was staying awake. A huge thermos of black coffee helped. Our shifts were constantly rotating. Once, for instance, I woke up, had a hasty breakfast, and took a cab to Covent Garden just in time for the opening curtain of *Boris Godunov*. Toward the end of the last scene I began to pray that I wouldn't have to leave the theater before Nicolai Rossi-Lemeni's death scene. Thanks to a fairly lively tempo, the opera ended a few minutes before midnight and I arrived at my job on the dot.

I couldn't help burning my candle at both ends. London had so unbelievably much to offer. Forty legitimate theaters in London alone, not to mention the Shakespeare season at Stratford-on-Avon. I saw Gielgud in fabulous productions of *A Winter's Tale* and *Much Ado about Nothing*. Claire Bloom was an exquisite Juliet. I lapped up all the great classics. Then there were four symphony orchestras in town. I was keen to hear a concert by Sir Thomas Beecham. Most of the time when I was stationed in London he was active somewhere else. Finally a Beecham concert was advertised. I ran out and bought a ticket. I arrived at the Royal Festival Hall early and sank into one of the comfortable seats. Next thing I knew, everyone was applauding. It was not his entrance; it was the end of the first half of the concert. Too much candle-burning on my part. I was loath to insult Sir Thomas by falling asleep again, so I left during the intermission.

Recitals? Dietrich Fischer-Dieskau sang the *Winterreise*. Tito Schipa, Gigli, Marian Anderson, Flagstad, Boris Christoff, Helen Traubel, the list is endless.

At the end of the Traubel recital at the Royal Festival Hall I was so proud of a fellow American that I felt like jumping up and croaking the Star-Spangled Banner. With the piano lid in its totally opened position that grandmotherly woman in a hair net let loose with Isolde's Narrative and Curse. What an enormous outpouring of sheer, thrilling tone! Then, as a sly, stunning contrast, she sang Brahms' Lullabye—*pianississimo*—as an encore. The audience went wild.

What I remember best about Boris Christoff's recital is my shock at the end of "The Erl-King": he had barely finished singing the tragic final line, "in his arms the child was dead," when, anticipating tumultuous applause, the singer broke into a broad grin and began to bow before the last chord had died away. The effect was grotesque. But Christoff was the best Boris since Chaliapin and I was moved to tears by his death scene.

I feasted on the Royal Ballet and the Sadler's Wells. Gorgeous productions! Margot Fonteyne's starry brilliance! Lovely Moira Shearer! *The Sleeping Beauty*, *Sylvia*, *Daphnis and Chloe*....

Kathleen Ferrier as Orfeo, her last role

And *two* opera companies. I saw every opera at least once during each season. A seat in the third row of the "stalls" at Covent Garden cost only one pound in those days, then about $2.80 (a ticket for that loca-tion would now be close to $200). Especially memorable were Kathleen Ferrier's Orfeo, shortly before her career was cut short by cancer, and the famous *Norma* that introduced Maria Callas to London. Actually I was more impressed with Ebe Stignani, the Adalgisa, than with Callas herself, though I was intrigued with her sometimes strangely curdled sound and impressed with her fluent coloratura. I would like to dispel one myth. Callas was not obese before her astonishing weight-loss. I would call her statuesque, full-bodied. But not obese. Nevertheless, she was not yet the sensational actress she later

Maria Callas as Norma
in London

became under the guidance of directors like Luchino Visconti. Her gestures struck me as rather semaphoric, and her stride was that of a burly truckdriver. Stignani, on the other hand, looked like Norma's mother and didn't bother to do much acting at all; but her voice was phenomenal from top to bottom, and gloriously huge.

The Navy was generous with leave. I was able to attend four of the leading summer festivals, Glyndebourne, Edinburgh, Bayreuth, and Salzburg. On my arrival at the last named, I checked in at a modest guest house in the suburbs and took off for the opera. After the performance, on my way back to my room, I was stopped by the American military police. "You can't go there, Sir; it's off-limits to U.S. servicemen." Why? "Because it's the local head-quarters of the Communist Party." For the rest of my stay in Salzburg I wore civilian clothes. Every other place in town was booked up for the duration of the festival.

Each of those festivals was an enriching experience. Glynde-bourne is situated in a lovely part of the English countryside. There are many beautiful gardens, each with a different color scheme, on a private estate. One can picnic on the grounds during the long intermissions. Sena Jurinac as Fiordiligi and Ilia made the most lasting impression on me with her pearly voice and cameo-like beauty.

I had already visited Edinburgh as a midshipman. I was in awe of the dark castle atop that huge crag rising above the gardens of Princes Street. I visited all the sites that had played a part in the tragic story of Mary Queen of Scots. At the festival, I heard Lisa della Casa for the first time, as Sophie in *Der Rosenkavalier*. Eighteen years later, when she had become a famous Marschallin and *the* Arabella, I had the great pleasure of coaching her in the title role of Handel's *Agrippina*. By then she had a castle on the Rhine. My wife and I had lunch with her and her handsome husband there.

But now: back to 1952. At Bayreuth I was overwhelmed with

Astrid Varnay's magnificent Isolde—the voice of a Flagstad, the expressive intensity of a Lotte Lehmann. The production was by Wieland Wagner. A nearly bare stage —but what miracles he achieved with light alone! At the beginning of the second act, for instance, one saw only a diagonal ray of flame-colored light slashing across a black stage. When Isolde doused the torch, all was plunged into darkness. Then, as our eyes made their gradual adjustment, we could see the lovers floating about in opalescent

Astrid Varnay as Isolde

clouds. It was one of the most poetically beautiful images I had ever seen in any opera.

On to Salzburg, a picture book of a town, nestled in the curved embrace of sheer cliffs, with its fortress towering above the towers, domes, and spires of many churches, and a jade-green river rushing through the city. There I saw Ramon Vinay as a powerful Otello and the premiere production of Strauss's mesmerizing late work, *Die Liebe der Danaë*, which combines two ancient myths, the golden touch of King Midas and Jupiter's wooing of Danaë in a shower of gold. The last act was hauntingly beautiful, Strauss at his autumnal best.

I owe so much to the Navy! During my ten years of service, I learned the three essential operatic languages, Italian, French, and German. I soaked up the art and the history of Europe, the background atmosphere of so much of the core repertoire. I had the chance to see and study the work of great conductors, singers, actors, and stage directors. And I was able to keep active as a musician, without jeopardizing my varied jobs as an officer, which included gunnery and engineering as well as those already mentioned.

After my stint in London, I was sent to San Diego, to be the executive officer on an LSM. Culturally there was quite a contrast, at least in those days. My link with opera was maintained at a rather unusual night club and restaurant called "The Opera Café." The juke box played a choice selection of arias. The main attraction was an authentic diva, Ina Souez. Her name was known to all seri-

Ina Souez

ous record collectors in those days. She was Donna Anna and Fiordiligi in the first complete recordings of *Don Giovanni* and *Così fan tutte*, conducted by Fritz Busch. She had been the star of the Glyndebourne Festival from its inception until World War II. She had sung at Covent Garden. The war put an untimely end to her career in Europe. Back in America—she was a Colorado girl—she had little luck. For a while she toured with Spike Jones and His City Slickers, playing a caricature of a prima donna. But her still rich voice and her big, colorful personality made her a hit as a night club entertainer. I became her accompanist and performed with her whenever my ship was in port and I was free to go ashore for an evening. She sang all the major soprano arias for the dinner guests. Between numbers she would go to the kitchen and cook a batch of her special spaghetti sauce.

When the Korean War ended, I was free to resign from the Navy. I had served during two wars, from April 1944 till July 1954, without seeing any combat. Now I wanted to see what else life might hold in store. I was temporarily transferred to a cargo ship headed for San Francisco. The evening before our arrival, the ship's movie was *San Francisco* with Jeanette MacDonald and Clark Gable. I hadn't seen it since I was in grade school. How I had loved those scenes from *Faust* and *La traviata*! I was happy to see that film again. Then we approached the Golden Gate Bridge just at dawn. That was a thrill. I fell in love with the bay area and decided to make it my home, which it was for the next three years.

I was transferred from the regular Navy to the Naval Reserve at Treasure Island. Ever since leaving active service I have had a recurrent dream: I have been called back into the Navy. I suddenly realize that my cap cover is stained, my shoes are not shined, I have lost the gold buttons or the shoulder boards for my uniform. I can't find the plan of the day and don't know whether I'm supposed to be on watch at the moment. All the equipment is new and I don't recognize anything. I can't find my quarters; I am somewhere amidships and don't know which way is fore and which is aft; I've lost my orders.

## Life as a Civilian Again

Elisabeth Schwarzkopf
as the Marschallin

San Francisco was rather close to Paradise. Beside the scenery, there was a great opera company. Quite a few major stars made their American debuts there, before they moved to the Met. Renata Tebaldi, Elisabeth Schwarzkopf, Leonie Rysanek, Boris Christoff, and Birgit Nilsson, to name just a few. What a feast! Nilsson, Rysanek, and Hans Hotter in *Die Walküre*, Schwarzkopf as the Marschallin in *Der Rosenkavalier* (I fell in love with that beautiful face before the curtain was raised six feet!), Christoff as Boris, Tebaldi as Tosca (she sang "*Vissi d'arte*" twice that night), Jussi Bjoerling in *Rigoletto, Don Carlo,* and *Manon Lescaut,* Licia Albanese as Madame Butterfly. There was a gala concert in which Tebaldi and Schwarzkopf sang the "Letter Duet" from *Le nozze di Figaro.* Concerts and recitals galore! Gina Bachauer, Dame Myra Hess, Wilhelm Backhaus, among the pianists who most impressed me. Risë Stevens moved me at her recital with her sensitive interpretation of Brahms' song "*Dein blaues Auge,*" and taught me a lesson at the end of the spiritual "Were You There." At the words, "tremble, tremble, tremble," her voice became softer and softer; and, as it did so, a unique hush came over the audience: no one dared even to breathe. It was a magical moment I shall never forget. She kept that entire audience spellbound until the very end of the last verse—and beyond.

San Francisco was full of aspiring musicians who had no place to practice. I decided to buy a large house on Fell Street, opposite the "panhandle" of Golden Gate Park, and convert it into a boarding house for musicians, where they could practice to their heart's content. I soon had three sopranos (two of them pregnant), a violinist, a trumpeter, a flautist, and five pianists. Every week we had a house concert. During the opera season we had several sub-scriptions, and I would give an in-formal talk about the opera we were about to see, with musical examples from our home tal-ent.

The boarding house for musicians on Fell Street

It was an odd house. When I first moved in, I discovered that the closets could only be locked from the inside, the bathrooms only from the *outside*!! The former owners were two sisters who never spoke to each other, so there were two separate entrances. I was told that the family jewels were still hidden somewhere in the house. So one evening, after a few glasses of wine, we all went on a treasure hunt. We found a trail of candle wax drippings that led to an old sofa in the basement. In high excitement we ripped open the upholstery. Something was wrapped in tissue paper. We held our breath. Then we held our noses. It turned out to be an old, moldy sandwich.

Meanwhile, thanks to the GI Bill, I was taking courses, first at San Francisco State College (as it was called at the time), then at the University of California at Berkeley. I studied literature and linguistics, Shakespeare and Chaucer. I took an advanced course in Italian, which led to my being cast in the leading role of a play, which we performed in its original Italian. My professor, Vittoria Colonna (named after Michelangelo's lady friend and from the same aristocratic Roman family), drilled me in the correct accent and idiomatic speech melodies. Nothing escaped her sharp ear. The play was fascinating, *Legittima difesa*, by Paolo Levi. My character was shot in the opening scene, then resurrected in a series of playbacks, as every other character gave his or her version of what actually happened. No two versions agreed, of course. Pirandello and *Roshomon* were the godparents. The director knew his business, and I learned a lot.

Just as well, because a few months later I received a telegram from the Northwest Grand Opera Association in Seattle, asking whether I would accept a contract as stage director for a production of *La traviata* with Dorothy Kirsten of the Metropolitan as the star. It seems that Glynn Ross, their usual director, had a sudden engagement elsewhere; and I had been recommended by a member of their team who had met me in San Francisco and been impressed with my enthusiasm for opera.

The fact is, my previous directing experience was limited to that navy show I had written and put on in Virginia a few years before.

So I had a problem with my conscience. On the other hand, this opportunity seemed like a gift from heaven that dropped into my lap. And I had certainly seen plenty of Traviatas, in New York, in Paris, and in San Francisco.

So I telegraphed my acceptance. I might not know much about stage directing, but I would make it my business to know everything about *La traviata*. So I memorized the whole opera, chorus parts and all. Meanwhile, I went to the San Francisco Public Library and checked out every book on stagecraft, acting, and directing that I could lay my hands on.

People arrived in Seattle according to a strict pecking order. I was the first "outsider" to check in. Then, a week before the dress rehearsal, we were joined by the tenor, Rudolf Petrak of the New York City Opera. The baritone, Giuseppe Valdengo, who had recorded Iago and Falstaff with Toscanini, showed up the day of the dress rehearsal. When I tried to discuss the blocking with him, he simply shook his head, sat down on a couch on the stage, sang his lines while staring at the conductor, and never made a move until the act was over. As for Miss Kirsten, our star, she arrived with her secretary the day *after* the dress rehearsal. We were already in Spokane, the first stop on our tour. There she walked through her part in the gymnasium of a convent. That night she gave a gorgeous performance.

Mr. Petrak was a great help to me during the week of preparation. He watched my work with the chorus and made some very practical suggestions. For instance, at Violetta's first entrance he would have

Dorothy Kirsten and Rudolf Petrak

them all inhale her perfume as she passed by. That detail immediately created a tangible aura for the character. You could sense that everyone present was falling under her spell. For Petrak, everything was "pictures, pictures," even when the resulting action wasn't totally logical. But I did gain a good sense of what works in the theater and what doesn't. I had rightly assumed that our star would do her own thing; so I concentrated on the chorus and all the little parts, Flora and all those barons, marquises, viscounts, and doctors, who are usually hard to tell apart, especially when the gentlemen are all wearing identical evening clothes. I tried to give each minor role an interesting profile. The most minor of all is the servant who has only one line: "*La cena è pronta*" ("Supper is served"). Unfortunately, he never did get it right. He would stand in the wings before his entrance, mouthing the words a thousand times. Then step on stage and freeze. Violetta's maid, Annina, was exceedingly conscientious. While the stagehands were setting up the last scene, during the intermission, she would dash about trying out the door as soon as it was in place, then the window shutters, then the drawers in the commode by the bed. At the same time she was singing the appropriate lines, cues and all, to the accompaniment of some hammering and a few muttered swear words. "What's the matter? Don't she know her part yet?" was the chief carpenter's comment.

The reviewers liked my work. I was clearly off to a good start. Beginner's luck!

The tour was fun. In the train, Miss Kirsten read movie magazines to keep up with her Hollywood friends. The rest of us got to know each other better. When we arrived in Vancouver, some of the singers worried about the effect of Canadian winter weather on their priceless throats. To protect her husband's, Mrs. Valdengo orchestrated quite a spectacle in the hotel lobby. Someone was recruited to keep clear the parking place directly in front of the hotel. The doorman and the bellhops were at their assigned posts. When her husband was ready to go to the theater, the taxi would be in place at the precisely prescribed time. A bellhop would be waiting to help him out of the elevator, another one at each of the glass doors, and the doorman would be poised to open the taxi door. Mrs. Valdengo stage managed a rehearsal of the whole porcedure, timed so that nothing could possibly go wrong. Then everyone held his breath. Finally the star baritone made his appearance, swathed in fur and mufflers; only his eyes and the tip of his nose were visible. He was hustled from bellhop to bellhop to doorman and into the taxi without more than a second's exposure to the icy outdoor air or a stray draft in the lobby.

What impressed me the most at the theater that evening were the stagehands. During the performance they took every opportunity to watch the singers from the wings, whereas in the U.S.A. the union stage crews couldn't have cared less and went out for a smoke or a card game between shifts. I observed the same phenomenon in Victoria the next season.

Back in San Francisco, more and more singers asked to coach with me. And the San Francisco Musical Club invited me to stage some operas for them. *Carmen* came first. The club members were all women, so they engaged guests as Don José and Escamillo. Their mezzo had learned her part all alone by listening to a complete recording of the opera. She herself didn't know a word of French. When she came to her first musical rehearsal I was appalled. I undertook to correct all the mangled language. She was a hard worker, and she wanted to get it right. So we spent hours going over every phrase, word by word, until it sounded about as acceptable as what often passed for French at the Met. Unfortunately, under the stress of performance, she forgot all the corrections and relapsed into all her old mistakes. Still, she put over her part, and our *Carmen* was a hit. So they asked me back for another opera. I chose Gluck's *Orpheus and Eurydice*, for its all female cast, so that no outside singers would have to be engaged; and I made a new English singing translation, trying for naturalness, understandability, and faithfulness to the rise and fall of the music. The score was arranged for string quartet. A soprano with an incredible upper range sang the famous flute solo in the Dance of the Blessed Spirits. The chorus ladies loved being Furies and raged up a storm in their fright wigs. *Faust* came next, at a legitimate downtown theater. Each production was more elaborate than the last.

Meanwhile, I had survived my second season with the Northwest Grand Opera, an unfinished season that came to an abrupt stop when the company went broke.

Suddenly out of a job, I returned to my home in San Francisco. As I walked in the door, I heard the phone ringing. It was a baritone whom I had coached in the *Winterreise* and *An die ferne Geliebte*. He was now a pupil in Lotte Lehmann's master classes at the Music Academy of the West. He said: "Beau, dash to the airport immediately and take the next plane to Santa Barbara. Mme. Lehmann's accompanist is leaving to go to Europe, and you have to get this job." I didn't even take off my winter coat. I did exactly what he told me to. Mme. Lehmann gave me a ten minute interview. Then she invited me to come and audit her classes.

By this time I had sold the boarding house to concentrate entirely on my new status as a professional opera coach and stage director. I pulled up stakes in San Francisco and moved into a little cabin high up in the mountains above Santa Barbara. The view was magnificent, and the spot was so isolated that I could run around stark naked when the weather was warm enough. It was a nice feeling. Once in a while a tarantula would pay me a visit. Otherwise I lived up there completely alone, studying music and reveling in the lush nature all around me.

Incidentally, that telephone call that had brought me to this Paradise was based on false information. Lehmann's accompanist was not leaving. There was no actual opening at all at the moment. But I sensed that destiny was at work, nevertheless. So I stayed on.

Twice a week I would go to the Music Academy to attend Mme. Lehmann's classes. They were a revelation to me. She would

Lotte Lehmann, inscription:
"For Beau, to remember the happy years of our work together, with much appreciation and affection"

demonstrate her interpretations of the lieder being studied, and would act out all the roles in the opera scenes. When she stepped in as Micaëla, for instance, she instantaneously transformed herself into a wholesome young girl from the country. Gray hair and wrinkles disappeared as if by magic. Or she would turn into the most hilarious Baron Ochs I had ever seen, snatching the wine away with a poisonous look of frustrated lechery when "Mariandel" was becoming too maudlin in her cups. I admired the elegantly off-hand way her sophisticated Tosca removed her gloves. Every character came to life in a uniquely believable way. The greatest privilege of all was to see her re-enact her world-famous Marschallin, with a thousand half-lights and nuances, "a tear in one eye and a twinkle in the other," as Strauss had prescribed. Nothing that she did ever had the stale whiff of "routine." Everything was freshly re-created, out of her mind and heart and soul, no matter how often she had performed it during a long career. Furthermore, she had the eloquence in her quaintly accented English to articulate her most subtle insights. Her students made fun of me because I used to write down all her comments in my scores. One day they presented me with a huge pencil, as a joke. But one of Lehmann's friends, who had dropped in for a visit, leaned over and whispered to me: "Someday you'll be very glad that you profited from her wisdom and experience;

someday you'll write a book about her." And thirty years later that is exactly what I did. My biography of Lotte Lehmann was published by Capra Press in 1988 in celebration of her centennial year.

One day Mme. Lehmann asked me to accompany her in two lieder. They were "*Auf ein altes Bild*" and "*Gebet*" by Hugo Wolf. The first was one of my favorites; the second was totally new to me, but it was not hard to play at sight, and a wave of inspiration seemed to guide my fingers. I was tremendously moved to find myself accompanying the greatest lieder singer I had ever heard. I felt a most reassuring rapport with her as we made music together. Evidently Lehmann was pleased with me, for she made a sudden, spontaneous decision. She announced that in the coming summer session she would have *three* separate master classes each week, instead of two. Jan Popper would continue to coach and accompany the opera class. Gwendolyn Koldofsky would continue to accompany the lieder class. And I would be the coach and accompanist for a third series, which would be devoted half to opera and half to lieder. I was overjoyed. I loved lieder just as much as I loved opera. And Lotte Lehmann was equally great in both.

So I spent my time preparing as much repertoire as I could, studying recordings, reading through opera scores and all seven volumes of Schubert songs, three of Schumann, four of Brahms, and all the many small volumes of Hugo Wolf.

My first assignment for the opera class was the scene between Hans Sachs and Eva from Act II of *Die Meistersinger*. I felt very privileged to be able to work on such a masterpiece. I threw myself into the preparation, played and sang the scene over and over until I felt that I understood the poetic and musical essence of every phrase. Then I coached the two young singers until they were able to sing everything faultlessly and by heart. Their voices were of course far too light for the roles they were singing; but the performance would be in a recital hall, not in an opera house, and with piano, not with an orchestra. The great day finally arrived:

my first public performance at a Lehmann master class. I started to play the opening music as I had rehearsed it a hundred times. "Louder, Beau, louder!" Mme. Lehmann called out. I started again, louder. "This is Wagner, not a Schumann *Lied*. Louder!" She sounded surprisingly impatient. I was devastated. During the course of the scene, Lehmann kept insisting on more volume. Must all of my exquisite details, the nuances I had come to love, be sacrificed to sheer loudness? I could hardly believe what was happening. When the intermission came, I slipped out into the garden, totally humiliated and demoralized. Fortunately for me, Gwendolyn Koldofsky came out and put her arm around me. "Don't let it get you down; we've all been through that at one time or another." I'll never forget her kindness. It took me a while to swallow my intense disappointment. I had so hoped to impress Lehmann with my interpretation of one of Wagner's great scenes! I'm afraid that I took out my resentment on an innocent baritone whose audition I was asked to accompany immediately after the master class. He had to bellow "*Nemico della patria*" over the loudest *fortissimo* I could pound out. When I was finally calm enough to analyze what had happened, a sense of perspective gradually returned. Obviously Lehmann, who had sung Wagner with all the greatest conductors in the world, whose teacher had actually sung the world premiere of the opera in question, must have missed something in the way I played that music. Who should know better than she how it was meant to sound? She expected a certain sonority, a certain deeper undercurrent, without which even the most refined nuances would count for nothing. It was a painful but valuable lesson. In retrospect, I am very grateful.

During that first summer I was one of three coaches. During the other three seasons of the next two years I was the only one. After that unfortunate experience with *Die Meistersinger*, I must have drastically improved, for Mme. Lehmann and I developed a warm, harmonious relationship as I gradually earned her trust. She saw that I worked well with her students.

Luba Tcheresky was one of Mme. Lehmann's most talented

pupils. She had a lovely *spinto* voice and lots of Russian temperament. Before one important sing, Lehmann had invited her to spend the night at her house, to get a good rest. Luba was surprised and touched when Mme. Lehmann herself served her breakfast in bed. Years later, when I was with the Zurich Opera, Luba came there to sing Donna Anna and Micaëla.

Another very gifted pupil was a baritone named Douglas Miller. His idol was Dietrich Fischer-Dieskau, and he took to lieder as a duck to water. I accompanied him in a recital that featured Brahms' "Four Serious Songs" and Ravel's "*Don Quichotte à Dulcinée.*"

But the star of the Lehmann classes was undoubtedly Grace Bumbry. She was on the threshold of a big career. Mme. Lehmann reveled in the glorious sound of her voice and was enormously proud of having discovered her and having released her innate talent.

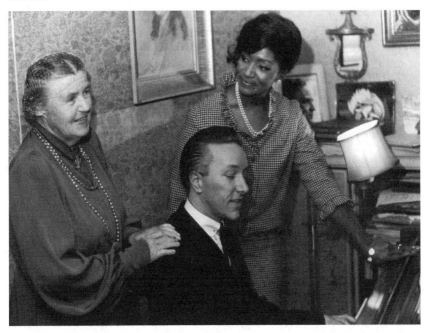

Lotte Lehmann coaching Grace Bumbry while I accompany the lesson

Lehmann did not teach voice as such, only interpretation. For vocal lessons her students were sent to Pasadena to work with Armand Tokatyan, a former tenor of the Metropolitan and an excellent voice teacher. His pupils all swore by him.

One of my odd jobs by then was to chauffeur the singers to and from their lessons with Mr. Tokatyan. One miserably rainy night I was driving them back to Santa Barbara. We were rounding a curve at a cautious speed when suddenly I saw a car speeding toward me in *my* lane. There was a mountain on one side and the ocean on the other. I had less than a second to choose. The next thing I knew I was spitting out teeth, half my lower lip was torn away, and the steering wheel was an outsize pretzel pressed against my jaw. The young baritone in the passenger seat was blinded by blood from his forehead. Grace Bumbry was unconscious on the floor of the back seat. My first thought was that the car might suddenly burst into flames, as I had seen in so many movies. I had somehow to get Grace out of that car, and in a hurry. I staggered out the door and found I could hardly walk. I slid around the side of the car and tried to drag Grace out, but I had no strength at all. Meanwhile a large crowd had materialized out of nowhere. Curious strangers stood around and gaped at me. Desperate, I begged for help. Finally a nurse appeared and we managed to get Grace out and all three of us into an ambulance. The baritone and Grace were soon released. She had only a small cut between her eyebrows. She had been sleeping in the back seat, and that had saved her. The scar is there to this day. As for me, my jaw was broken and had to grow a new hinge. And muscle trauma in my legs kept me on crutches for several weeks.

There is an uncanny aftermath to that story. Four years later I reported to a U.S. Navy hospital for a final physical before being discharged from the Naval Reserve. I told the examining physician about my accident in some detail. He took me to another room in which enlisted men were waiting for their discharge documents. He pointed to one poor wretch whose face looked like a patchwork quilt, all scars and the traces of stitches. "There's the man who hit you," said the doctor. He had checked the police report of our accident: that sailor had been doing ninety miles an hour. The whiskey bottle was still clutched in his hand when they found him. I was flabbergasted at the coincidence. Two ex-navy men, both to be discharged on the same day. And both examined by the same doctor!

A month after my car accident, I met my future wife. I was still on crutches, four front teeth were missing and my jaw was wired shut. She was absolutely gorgeous (still is, forty-seven years later). I

Evangeline Noël, my lovely wife

first laid eyes on her when she came to audition for Mme. Lehmann. I, as usual, was the accompanist. The first thing I heard Evangeline sing—omen of things to come!—was Grieg's "I Love You," in German, the nearest thing to a *Lied* that she knew by heart at the time. Then she let loose some glorious, full-blooded high notes in Santuzza's aria. Mme. Lehmann accepted her as a pupil. And I scheduled her coaching sessions as the last in the day, so that I could have as much time with her as possible, with no interruptions from other students arriving for their lessons. We worked on arias from *Lohengrin* and *Tosca*, then went for long strolls in the beautiful gardens that surrounded the Music Academy. We had met in January, became engaged in March, and were married in June. Our daughter Melody was born the following March, after her mother had performed a very pregnant Sieglinde under Mme. Lehmann's direction in Act I of *Die Walküre*. Her Siegmund was a young tenor with a powerful voice that had a timbre remarkably similar to

Our wedding, June 7, 1958

that of the great Lauritz Melchior. He was, however, rather green as an actor. During the introduction to Siegmund's "Spring Song," Lehmann asked him to lead Sieglinde toward the bearskin by the hearth. "But, Madame," he interrupted, "isn't this my big aria? You mean to say I have to sing and *act* at the same time?"

It was always an experience to be invited to the menagerie that Lotte Lehmann called home. Numerous dogs would beg for scraps at the table. We were encouraged to feed them, then to let them lick the plates. There were parrots, horses, all sorts of animals at one time or another. But my favorites were the talking Indian mynah birds. They seemed to know when their mistress was getting bored. They would say with uncanny clarity in a sing-song tone: "Time to go, time to go!" And we all had enough sense to take the hint.

Melody Glass, six weeks old

After our baby was born we left Santa Barbara's cozy Paradise for the real-life rigors of New York. Two years later, Lehmann invited me to come back and be her assistant in staging her final production, Beethoven's *Fidelio*. She was seventy-three at the time and troubled by arthritis. So she needed someone to move people around the stage while she worked on details of characterization with the individual singers. Besides helping with the stage direction, I was the chorus master and sang in the chorus myself. Evangeline participated in the master classes, making an outstanding impression in two scenes from *Die toten Augen* by Eugene d'Albert. One of Lehmann's greatest early successes had been the role of Myrtocle in that

The Prisoners' Chorus, *Fidelio*, I on the right

opera. She showed Evangeline how to mime the immensely moving climactic scene where her character blinds herself by staring at the sun during a long and powerful orchestral interlude, a *tour de force* as Lehmann performed it, and as Evangeline re-created it under her guidance.

**Off to Europe!**

Where to go next? A soprano, an opera coach / stage director, and a two-and-a-half-year-old child! Mme. Lehmann thought that Evangeline and I might both find work in Europe. She gave us each a fine letter of recommendation. So—without the slightest idea where we might find a job or how to go about looking for one—we booked a flight to Zurich. Why? Because Switzerland was at the hub of the European opera world (the "Iron Curtain" still cut off the East). Three of the four official Swiss languages are those that are indispensable to a career in opera. We would be within easy reach of Germany, Austria, Italy, and France, the surrounding countries in clockwise order.

While the soprano and the baby were in a hotel room recovering from jet lag, I went over to the opera house to see what might be playing. As I examined the poster by the stage door, I heard someone say: "Hi, Beau! What are you doing here in Switzerland?" It was Lotfi Mansouri, then a busy stage director, now famous also as the ex-head of the San Francisco Opera. As a tenor he had been one of Lehmann's students. I had coached him in a scene from *Der Freischütz* at the Music Academy. Now he was directing major productions in Zurich and teaching at the newly established International Opera Center there. "We could use you here," he said. He invited me to meet the musical director. I was asked to accompany a rehearsal of the "Presentation of the Silver Rose" from *Der Rosenkavalier*. Before I knew it, I had a job.

I was given a title—*"Studienleiter"*[*]—which at that opera school meant jack-of-all-trades. When Lotfi went off to stage an opera at Turin, say, I would take over his "opera dramatics" classes. When Hans-Willi Haeuslein, the musical director, was off in France conducting the *"Ring,"* I would teach his ensemble class. Meanwhile I was the coach for all the student singers (who then

included Gwyneth Jones and Felicia Weathers, both of whom went on to glory as international opera stars). I was responsible for the daily rehearsal schedules. And I staged scenes and one-act operas for public performances.

Stage Director Mansouri, Conductor Haeuslein,
and Jack-of-All-Trades Glass (on left)

At the Opera House—then still called the *Stadttheater* (Civic Theater)—I was Mansouri's assistant during rehearsals of *Le prophète*, starring James McCracken and Sandra Warfield, a husband-and-wife team who had already conquered Zurich in *Samson et Dalila* and *Il trovatore*, followed later by a joint triumph in *Aida*. Both were highly committed, exciting artists. At the *Prophète* rehearsals, I was impressed with the way Jimmy would "mark" vocally—that means he would sing softly and

---

[*] Later, I earned that title in its usual sense: I became the head of the coaching staff of the Zurich Opera, responsible for the musical preparation of all the operas, assigning the other coaches their particular tasks, and arranging all the rehearsal schedules.

perhaps an octave lower—but with full intensity of expression and diction. He never spared himself by "marking" the acting. By the time I arrived in Zurich he was already a famous Otello in Europe, and he soon made a sensation in the role at the Metropolitan Opera. He and Sandra brought distinction to every performance they gave.

James McCracken and Sandra Warfield
in *Samson et Dalila*

My six years of German hadn't taught me the musical terms or the theater language. But I soon learned the lingo, and the day-to-day back-stage routine of a German-speaking opera company. Before long I was a full-time member of the coaching staff of the Zurich Opera House. Thirty-five operas were in the repertoire at the time. Before my official duties began, I asked the General Music Director which of them I should prepare first. "All thirty-five," was the straight-forward answer.

My first assignment was *Night Flight* and *The Prisoner* by Luigi Dallapiccola. Then came an operetta, *The Opera Ball*. The cast liked my way with a waltz, so for several years I was drafted for operettas on the one hand and anything atonal on the other.

Evangeline and I were able to attend as many rehearsals and performances as our busy schedules would allow. We took Melody to see *Amahl and the Night Visitors*, her first opera, at Christmas time. I can still see her, leaning back in her box seat to drink from her milk bottle, her feet propped up on the railing. When she was three she saw *The Magic Flute*. She loved Papageno and practically everything else in the opera. But every time Sarastro opened his mouth to sing one of his slow, sublimely solemn arias she had to go to the ladies' room. And every time she had to go to the ladies' room, the door to the box would open and a shaft of light would fall onto the stage. Then the ladies with the imposing title of *Logenaufschliesserinnen*—"box-unlockers"— would scold me as only a Swiss *Logenaufschliesserin* can scold. It was the same story at her next opera, *Der Freischütz*: she was at the edge of her seat, drinking it all in, until Agathe had one of her *adagio* arias to sing. Then, of course, Melody would have to go to the bathroom.

We enrolled her in an English-speaking pre-school first. We were startled to hear from her that her classmate Alexander Hamilton had shown her his penis under the "nature table." That soon became a family joke. When it became clear that we would be staying in Switzerland for a while, we sent her to a Swiss Kindergarten. I used to drop her off there on my way to the Opera House. As we neared the neighborhood she would say: "Talk about opera, Daddy." I would start to tell her some story and before we knew it I would have driven far past the dreaded Kindergarten, where when seated she had to keep her knees pressed close together like a proper little lady or get a box on the ears.

Before long, she was in the children's chorus, sharing the stage with Birgit Nilsson in *Turandot* or playing a grasshopper in *The Cunning Little Vixen*. When she wasn't actually on stage during one of her performances, she would be exploring the opera house. I got used to hearing "Melody Glass, please come to the stage immediately!" over the intercom. Somehow, she always made her entrance just in time.

That is more than I can say for some of our adult performers. Our leading soubrette sang Valencienne in the premiere of *The Merry Widow* and in the first few performances. Then she went off to make a movie in Germany and another singer temporarily took over her role. While our first-cast Valencienne was away, a long, interpolated ballet was cut from the show, just before her big can-can number in Act III; but no one thought to tell her. She rejoined the cast. During the second intermission she had to go to the toilet. Just enough time, she thought, thanks to that long ballet. Imagine her reaction when she was ensconced in a stall and heard her entrance music over the intercom! She finished what she was doing as fast as decently possible and flew down the stairs to the stage. Fortunately the leading lady, who had sung the part of Valencienne in earlier productions, still remembered the lyrics and sang the song until our mortified soubrette showed up, panting, perspiring, and too weak in the knees for the high kicks in the final chorus.

Our leading operetta tenor was a very witty, urbane English aristocrat, Nigel Douglas. We worked together on several Benjamin Britten roles as well. Later he wrote some wonderful books on opera and great singers as well as the best operetta translations I have ever discovered.

Another of our divas completely missed a performance of *Die Fledermaus* in which she was to have sung the leading role of Rosalinda. It was a matinee. She thought it was to be in the evening. When she failed to show up in her dressing room, the frantic director called her home. The maid said she'd gone to the movies. No one had any idea *which* movie. Zurich has quite a few different cinemas. So the house librarian searched for the orchestra parts of as many operetta numbers as she could find and we improvised a variety show.

That soprano wasn't the only opera singer to get confused about performance dates. One evening our handsome leading tenor, Glade Peterson, was sitting down to dinner with his family when he got a call from the theater in Schaffhausen, a Swiss town on the German side of the Rhine, quite a long drive from Zurich. They had just started a performance of *Fidelio* and the tenor lead was not in the house. Could Glade take a taxi immediately and come to save the show? The famous *Heldentenor* Wolfgang Windgassen had been engaged to sing the role of Florestan as a guest artist. Florestan does not appear until the second act; so when *Herr*

*Kammersänger* Windgassen did not show up before the overture, they assumed he was simply exercising his prerogative as a star tenor and planning to arrive a bit late. They telephoned his home in Stuttgart to make sure he had left in time. He took the call and calmly told them that he had thought the performance was for the following evening. He couldn't possibly come from Stuttgart to Schaffhausen in time. Very sorry. So Glade got his taxi driver to break all speed records, reviewed Florestan's part with a flashlight in the back seat, was hustled into a costume on arrival at the theater, and saved the show.

I'm a fine one to talk! I, too, missed a performance. I was to play the organ in Wagner's *Die Meistersinger*. The opening scene takes place in a church in medieval Nuremberg. The first note of the organ is the last note of the overture. Because *Die Meistersinger* is a very long opera, the performances always began at 6:00 p.m. A colleague of mine asked me to take over a 4:00 o'clock rehearsal of *Rusalka* on the rehearsal stage next door. He promised to relieve me at a quarter to six. I became involved in *Rusalka* and forgot to keep an eye on the clock. My colleague was late. It was already 6:15! I dashed across the street and into the organ compartment, just above the orchestra pit. But of course the opening chorale—*a cappella* that evening—had long since come and gone. I had no choice but to wait for the conductor to return to his dressing room at intermission, make my abject apologies, face the music and take my punishment. Ferdinand Leitner, our General Music Director and the conductor of that performance was slumped in a chair with the most despondent look on his face I had ever seen. "In all my years as a conductor..." he began, in an ominously soft voice, each word squeezed out *lentissimo*. I swallowed hard. "Such a thing has never happened to me! I look up to give the cue and the organ loge is empty." I expected all hell to break out. Instead, after I had explained what had happened to me at the *Rusalka* rehearsal, he was silent for some moments, then— surprise!—praised me, if glumly, for not being one of those employees who are always looking at the clock. I assumed that I had been forgiven and backed out of his dressing room, my tail between my legs. One of life's darkest moments, for both of us.

Although my main duty was to coach solo singers in their assigned roles, I was pressed into service for many other tasks. In *Wozzeck*, for example, I had to climb high up on a pole, offstage, hang on with one hand, and, with a pocket flashlight in the other, conduct an onstage orchestra, by heart, in a piece with a constantly changing time signature, while keeping my eye on an offstage monitor to coordinate my beat with that of the conductor in the pit, where totally different music was being performed. Then I played a deliberately out-of-tune piano onstage and in costume for another tavern scene (also by heart, since I had to start in the dark, during a scene shift). And finally, I cued the little child who appears in the final scene and has to know when to sing "hopp-hopp!" as he rides his hobby horse, while the other children run off to see the corpse of his mother, who had been murdered by his father the night before.

In *Don Carlo, Tannhäuser, Lohengrin, Rosenkavalier*, and *The Love of Three Oranges* I had to conduct offstage instrumental groups, watching the monitor for the conductor's beat and then trying to anticipate that beat by a fraction of a second, so that the sound from backstage and the sound from the pit would reach the audience simultaneously.

In operas by Monteverdi, Handel, Mozart, and Rossini I accompanied the recitatives on the harpsichord. In *Tosca, Der Rosenkavalier, The Magic Flute* (Papageno's silver bells) I played the celeste. In *Ariadne auf Naxos* it was the harmonium. In *Cavalleria rusticana, Tosca, La forza del destino, Faust, Manon, Die Meistersinger*, and *Lohengrin* it was the organ. In *Parsifal* it was the big bells. In one modern opera, *Figaro Gets a Divorce*, by Giselher Klebe, I had to play the onstage piano in "Cherubino's night club," a cigarette dangling out of the corner of my mouth.

My most startling experience as a pit musician was in *Il re cervo* by Hans Werner Henze. The composer himself came to conduct us. At our first rehearsal in the pit I was seated at the harpsichord, confronted with a part full of tone clusters that called for the use of more than ten fingers at once (in other words, several fingers had to strike more than one key). I struck one particularly opaque chord in the bass. Henze stopped the rehearsal. "*Herr* Glass," he said, "the lowest note of that chord is C natural, not C sharp." I looked down at my hands. True, my left little finger was resting on C sharp. How in the world could he have heard that? On the harpsichord the whole cluster chord sounded like a tinny jangle, with no recognizable pitch at all. But Henze knew the sound he wanted. The C natural was important to him. What an ear!

At the premiere the lights in the pit suddenly went out during one of the scenes, whereas the onstage lighting was unaffected. All of us musicians simply improvised until the lights came on again. Henze blew us a kiss, delighted that we hadn't stopped the flow of the music. Later, we found out that no one in the audience had noticed the two or three minutes of music spontaneously improvised by a pit full of musicians in the dark. Thank God the opera was basically atonal to start with!

Sometimes I only had to give some cues, without playing or conducting anything myself. Act II of *The Girl of the Golden West* plays in a cabin high up in the Sierra mountains of California during a snowstorm. Every time someone opens the cabin door, we are supposed to hear the sound of the blizzard outside. The opening and closing of the door is precisely timed by the musical score. In one production, we had a tape recording of a simulated blizzard. My job was to give the musical cues to the technician operating the tape recorder. After each bit of blizzard I'd say "stop and rewind," then wait for the next cue. Seven performances went without a hitch. Just before the eighth, the technician said: "Mr. Glass, you really don't need to keep saying 'rewind'; there's always plenty of tape, enough for all the blizzard sequences and then some." So I didn't say "rewind." All of a sudden, during a particularly serious scene I heard uproarious laughter. What can have happened onstage? Why is the audience laughing? Then we heard the raucous voice of a comedian telling jokes—someone had recorded a comedy show on the second half of our blizzard tape! Of course the tape was turned off as soon as we realized what had happened. But it took a few seconds, and those seconds seemed an eternity!

I was often assigned to accompany auditions. For the most part I enjoyed doing it, and took pride in trying to play each accompaniment as beautifully as I could. Once, early on, a soprano decided to offer Brünnhilde's Immolation Scene. Since *Götterdämmerung* was not in our repertoire, and since Evangeline had not yet begun to study the heavier Wagner roles, I hadn't looked at the music in years. All would probably have gone well if the soprano had been allowed to start at the beginning. But instead they asked her to plunge in at the most hectic part, at "*Fliegt heim, ihr Raben!*" I took a hasty look at all those chromatics and black notes and panicked. That poor woman! I rushed unmercifully, and she was forced to race along with me. She barely had time to gulp for breath, and the frequent high notes were yelps and squeaks. She must have been as nervous at the start as I was, otherwise she would have found a way to slow me down, or would have simply stopped and asked for a more reasonable tempo.

When at another audition a young lady laid "*Lulu's Lied*" before me, I sensibly advised her to pick something else, since without a rehearsal we would both have made a hash of it. I'm happy to play even the most demanding accompaniment, if only there's the possibility of rehearsing it beforehand. Singers who plan to audition with non-standard arias or pieces with particularly difficult accompaniments should bring their own accompanists. Whenever possible, I tried to get leave to accompany Evangeline at her auditions. One of the few times I wasn't able to, an inept accompanist ruined her audition at Graz by making a mess of Amelia's big aria from *Un ballo in maschera*.

Once Evangeline had an audition date in Bremen. She flew the day before, to be well rested for her taxing arias. Since I had to work that day, I planned to fly on the day of the audition. Unfortunately the first plane I had to take was delayed. I missed a connection at Frankfurt. The only possibility was to fly to Hamburg and try to get a train from there. When that plane was also late and I missed the train, I had no choice but to hire a taxi to drive me from Hamburg to Bremen. If I couldn't arrive there in time for the five o'clock audition, all the expense of the round trip flight would have been for nothing. So the driver and I took off down the *Autobahn*. Wouldn't you know. He had a flat tire half way to Bremen. While he was changing to his spare, I cooled my heels by watching the biggest pigs I had ever seen. At first I thought they must be cows. But no, they were pigs all right. Monster pigs. If you ever want to see really huge pigs, try the *Autobahn* between Bremen and Hamburg. Believe it or not, I actually arrived at the stage door at one minute to five, and the audition took place as planned. Germans say that pigs bring luck!

Dusolina Giannini as Santuzza

A major artistic influence in our lives during our Zurich years was the great Italian-American soprano Dusolina Giannini, who had been invited by Herbert Graf to teach "stylistic interpretation" at the International Opera Center. One of my early duties was to accompany her master classes. Her remarkable musicality and stylistic versatility impressed me enormously, and I fell under the spell of her big, big personality. When she expressed an opinion or a judgment in class, she would turn to me and loudly ask: "Am I right, Beau?" I don't know what would have happened if I had ever had to answer: "Sorry, Mme. Giannini, but I don't think so." She was not accustomed to contradiction. In any case, I decided almost immediately that Evangeline should study with her. I knew that she would be a great inspiration. Giannini took an almost motherly interest in Evangeline after a few lessons, and often invited her to stay with her in Monte Carlo or Baden-Baden. Everywhere she went she was treated like a queen. Although she had sung with success at the Metropolitan Opera, her competition there had included Rosa Ponselle and Elisabeth Rethberg. She was far more famous in Europe than in America, having been a great favorite in Hamburg, Berlin, London, Salzburg, and Vienna, before—and again just after—World War II. Her roles included Aida, Tosca, Butterfly, Santuzza, Donna Anna, Rachel (in *La juive*), Leonora (in *Forza*), and Carmen.

In 1944 she had taken the New York City Opera under her wing and agreed to sing Tosca in their opening performance. Sometime after that Dorothy Kirsten was assigned to the title role in *Traviata*; when she arrived she asked for directions to the star dressing room. Dusolina said: "Miss Kirsten, there are no stars at the City Center—and if there *were* one, it would be *Giannini!*" (She always referred to herself that way, in the third person!)

When she was singing Donna Anna opposite Ezio Pinza at the Salzburg Festival, Pinza's wife buttonholed her in an elevator and begged her to keep an eye on her husband, who was notoriously unfaithful, a real Don Giovanni offstage as well as on. Dusolina's response: "*Signora*, you can look after your **own** *gallo* [= rooster]!"

Her self-confidence was gigantic. One day Federico Fellini was staying at the same hotel. Though they had not been introduced, Giannini barged over to him and started to scold him for the indecency and immorality of one of his films. He took the barrage like a man. I wonder if he had a clue who she was. Evangeline was an eye-witness of the encounter.

We were both in awe of her artistry and the sense of authority and inevitability in her interpretations. Like Lotte Lehmann, she seemed to become each of the characters she was portraying. One day, when Evangeline was preparing the role of Butterfly with her, Dusolina demonstrated how she herself had sung "*Un bel dì*." Neither of us shall ever forget it. Without a single gesture she had us absolutely mesmerized by vocal inflection and confident posture alone. Through her we could actually "see" Pinkerton's ship arriving and all the action that followed. But she hardly moved a muscle. It was a *tour de force*. It proved to me that a great operatic artist can stand absolutely motionless and still project immense intensity. Astrid Varnay also had that gift. It was riveting. Unfortunately we had never had the chance to see Giannini on the stage, though I had been collecting her recordings ever since I was a boy.

She had started singing opera as a child. Her father, Ferruccio Giannini (who had been the first to sing Massenet's Des Grieux in America) was her first teacher. He had his own little opera stage in Philadelphia. Barely in her teens, she had sung Azucena to his Manrico, Santuzza to his Turiddu. Then she was sent to New York to study with Marcella Sembrich, the versatile coloratura who had been a great favorite at the Met since its very first season. Beside giving Dusolina an enviable technique, Sembrich also saw to it that her pupil's career would be properly launched. Before long she was singing Aida opposite Aureliano Pertile and an otherwise all-Italian cast in a famous recording of the opera. Her colleagues, all active at La Scala, resented that an American who had not yet made her mark in Italy should have been given the title role. They strongly suspected some involvement of the mafia.

When she sang Donna Anna at Salzburg, later, Bruno Walter described her singing as "molten lava."

Giannini was very attached to her mother, who accompanied her all over the world during her career, even though that meant leaving a husband, two sons, and another daughter back home. When Dusolina was singing the treacherous off-stage high B in the third act of *Butterfly*, Mamma would be holding her hand in the wings. Cio-Cio-San was her most exhausting role. She always spent the following day in bed. Tosca, in contrast, was a snap. She could give free rein to her fiery temperament and give God a piece of her mind.

She was magnetic, she was intense, she would hold Evangeline's hand, look into her eyes, and swallow her whole. She would say: "Don't listen to coaches! Don't listen to husbands! Giannini will give you everything you need to know!" Her own husband, a Christian Science practitioner, was the ideal consort for a prima donna, very self-effacing, unruffled, a serene, calming presence, so considerate that he chose a night when she was having dinner with us to die. We found the body when we brought her back to her hotel room. Evangeline spent the night with her and never left her side during the next two weeks.

Working with Mme. Giannini gave Evangeline new inspiration. Soon she was ready for the next chapter of her career. Dr. Herbert Graf asked her to sing Musetta in *La bohème* at the Grand Théatre of Geneva. Evangeline felt a great rapport with Nello Santi, who conducted the first four performances. When Maestro Santi broke his leg, Lamberto Gardelli took over the rest of the run. Dr. Graf told Evangeline that she was the best Musetta he had ever seen. She later sang the role also at the Zurich Opera.

Evangeline Noël as Musetta

76

Evangeline as the Marschallin

Because Evangeline was always studying new roles and often had to be away for guest engagements or auditions, it was essential that we have someone living with us who could take care of our little daughter and keep house for us. Over the years we had seven, and a colorful lot they were. The first was an aging Polish refugee who broke down every holiday, scarred by the past. The second—the only good one and one of our best friends to this day—eloped with a slick-talking young man who turned out to have another wife and several kids in Germany. He abandoned our girl in Holland, with a new-born baby. She returned to Zurich and started to work for an actress who lived just across the hall from us. Since the actress needed peace and quiet, the baby came to live with us. When she was old enough to talk, she always called me "Daddy." I'm sure that everyone in that house thought I was really the father. Our third maid was a very young German who was picked up by the police and shipped back home soon after she had started to work for us. We never did find out the reason. The fourth wore a towering "beehive" hairdo and would leave brooms and dustpans lying around in strategic places to give the impression that she had at least contemplated doing some housework. Our most memorable experience with her was during a flight from Salzburg to Vienna. It was her first time on a plane. The poor girl became literally paralyzed with fear, every muscle in a spasm, a horrifying grimace on her face, her fingers splayed and extended to their utmost stretch. She couldn't utter a sound. We had never seen anything like it. I had to spend our entire time in Vienna making arrangements for her to return to Zurich by train. Next came a German woman who had a grown-up son and a drinking problem. The son came to spend New Year's Eve with his mother at our house. The next day we asked her to read a story to our daughter. "Oh Mr. Glass, I'm just too tired!" —"You can sit in the rocking chair." —"I'm too tired to do anything..." Well, that was the end of her. We found two dozen *Schnaps* bottles under her bed. The sixth started by calling Melody her "little sister"; ended by fighting with her and slapping her black and blue. The last was an English nanny. When Evangeline showed her her room, she announced that when she worked for the Honorable Lady So-and-so, her bed was always made for her. Evangeline wondered whom she expected to do it here. Children made her nervous; whenever things got a bit too lively she would run to her room for a tranquilizer. Poor Melody! And poor Evangeline! When she was away, singing a guest engagement somewhere, there was sure to be a crisis back home.

Opera brought us most of our closest Swiss friends. Astrid and Carmen Nussbaumer happened to share a box with us one night; our enthusiastic sharing of impressions was the beginning of a long, precious friendship. Soon after that first evening together, we met their brother Harry, a distinguished scientist whose specialty is the study of the sun, but whose passions include opera and ballet. The Nussbaumers have remained dear friends, along with Harry's lovely wife Elfried.

The most extraordinary friend of all was Erna Mende. She was close to eighty when we first met her, well into her nineties when she died. She never missed an opening night. Her seat was always in the front row, and that's where we always preferred to be, so it wasn't long after our arrival in Zurich that we first struck up a conversation. And soon she became *"Tanti"* ("Auntie") to us. Her father had been a famous homeopathic physician. Letters would arrive addressed simply "Dr. Mende, Zurich," or even "Dr. Mende, over the Gotthard Pass." Russian grand dukes, the Queen of Romania, and Mattia Battistini, prince of baritones, were among his clients. As a young girl her family had attended the Bayreuth Festival every summer. They would spend the mornings studying the scores, discussing the stories, and learning the "leading motives." They knew all the singers personally. Soon Erna developed into a very beautiful young lady and a singer herself. She showed us a gorgeous photo of her as "the Beautiful Galatea" in Franz von Suppé's operetta, which she had sung at the Zurich Opera before World War I. The infante of Spain fell madly in love with her (as we learned from her relatives at her funeral). In any case, she gave us some beautiful cushions that had been handmade for her by the infanta. Well into her nineties she loved to travel, and we made many trips together. When we arrived to pick her up she would be in a tizzy, ordering a flustered helper about, as she supervised the packing of half a dozen bags, the green one with her favorite car pillow, the blue one with a spare pair of walking shoes, the yellow with extra sweaters or scarves, the black with maps and addresses, the red with the special Milanese cookies she loved, and the gold one full of chocolate. Woe to the companion who packed an item in the wrong bag! A very smelly cocker spaniel named Nana often had to come along too, until the poor dog died of old age. Tanti loved to take advantage of every possible excuse for a celebration, the arrival of the new asparagus crop, the new grape juice or apple cider—in Switzerland every food or drink has its season—or the tulips on an island in the Rhine. When Evangeline accompanied her on an excursion to Bayreuth, they partied at the "*Eule*" after an exciting performance of *Die Meistersinger*, Tanti enjoying a cigar along with her beer as she reminisced about the festivals of long-ago summers. Her annual Christmas tree was only slightly less tall than the one in Rockefeller Plaza. She decorated it with tangerines and one hundred orange candles. Nearby was a long pole with a wet sponge at the far end. She and Evangeline would sit on a couch and admire the tree for hours. The candles would burn lower and lower, until I was afraid the dry branches would catch fire. But every time I went to put out one of the guttering flames, Tanti and Evangeline would moan and groan piteously, begging me to wait just a little bit longer.

Tanti had a splendid old house in town and a delightful vacation retreat a half hour away, on the lake, with a charming garden and a marvelous view of distant mountains. We eventually bought that second house. After her death, it became our home for our last four years in Switzerland.

Before that move, we had lived for fourteen years in an apartment house. Among our neighbors there, there was a certain very quiet Mr. Helmisch. For years he and I would nod to each other in the hall and mumble "Good morning" to each other. One day he came up to me and told me with some pride that he had just bought a subscription to the opera. Poor Mr. Helmisch! It was just his luck that the Zurich Opera House had scheduled not one but *three* contemporary atonal operas that season, and one of them happened to be the first performance on his subscription series. I was walking along the corridor outside the boxes just as the first act ended. Right in front of me, the door to a box flew open with a bang. There was Mr. Helmisch, ready to explode with rage. His face was purple, the veins were bulging out. I thought he might be on the verge of apoplexy. "*Das ist ja eine Katastrophe!*" he shrieked, "That is a catastrophe!" as he ran for the nearest exit. From that day onward he never spoke a single word to me. No more "*Guten Morgen, Herr Glass.*" In his mind I was a representative of that crazy opera house that his tax money was being squandered to support. I'm sure that he never forgave me.

Those contemporary operas were invariably thrown at *me*, since none of my more senior colleagues wanted anything to do with them. When you first struggle with the score you wonder how in the world anyone is going to learn that stuff. The more you work at it, the more you find yourself beginning to like a phrase here, a pattern there, a combination of notes somewhere else. That's the insidious part of it. Because the audience doesn't get that chance. They hear the piece once and don't generally come back for a second helping. In my opinion, every work of art should at least make some positive impression on first acquaintance. Later one can explore the subtle hidden beauties. In any case, I can still see all those singers lined up in the wings with their pitch pipes, hoping to keep their starting pitch in mind as they make their entrances. They knew enough not to count on taking the pitch from the cues provided by their colleagues on stage, who were just as unsure of the notes as they were (or, for that matter, from the instruments in the pit).

One of my most gratifying assignments was the musical preparation of Handel's *Agrippina*. The Zurich Opera borrowed beautiful sets designed by Jean-Pierre Ponnelle for the Munich National Theater. Lisa della Casa, a glamorous Swiss soprano and a major international star, was engaged to sing the title role. The conduc-

Lisa della Casa and Marga Schiml in *Agrippina*

tor, Alberto Erede, had a flattering confidence in me. He gave me *carte blanche* for the musical preparation. My job was to create the ornaments, cadenzas, and *da capo* variants that the singers of the Baroque era were expected to improvise. I also arranged an accompaniment for the recitatives, playing the harpsichord myself, supported by cello and double bass, with an occasional use of the harp or the guitar. The orchestral material we received was in a shocking condition; besides innumerable errors and misprints, there were many cuts and transpositions that had been made for other productions. Some parts had been altered or obliterated entirely. Fortunately I had an eighteenth century edition of the full score, and could make the necessary corrections, with much cutting and pasting. It was an enormous lot of work, but I found it very enjoyable, even though I overheard one of the Swiss violinists say to another just before the first orchestra rehearsal: "today we'll be playing Handel *all'americana.*" That took the wind out of my sails for a moment or two. It reminded me rather painfully that many Europeans look down on us Americans as culturally illiterate.

Miss della Casa invited me to come to her castle on the Rhine to coach her in her part. The historical castle, Gottlieben, had once housed John Huss. Napoleon had torn down one wall to create a garden. Of course, Evangeline wanted to have a peek at the castle, at least from outside, so she accompanied me on the drive from Zurich. When we arrived at the castle gate, she got out of the car and agreed to wait for me at the nearby inn. The gate was opened by a pretty barefoot girl, and I drove up to the main entrance. I was met there by Miss della Casa and we had a very pleasant, productive rehearsal. I was only too happy to adjust the variants in her arias according to her very appropriate suggestions. After the rehearsal, she invited me to lunch. I thanked her, but told her that someone was waiting for me elsewhere. Her daughter, the pretty girl who had opened the gate for me, was sent to fetch Evangeline from the inn and we both had the unexpected treat of dining with Miss della Casa and her genial husband on a balcony overlooking the Rhine. Evangeline and I are confirmed vegetarians, but our hosts had little individual cheese pies, a Swiss specialty, already warmed up for us.

Rehearsals at the Zurich Opera always began with an obligatory routine. No matter how many people were present—cast, conductor, stage director, coach-accompanist, stage manager, prompter, lighting designer, prop man, whatever—one had to greet by name and shake hands with every single person there. Every time a new arrival entered the room, the rehearsal had to stop and the entire procedure had to take place anew. If one of us would forget, or simply be reluctant to interrupt everyone's concentration, then someone would be sure to come over and remind us that we hadn't yet greeted one another *comme il faut*. "*Herr Glass, wir haben einander noch nicht richtig begrüßt!*"—"We haven't properly greeted each other"—Oh dear, what a *faux pas*!

One lesson I learned early on: never ask anyone how they are. They may take the time to tell you. Every day I would pass a certain cleaning woman on my way to some rehearsal. "*Grüß Gott, Frau Sigrist,*" I would say. "*Grüss Gott, Herr Glass,*" would come back, all nice and friendly. One day, still in a hurry as usual, I made the big mistake. "*Wie geht es Ihnen?*" ("How are you?") —"Well, Mr. Glass, my back is killing me, my arthritis is acting up, I have a pain in my knee, a headache, and I think I'm coming down with a cold. My son is driving me into an early grave. He spends my money faster than I can make it. He just bought two new suits that I can't afford. I can't do anything with him. And he drinks, Mr. Glass! Oh, if you only knew..." etc., etc., etc.! Poor dear, my heart went out to her; but, try as I might, I couldn't seem to convey to her in any reasonably polite way that I had to be somewhere else and soon. So after that I went back to "*Grüß Gott, Frau Sigrist.*"

For all that European formality, sometimes there were lapses. Guest artists expected to be officially greeted on their arrival, understandably. I can still see the grim look on Birgit Nilsson's face as she slowly mounted the steps to our rehearsal stage. "I had to find this place by myself," she muttered. "No one from the Direction bothered to meet me."

Glamorous guest stars were always a treat for us, a chance to work with some of the most famous singers in the world. José Carreras and Teresa Berganza came to sing in our production of *Werther*. The role of Charlotte was new to Miss Berganza. I had the enormous pleasure of coaching her in the part. She took care to refine every nuance and graciously accepted every suggestion. (Later she also studied Schumann's *Frauenliebe* Cycle with me.) Mr. Carreras, on the other hand, had already sung his role elsewhere. When I pointed out to him that he was mispronouncing all

Teresa Berganza and José Carreras in the final scene of *Werther*, Zurich Opera

the French words that called for a "closed" e (*aigu*), and that it often altered the meaning, he seemed utterly unconcerned. He had sung it that way with success; why should he bother to change anything?

Another guest artist who, like Teresa Berganza, took pains to master the sounds of the French language was Ruggero Raimondi, who came to us to sing his first Don Quichotte. He had one problem. In the dialect of Bologna, his original home town, it seems that there is some confusion between the sounds of "s" and "sh." In those days, even when he sang Italian roles, one could sometimes hear an "sh" creep into a word that called for an "s." Now Don Quichotte often has to call to his companion Sancho Panza and ask for his lance. In Raimondi's then-current version of French that oft-recurring phrase, "*Sancho, ma lance!*" would come out in several variants, as, for instance "*Chancho, ma lanche!*" or "*Sanso, ma lance!*" At the dress rehearsals and at every performance I would have a notebook with me in my box and make note of his errors. In the interval or after the performance I would give him the list. He was very conscientious and made a real effort to

Ruggero Raimondi (with "lanche")
as Don Quichotte, Zurich Opera

correct all the little mispronunciations. Even then, in his first production, he was a wonderfully moving and totally convincing Don Quichotte. By the time he had finished the run with us, his French was excellent, and he is now *the* leading interpreter of the role, which has been revived for him in many theaters.

One of my favorites among the great stars who came to sing at the Zurich Opera was Astrid Varnay. The unbelievable intensity of her Isolde kept us riveted to our front row seats, scarcely daring or able to breathe. Her Kundry was miraculous. By the 1960s she was no longer the slim young woman I had admired years before at the Met. But in the second act, by some secret alchemy, she created an aura of seductive beauty through the way she moved, the way she held her face to the light, not to mention the honeyed, caressing tones in her voice. Then, when the convulsive laughter began to rise up from deep inside her, every note that Wagner scored for that passage could have been conceived especially to underscore her phenomenal acting. It is a sad loss to the world that no videotape exists to preserve her infinitely subtle, inspired interpretation.

I had admired Cesare Siepi's definitive Don Giovanni at the San Francisco Opera and at the Met. Now here he was at my home theater, and I was accompanying his rehearsals! He was engaged to sing the first three performances. The trapdoor operator sabotaged all three. At the first, Mr. Siepi stood on the right spot and waited to be taken down to hell. Nothing happened. Finally he had to walk offstage. He couldn't very well have stayed there while Leporello was telling the rest of the cast that he'd gone to his just reward. At the second performance the trapdoor operator was so nervous that he started the descent far too early. Siepi had to

Cesare Siepi as Don Giovanni

leap in, long before the proper cue, and sing his last line from the underworld. By the third evening everyone was tense. The stressed-out operator pulled the wrong rope, or the right rope the wrong way. Before the mistake could be corrected, Don Giovanni started to ascend to heaven—much to the all-too-earthy delight of our audience.

After Mr. Siepi's departure, our house baritone took over as Don Giovanni. He was also singing the role in Cologne during the same period. Our conductor, Ferdinand Leitner, asked for lots of appoggiaturas. The conductor in Cologne, István Kertész, despised them. Our baritone was alternating performances, sometimes two or three times a week, between the two houses. He constantly had to remember which version he was supposed to be singing, a very confusing problem, since the recitatives, especially, sound almost totally different—same words, another melody. Woe to him if he inadvertently sang a banished appoggiatura in Cologne, or omitted a prescribed one in Zurich! Even if the conductor didn't fume, the colleagues on stage would be thrown off by unfamiliar-sounding cues. That is a problem for all singers who are learning Mozart roles, and for the coaches who are trying to help them. Some conductors, like Sir Charles Mackerras, whom I had the privilege of assisting at Aix, expect a cadenza if there is a *fermata* in the score, and compose elaborate variations for the singer when a melody is repeated. On the other hand, there is not a single appoggiatura, even at the end of a recitative, in the historically famous recordings of *Don Giovanni* and *Così fan tutte* that Fritz Busch conducted at Glyndebourne in the 1930s. Erich Leinsdorf's recording that features Cesare Siepi, along with Birgit Nilsson and Leontyne Price, is an interesting case: the three women all sing a generous number of appoggiaturas, the four men almost none at all. By now modern scholarship has well established that 18th- and early 19th-century composers respected the tradition of adding unwritten appoggiaturas, cadenzas, and variations. Those expressive "ornaments" were fully expected. Appoggiaturas are not only authentic, the accented dissonances add a richer expressiveness to words and music. Among conductors, Sir Charles Mackerras was one of the pioneers. He was kind enough to share with me a vast amount of his research.

Zurich was a truly international house. We had Swedes, Finns, Dutch, Welsh, Scots, Greeks, Poles, Czechs, Hungarians, Romanians, and Russians among our leading singers. We even had a spy! She was a glamorous red-haired Romanian. The Swiss caught her taking photos of one of their military installations. That very same day she was hustled onto a plane and shipped back to Bucharest.

The chorus, too, was a mini-UN. One of my amusing jobs was to teach them to sing American Southern dialect in *Porgy and Bess*, which we performed in English. The opera was a sensational success, performed more often than any ten others during two seasons. Even when a touring company presented *Porgy* in competition with us, both companies played to sold-out houses.

As a stage director myself, I was always interested in observing the work of the well-known directors who were engaged to stage our productions. One of the most famous at that time was Günther Rennert. He came to direct Hindemith's opera *Cardillac*. There is one scene in which a woman is in bed with her lover. At the first rehearsal of that segment *Herr* Rennert seemed to be getting quite excited. He crouched near the bed and kept yelling: "*Arbeiten Sie, Herr Ek, arrrbeiten Sie!*" ("Work at it, Mr. Ek, *work* at it!") at the poor, embarrassed tenor who was doing his best to simulate a hot love scene that was never ever sizzling enough for the director. In the performance, the very attractive mezzo-soprano upon whom our tenor was "working" had to play the scene with a bare bosom, except for a scrap of black lace that was a grudging concession to her modesty. I can still hear those rolled, uvular Rs and the irritable, greedy impatience of that "*arrrbeiten Sie!*"

Accompanying the rehearsals of Jean-Pierre Ponnelle was a great learning experience for me. In Haydn's "*La fedeltà premiata,*" he was guided by the shifting musical patterns of the ensembles in his imaginative visual recreation. Whenever the voices combined in a different configuration, Ponnelle found a convincing motivation for a corresponding action on stage. "Deeds of music were made visible," to paraphrase Wagner's ideal.

Another director came to us from the Zurich *Schauspielhaus*, the theater for spoken drama that had earned a great reputation during the Nazi era, thanks to the many fine actors who had fled the German *Reich* and found refuge in Switzerland. The director to whom I am referring was engaged to stage Massenet's *Manon* but showed up thinking it was to be Puccini's version. At the first rehearsal he was utterly baffled to hear a totally different opening scene. He hated it, calling it a "*Musical-grusical*" ("ghastly musical"), but he was stuck with it. So he began to find motivations for the characters. He had one all-purpose phrase to express intense emotion. When the young Chevalier des Grieux first sees the lovely heroine of the opera his reaction is: "*Oooh du grooosse Scheisse!*" (Forgive me, dear reader, but that means "Oh you big shit!" The director always said it with an expression of over-whelming wonder.) Then Manon notices the handsome stranger who is admiring her, and of course she says to herself: "*Oh du grosse Scheisse!*" Whatever the situation, all the characters were supposed to be thinking: "*Oh du grosse Scheisse!*" at the moment of peak emotion. Finally the leading lady had enough of that. She said: "I don't think Manon is thinking that at all—and I'm thoroughly tired of hearing that crude obscenity as if it were some great artistic inspiration." That cleansed the air, at least.

My years in Zurich coincided with the emerging trend to hire stage directors from the theater or the movies, rather than those who specialized in opera. The results were all too often anti-musical. The new breed of directors would work from the libretto, not from the score. If a cast member or the conductor would call their attention to what the music seemed to be expressing, the exasperating answer was invariably something like this: "Oh, it's much more interesting to act *against* the music rather than with it; it's better to set up a dramatic counterpoint." Baloney! Music has its own language and the glory of opera is the expressive power of music. The music tells us when to move, when to be still, what to feel. The great composers have visualized the dramatic action in their music. When tin-eared stage directors are insensitive to what the music is telling us, then "*gegen die Musik*" ("against the music") makes a convenient excuse.

Each conductor had an individual approach. Ferdinand Leitner, for instance, would meet with the coaches early on and brief us with his special wishes regarding appoggiaturas, etc. There would be an ensemble rehearsal with the singers, once they had learned their roles. Then we wouldn't see him again until the orchestra was in the pit. Nello Santi, on the other hand, rarely missed a single staging rehearsal. He was always there, in absolute control of the flow of the music, accustoming the singers to his beat, even conducting the cadenzas. Armin Jordan, one of my favorites, had the good sense to solicit suggestions from the coaches, since he recognized that they had spent long weeks preparing the singers, noticing their strengths and weaknesses, and delving into the hidden beauties of the score as day by day their acquaintance with it deepened. He was very receptive to whatever insights we may have gleaned along the way.

In America I had become used to "instant opera." Few if any orchestra rehearsals for the singers, often only two or three days in which to block all the staging, maybe a week of rehearsals before the first performance. Sometimes the leading lady would show up the day of the dress rehearsal, sometimes—as in my first *Traviata*—the day after. While I was with the New York City Opera one young lady had to make her debut as Musetta after only one rehearsal with the Alcindoro and none at all with her Marcello. I already mentioned, above, the production of *Pagliacci* in which only the first act was rehearsed by the stage director, who left my wife, the Nedda, and her colleagues to improvise the entire second act without his dubious guidance. I'd like to quote here from a letter that the well-loved movie-star soprano Jeanette MacDonald sent to Lotte Lehmann after Miss MacDonald's performance in Cincinnati of Marguerite, a role that she had coached with Lehmann in illuminating detail.

> The way these things are thrown together is appalling. There was at no time any attempt to rehearse the stage business— not a sign of a prop. When I asked the (so-called) stage director what the sets would look like, and where the benches, doors, etc., would be, it was as though I had committed a *faux pas*. The truth of the matter was that he didn't know himself, and it wasn't until the actual performance (before each act) that I was able to find out and look the situation over. I might add that I even took the liberty of placing the furniture for my own convenience! Actors and actresses had no idea which side of the stage they were going to be on until the time arrived. The Church scene of "Faust" was an unholy mess, with the chorus picking up the wrong cue for the prayer, which meant that the orchestra and I were doing one thing and they were singing another. It was

pretty ghastly, to say nothing of being very confusing to me, and, since they were singing so loud, I had to stop to be sure that I was with the orchestra. (You know how difficult it is frequently to hear the orchestra.) The prompter had left his box in order to play the organ back-stage, and the stage manager was in his place. He, in turn, knew no more about prompting than little Mousie [*Lehmann's dog*]. So, all in all, the effect must have been like a cat and dog fight. Ultimately, however, the chorus, realizing I had stopped singing, took their cue and stopped also. I then proceeded with the orchestra alone. At any rate I won!

Well, in European opera houses—at least in the German-speaking countries—a new production gets a month of daily stage rehearsals, several rehearsals with the orchestra in the pit before the *two* dress rehearsals with orchestra that follow a dress rehearsal with piano. Before the first staging rehearsal, the house singers will have been coached for at least a month in the music and words of their roles. Preparation is unhurried and thorough. The conductor is often present at the staging rehearsals, to accustom the singers to watching the baton without seeming to, and to settle any disagreements about tempo. What luxury! And the seasons are generally forty-six weeks long, with a six-week paid vacation.

Oh, those vacations! It was so much fun to plan them, to pick out the country we wanted to visit and to study the history of each place! We made a special point of visiting sites that played a part in opera. In Venice, for instance, we pictured Act I of *La Gioconda* taking place in the courtyard of the Doge's Palace, and Act III in the beautiful Ca' d'oro. In Rome

Evangeline and I doing research for
*La Gioconda*

we visited the three settings of *Tosca*, along with all the other obligatory sights. Verona offered "Juliet's balcony, Romeo's house, and Juliet's grave," thanks to a shrewd tourist industry there. And in Mantua we could visit an authentic ducal palace, even if the original setting of *Rigoletto* was supposed to be the court of Francis I in France (of course we eventually had to see *his* castle Fontainebleau too).

In Spain we thought of *Don Carlo* at the Escorial, where life-sized golden statues of Philip II and his four wives face the emperor Charles V (*Ernani*'s Don Carlo) on opposite sides of the main altar. Philip, eventually too lame with gout to walk, had a hole made in the wall by his bed, so that he could hear mass in the cathedral adjoining his room. In Saragossa we saw the "Troubadour's Tower" in the castle of Aljafería, setting of several scenes in *Il trovatore*. Seville, of course, is one of the most popular locations for operatic plots. Carmen's cigarette factory, at least, is still there. We visited Montserrat, thinking of *Parsifal*. In the cathedral of Valencia I noticed a long line of people waiting at a side chapel. I wanted to investigate, but Evangeline and Melody had already left the building, and by the time I found them it was time to move on. Imagine my chagrin when I later read in the guide book that one of the attractions of Valencia is the "Holy Grail" in that side chapel I had missed!

In Scotland we searched for traces of Macbeth at Glamis Castle, Cawdor, and Inverness, and visited all the places associated with Mary Stuart. In France it was Joan of Arc, from her father's farmhouse at Domremy, via the ruins of Chinon, to the cathedral of Rheims, the tower in Rouen where she had been imprisoned, and the spot on the public square where she was burned at the stake. We fell in love with Chenonceaux, the setting for Act II of *Les Huguenots* and its ballet of bathing beauties. We were moved by the Conciergerie, the prison where Marie Antoinette had waited for the guillotine. We were shown a little note that the doomed queen had tried to smuggle out. Since all writing implements had been taken from her, she pricked out the message with a pin.

Though André Chénier's prison was St. Lazare, we could easily imagine the atmosphere there.

As a died-in-the-wool Wagnerian, I had to visit Drachenfels, said to be the site of Siegfried's famous battle with the dragon, and Xanten on the Rhine, where he was born, according to the *Niebelungenlied*, one of Wagner's sources. Evangeline and I spent hours at the ruins of Tintagel Castle in Cornwall. In Gottfried von Strassburg's version of the legend, that was King Marke's castle. Perched on a rock overlooking the sea, we listened to a tape recording of *Tristan und Isolde* and soaked up the potent atmosphere. We even discovered the little brook that Isolde hears while Brangäne is listening to Melot's hunting horns. We paid our respects at Tristan's grave stone, a sixth-century monolith standing alone in a field. According to the inscription, "Drustan" seems to have been the *son*, not the nephew of King Marke.

Tristan's gravestone

As we were leaving Tintagel, we happened to notice that the souvenir stands were all featuring "pixies," apparently the local specialty. So we bought one, innocently enough. That turned out to have been a dangerous mistake. Almost instantaneously the weather—which had been balmy—changed to a downpour. The following morning we woke up, looked out the window of our lodgings, and saw absolutely nothing but an opaque sheet of rain. So we decided to stay in our room, write a few postcards, and read about the local attractions we would be missing. The children, Melody and a younger friend from Switzerland who was making the trip with us, were bitterly disappointed; they had been looking forward to patting all the farm animals that belonged to the house. So we tried to persuade them to spend the rainy day writing down their impressions of the places they had visited. We had enough food with us, we wouldn't need to go out into the storm—or so we thought. Our landlady would have none of that. She was very proud of her 16th-century "manor house." Queen Elizabeth I had slept there on one of her famous "royal progresses" (her coat-of-arms had been painted above the living room couch to prove it).

So, although we had booked three nights with her, she insisted that we leave the house right after breakfast and stay away until the evening. That, she said, was a rule in English bed-and-breakfast establishments. I told her we would make our own beds and wouldn't stir from our room or cause her any trouble at all. She objected that we would undoubtedly be using her toilet paper and flushing too often. She was adamant. So we had no choice. Evangeline and I piled the children into our VW bug and we slowly drove out into the deluge. Sight-seeing was obviously out. We decided to head for the only movie theater in the area. We had read that there would be a matinee of *The Bridge on the River Kwai.* Since I was essentially driving blind, I hadn't gone very far before I bumped into a low stone wall. As I was backing away from that accident, I banged straight into a passing taxi. The driver was not convinced that my insurance would take care of the damage. He and I spent an hour or two looking for a mechanic to get an estimate. It was Sunday. Every garage was closed. Finally we found someone whose opinion he trusted and I paid him what he wanted. There was still just enough time to get to the matinee. I found the cinema and risked drowning to get out of the car and buy our tickets. Then I saw the sign: "Closed today." By this time I was sure that the pixie was responsible for all our troubles. I set him down on the counter of the box office. At that very instant the ceiling of the rain-soaked marquee collapsed in front of me. Several square yards of plaster crashed at my feet. Now the theater had the bad luck instead of me. Sure enough, the sun came out on cue and we were able to enjoy a delightful visit to the local castle. Never underestimate the power of Cornish pixies!

In 1967 I accompanied Martina Arroyo on a short concert tour in Germany. Our first recital was in Nuremberg. The morning after,

Martina Arroyo as Madame Butterfly

I wandered around the town a bit, to catch a few of the sights before we had to move on to our next stop on the tour. When I returned to the hotel, I noticed a postcard rack on the reception desk with a photo of Hans Sachs's house! There was no more time for sight-seeing, the bus was ready to leave. I was devastated to think that I had missed what for me would have been the most fascinating thing in Nuremberg. Some years later I finally had a chance to return to the city. Naturally the first thing I wanted to see was that house! Alas, there was only a plaque to show where it had stood. That postcard had been an old one from before the war, kept by the concierge as a memento of the past.

Until a year before she died, Lotte Lehmann used to spend her summers in Europe, where it did her heart good to see herself remembered with affection and great respect. The first time she returned to Austria after the war, she was overwhelmed with the warmth of her reception everywhere. When she entered a restaurant the orchestra would play melodies from her most famous roles. Her hotel rooms were always full of flowers. She invariably invited us to visit her at whatever beautiful spot she had chosen that year. Like many Europeans she had great faith in the curative powers of "the waters." Often she went to Bad Gastein, hoping it would help relieve her arthritis. In Salzburg Hilde Gueden studied

Strauss lieder with Mme. Lehmann and I accompanied her lessons. Other summers we might meet in Schruns—where Elisabeth Schwarzkopf was also staying—or Lucerne. One year it was Vienna. She invited us to a *"Heurigen"* party— celebrating the new vintage of wine—at a little restaurant near the Vienna Woods. Among her other guests there were three internationally famous opera stars, Leontyne Price, Rita Streich, and Hermann Prey. Evangeline and I had been seated opposite Mme. Lehmann at a long table. At one

Lotte Lehmann, Hilde Gueden, and friends in Salzburg, taking a break between coachings

point in the general conversation I left my seat to go and pay my respects to Miss Price. While I was gone, Hermann Prey slipped into my seat to talk to Lehmann across the table. As it happens, Evangeline—involved in another conversation—hadn't noticed that I was no longer sitting beside her. Without turning her head, she put her hand on Mr. Prey's thigh, thinking it was mine, and gave a little squeeze. He turned purple and probably so did she. Ever since, "Prey's thigh" has joined "Alexander Hamilton's penis" as a family byword.

As soon as we had arrived in Vienna, I tried to call Lotte Lehmann at her hotel. I was as yet unfamiliar with the Viennese telephone system. I put coins in the slot and dialed the number. I got the front desk. They put me through to Mme. Lehmann's room. Her traveling companion answered and told Lotte who was on the phone. I could picture her struggling with her arthritis as she painfully walked across the room. Just as I heard her voice the phone line went dead. My money had run out. I felt terrible that Lotte had been disturbed for nothing, but I had to speak to her to find out when and where she wanted to see us. I dropped twice as many coins in the machine and tried again. The whole procedure was repeated. Once more I was cut off just after Lehmann's first words. How embarrassing! Then someone told me that it doesn't do any good to put in all your coins before you dial. Apparently you have to keep dropping them in, one by one, once the connection has been made.

You'd think I'd have learned my lesson. But years later, when I was gathering material for my biography of Lehmann, we were again in Vienna. A gracious, elderly lady, who had been one of Lotte's most devoted fans, had invited me to her apartment to see clippings, reviews, interviews, letters, and all sorts of interesting and—for my book—usable items. She and her husband had served us champagne and cake. She had suggested that we should all visit Lotte's grave in the Central Cemetery the following day, our last in Vienna. As it happens it was raining hard the next morning, so we decided to visit the art museum instead. So I called our new friend to make our excuses. When she answered the phone, I thanked her for the previous evening's hospitality and help, and explained why we had decided not to visit the cemetery. Suddenly she said: "The devil take you!" and hung up. I was devastated. What could I possibly have done to offend her? Was she annoyed that I had turned down her offer to accompany us to Lotte's grave? Did she take that as disloyalty to the memory of her idol, as a sign that I didn't care enough? I couldn't enjoy my hours at the museum at all. Evangeline said that I was as pale as a ghost when I returned from the phone booth. Well, when we got back to our hotel, the concierge told me that the lady in question had called while we were away and left a friendly message, wishing us a pleasant journey and expressing delight at having met us. I was totally flabbergasted. I told the concierge what she had said when I called her that morning from the museum. He laughed. "Did you press the red button?" What red button? It seems that on one kind of public telephone in Vienna the party you are calling can't hear you until you press a red button, even though you can hear her or him perfectly clearly. Obviously that had been the case. She hadn't heard a word I was saying and was simply tired of holding the phone for nothing. What a relief!

Looking back, it is the *mishaps* on our trips that provide the most amusing memories. One summer we took a young niece with us on a tour of France. Before we had even crossed the border she had already managed to lock herself into two toilets. The second time was on a mountain pass. We had just finished lunch in the garden of an inn. Robin had gone to the ladies' room. We waited and waited. Evangeline, Melody, and I passed the time imagining a postcard we might write her mother: "Dear Yvonne, Robin just fell off an alp." What *could* she be doing in there? Is she washing her hair? Finally I went to the door and called to her. "Uncle Beau, I can't open the door!" she sobbed. "Get me out of here!" So I summoned the owner. He couldn't open the door either. He sent someone to the nearest neighbor a half mile away who had a crowbar. Meanwhile he tried to instruct her in French—with me translating—how to climb up onto the sink and crawl out the narrow window; but she couldn't open that either. The crowbar finally arrived, just as Robin gave the doorknob another little twist and—miraculously!—it opened by itself.

Our next adventure was in Avignon, a picturesque walled city on the banks of the Rhone. In the fourteenth century its castle had been the official residence of the popes. We had a picnic lunch under the ruined bridge, the *Pont d'Avignon*, known to every child in France through a famous song. We had parked just across the street. As we picked up our things to go back to the car, a sudden gust of wind tore open Evangeline's purse and all of its contents went flying through the air like autumn leaves in a gale. Our passports, drivers licenses, Robin's plane tickets, and all the cash for our trip, in four different currencies, were whisked along ahead of us by the notorious *mistral*, a north wind that sweeps down the Rhone valley with indescribable force. We all ran after our indispensable valuables as fast as we could. I felt sure that some of them would inevitably be blown into the river, which was flowing by, just beside the road. I watched helplessly and out of breath as fifty-dollar bills flew through the ancient city gates and disappeared around corners. Incredible as it must seem, we actually retrieved absolutely everything, thanks to helpful passersby. I still had the lists from the bank of the exact amounts of foreign currencies we had purchased, including the dollars that Robin needed for her return home. Every single franc, both Swiss and French, every lira, every dollar could be accounted for. I consider that a miracle.

As we approached Paris, we began to look for hotels. We were all exhausted from a full day of sight-seeing. It was getting later and later, accommodations would be harder and harder to find. Melody, then about seven years old, remembered that when she had prayed to St. Anthony her lost cat had come back. So, having heard somewhere about St. Germain, she began to pray to *him*. Weren't we in France, and wouldn't he be a French saint? Well, saintly or not, he seemed to help us. She pointed out a hotel. We stopped. Yes, there were rooms available. Weary and relieved, we settled in. But we didn't get much sleep. It was one of those hotels where rooms can be rented by the hour. All night long we heard high heels tapping past our door, not to mention certain other sounds emanating now and then from other rooms.

On Montmartre we had a collision with another car. A busy intersection was blocked for what seemed like an hour. A lot of very upset Frenchmen were drowning each other out without accomplishing very much. The two insurance companies fought with one another for years, trying to figure out who had been at fault. In Luxemburg all our suitcases were stolen. With them we lost all our souvenirs, as well as the three little cloth lambs that Melody always took to bed with her. The case of wine we bought was spoiled by the time we returned to Switzerland, thanks to bumpy travel under the hood of a VW in July and August. Other than that, it was a fabulous summer.

Another visiting niece, a special pet of ours, gave us a few tense moments and a lot of laughs afterward. Laurel had just graduated from high school. Evangeline's mother offered to accompany her on a trip to Europe. They were headed for New York when Laurel inadvertently left her passport at a reststop. When the loss was discovered, my mother-in-law was able to call the place. Sure enough, the passport had been found and would be sent to them by overnight express. They made their plane just in time. The day after their arrival, we took them to see the Rhine Falls. Laurel left her new

Laurel and Evangeline's mother with us in Rome

wristwatch under her napkin at the restaurant where we had lunch. The next day I drove back there to fetch it. Then we went to Italy. In Venice she left her raincoat over her chair at an outdoor *trattoria*. We found it a few hours later. In Rome she left her camera, a graduation present, on a chair in the Piazza Navona. A kind waiter put it aside for her. And they tell women to watch their purses in Italy?! Incidentally, wherever we went, Laurel, a very attractive young lady, was the center of male attention. I imagine that helped rebuild her morale after the embarrassment of that colossal losing streak.

In the summer of 1965 I had the honor and the pleasure of accompanying Grace Bumbry in song recitals at two major international festivals, first in Amsterdam, later in Salzburg. It was a thrill to perform in the famous Concertgebouw. There was a hitch, however. The page turner was so entranced by Miss Bumbry, her

Grace Bumbry and I after a recital

glamorous appearance and her lively personality, that he forgot to look at the music. The first half of the program was devoted to the lieder of Brahms, and the opening song was "*Wie Melodien zieht es mir,*" one of everyone's favorites. There are graceful little garlands in the piano part from time to time. In the edition I was using they occur just at the page turns. And the mesmerized page turner was in another world. Well, I had not memorized those interludes, and I have no talent for improvising at the piano. The latter fact is unfortunately well documented. The program was taped for broadcasts. When I returned to Zurich, people were constantly stopping me on the street to say: "I heard you on the radio yesterday." I never knew in advance when the tape would be aired, so I never heard the performance myself;[*] but the Swiss radio must have repeated it frequently over a period of several weeks, thanks to Miss Bumbry's popularity.

---

[*] In early 2002 I learned through a friend that two groups from that recital and part of our Salzburg Brahms program are included in "Grace Bumbry—a Portrait," 2 *Gala* CDs, GL 100.539, via *Qualiton Imports*

Her engagement to sing Venus in *Tannhäuser* at the Bayreuth Festival had created a big splash. Luckily for Grace, forty people had written letters of protest to the management. "A black singer at the shrine of blonde German womanhood?" The fact that Venus was presumably Greek and not German didn't count. The ensuing publicity put Grace on the front pages all over Europe. When Evangeline and I first arrived in Switzerland her face was in every illustrated magazine. Grace and her new sports car. Grace shopping. Except she wasn't called Grace Bumbry in the captions and headlines: she was invariably identified as "the black Venus of Bayreuth."

Incidentally, she was neither black nor white in that production; she was painted gold and had to stay as motionless as a statue. She told us that her arms fell asleep in their propped-up position.

Our Salzburg Festival recital was a rather bitter experience for me. I arrived at the Mozarteum early enough to try to prepare myself inwardly for performing. Then I learned that the tickets I had ordered for my wife and for an important guest were not at the box office. Consternation! Evangeline had to rush to the office of the festival director, which was normally closed in the evening. Then I noticed that the step down onto the recital platform was an unusually big one. I couldn't believe that all the great divas who had performed there in their elaborate concert gowns would have had to face such a daunting plunge. So I asked that some portable steps be found, to help our soloist make a more graceful and dignified entrance. No one could come up with a solution. Meanwhile the ushers were already admitting members of the audience into the auditorium. Frustrated, I returned to my dressing room— to be faced with an enormous crack in the mirror, from top to bottom, bisecting my face. How could the Mozarteum demoralize us superstitious theater people like that? I tried to compose myself. Then out onto the battlefield. During the first song—"*Wie Melodien*" again—I heard a distracting, high-pitched squeal every time I moved. I saw a microphone about a foot away, so I was concerned that the squeal would be heard over the air. I soon realized that it was caused by my gold collar stud rubbing against the starched collar of my dress shirt. I didn't dare move my head for the rest of the recital. Unnerved, I hit a klinker in the postlude of "*Wir wandelten.*"

The *coup de Grace* came the next day. Besides the musical klinker, I had made a pair of political blunders. At Salzburg, one is expected to maintain an aura of success and to understand the intricacies of court etiquette. Error No. 1, I had disgraced myself and the prestige of a Salzburg Festival performer by booking a room in an inexpensive hotel. Then, most seriously, I had failed to pay my respects to the director of the festival on arrival. I had violated proper Austrian protocol. My career as Grace Bumbry's preferred accompanist was suddenly over.

Immediately on realizing my disastrous lapse of good manners, I raced over to the Festival Director's office. I told his secretary that

Evangeline with José Van Dam and Dr. Graf in
*La rappresentazione di anima e di corpo*, Salzburg Festival 1968

I had been unable to meet Dr. Nekola personally before the recital and wished to pay my respects to him before leaving Salzburg later that afternoon. So she asked me to wait. I sat there waiting for four hours. Finally, it was time to check in at the airport. I expressed my regrets to the secretary and left. Later, in Zurich, a kind Austrian lady helped me to compose a letter of appropriately abject apology, with all the requisite, figurative bowing and scraping. There was no response at the time. But three years later, when Evangeline was engaged by the festival to sing the role of "*Vita Mondana*" in *La rappresentazione di anima e di corpo*, Dr. Nekola welcomed me as if I were his long-lost brother.

My next festival experience—at Aix-en-Provence—was considerably less formal. I decided on no hotel at all, far less a fashionable one. Like Valerie Masterson and Robert Lloyd, two of the very finest singers in the festival, I took up residence at Camping Chantecler. The attractions were a large swimming pool and a fine view of Cézanne's Mont St. Victoire. I pitched my tent under two apricot trees. Other—non-operatic—campers nearby were startled to see me emerge from my tent in full evening dress, then tie my white tie while looking into a mirror that was hanging from a branch of one of the apricot trees. I saved the patent leather shoes for the car ride to the Archbishop's Palace, where our performances were to take place.

Four of my summers were spent at the Festival of Aix-en-Provence. The operas I was assigned to coach were *La clemenza di Tito, Don Giovanni, Così fan tutte, Alcina,* and

Alberto Erede and I during a rehearsal at Aix

*Dido and Aeneas*. All of those operas were rehearsed and performed in the open courtyard of the Archbishop's Palace. When the north wind was blowing, the notorious *mistral*, those early morning rehearsals in late June or early July could be surprisingly cold. I often played the piano with gloves on to keep my fingers from freezing.

For *Don Giovanni* a cellist and I had to don 18th-century costume and accompany the recitatives at a harpsichord in a special alcove at the side of the stage.

In the first performance, the Ottavio, a friend from the Zurich Opera, missed the high A in "*Il mio tesoro.*" He was booed. The shock literally put a sudden end to his—till then—promising career. From that night on, he never again made that A, and he was booed every single time. His confidence was utterly shattered. His singing became more and more erratic. Back in Zurich, where his Ottavio had originally led to his engagement at Aix, he was switched to minor roles until his contract expired. Jobs at lesser theaters were few and far between. Finally, tragically, he committed suicide. As far as I know, he was not yet thirty.

Booing can have comic as well as tragic consequences. During my first summer at Aix, I attended a performance of *Luisa Miller*. After the duet of the tenor and mezzo-soprano, two men booed. Suddenly the tenor appeared in the audience area and shouted in Italian: "Who yelled 'boo'? Who yelled 'boo'? The lady is an excellent artist!" He drew his sword, prepared to defend her honor. "We weren't booing *her*, we were booing *you*!" someone shouted back. The outraged tenor ran up the aisle, armed for combat. Then the audience took sides, half of them booing the tenor, the other half booing the booers. Everyone was shouting at once. In the midst of the uproar, a phalanx of gendarmes came running into the courtyard, to face an avalanche of booing, aimed at *them*. They backed up, stunned. I managed to slip outside during the ensuing mayhem.

One note in *Don Giovanni* destroyed a career. One unscored tone-cluster put an end to my summers at Aix. *Dido and Aeneas* was the opera. It was a very windy night. The open-air performance was being filmed for future telecasts. Dame Janet Baker was the star, Sir Charles Mackerras conducted the orchestra and chorus of Scottish Opera. We musicians in the pit had to keep our music open with wooden clothespins. Dido's first aria is accompanied only by the *continuo*—me and a cellist. Right in the middle of that aria, as my page-turner tried to turn a page, the clothespin slipped out of his hand, flew into the air, and landed with a hideous noise in the midst of the strings of the harpsichord, ruining the aria. At midnight, after the performance, the piece had to be filmed again, with the television crew and the orchestra (all but the guest harpsichordist) receiving expensive overtime. The fact that it was the page-turner, not I, who caused the unfortunate accident made no difference to anyone but me. I was still held responsible; it had occurred "on my watch." The next morning I happened to run into Raymond Leppard. "I hear you 'Scotched' it last night" —a reference to my Scottish colleagues in the pit—was his not very tactful little witticism.

The wind that caused havoc in *Dido and Aeneas* was again a leading player in a performance of *Norma* my wife and I attended in the ancient Roman Theater of Orange. The *mistral* was so strong that evening that the start of the opera was delayed for a full hour, in the hope that the near-tempest would die down a bit. No such luck! I felt sure that Montserrat Caballé would refuse to go on. I was wrong. Later, she called that evening *the* performance of her career. Her "*Casta diva*" became a duet for soprano and wind in counterpoint, the all slow *legato cantilena*, the wind *molto agitato*. Her veils and draperies were whipped about like sails in a gale, intermittently exposing some details of her anatomy that they had been designed to cover. I greatly admired her courage and sportsmanship. All through the performance, orchestra parts were flying about, music stands were falling down, and the pages of the conductor's score had to be held down with one hand to keep them from riffling. But Caballé sang and acted marvelously. The performance can be savored on video. If you knew where to look, you could even make out Evangeline and me in a shot of the audience.

During one festival, *Medea* was performed in the Greek amphitheater at Arles. Leonie Rysanek sang the title role, my good friend Costanza Cuccaro was the Glauce. Arles is very near the marshes

of the Camargue. Connie told me that either the *mistral* was blowing down her throat and she could hardly hear herself, or it wasn't, and mosquitos were flying in and—hopefully—out of her mouth every time she had to sing a long note.

During rehearsals for *Don Giovanni*, the cast and I decided to take a break and go for a swim. We found a pleasantly uncrowded little stretch of beach and enjoyed a communal sunbath. Those who ventured into the water noticed that it was rather slimy. When we returned

Costanza Cuccaro, inscription: "To Beau, you are the very "best" there is."

to our cars we saw a sign we hadn't noticed before. Bathers were warned that the main sewer of the city of Marseilles was disgorging its contents into the Mediterranean precisely at the spot we had chosen.

Our Elvira was Elena Mauti-Nunziata. She told me about a performance of *Madama Butterfly* that she had sung at La Scala. The child was restless during the third act, so someone backstage gave him a treat to quiet him down. Just as Butterfly was preparing to commit suicide, the child strolled onto the stage licking an ice cream cone. The audience giggled with delight and the tragic mood was shattered. Elena herself could hardly keep a straight face as she launched into her heart-breaking aria of farewell.

Some of the most hilarious operatic anecdotes concern Butterfly's child, appropriately named "Trouble" and a frequent source of problems. Once Florence Easton was given a doll; its arm came off in Sharpless's hand. Another time the "child" behaved perfectly, responding affectionately to every caress. After the performance Miss Easton asked sweetly: "how old are you, dear?" A deep bass voice growled the answer. They had hired a midget. My all-time favorite was told me by Lotte Lehmann. At the Vienna State Opera, in the middle of the second act, the baby suddenly called out: "*Frau Butterfly, ich muss Pipi machen!*" ("Mrs. Butterfly, I have to pee!") How endearing, "Frau Butterfly," instead of "Frau Lehmann"!

The Chantecler at Aix was of festival standard, compared to some of our other camp sites. When Evangeline first suggested that we buy a tent, I predicted that she would last just one night in one. How wrong I was! She loved outdoor living, especially in the

Melody and Evangeline camping out in nature

warm Mediterranean climate, and took every inconvenience in stride. My inexperience was obvious in the very first try. The three of us—Melody was just ten—were on our way to Italy, via the Saint Gotthard Pass. I waited too long to look for a *campeggio*. It was already growing dark, and I had never tried to set up a tent before. It had looked so simple when the salesman demonstrated the procedure at the store! Blowing up the air mattresses seemed to take forever. Without the kindly help of a fellow camper we would have spent the night under the stars. As it was, the wind that rushed down into the valley from the mountain pass kept the tent flapping and rattling all night, so no one got much sleep. By the time we reached Florence, where we camped in an orchard at the feet of the colossal David of the Piazzale Michelangelo, we had at least mastered the fundamentals.

Greece was Paradise. Living outdoors seems so natural there! By sheer dumb luck, we arrived just outside Athens on the first night of the full moon. In those days, one was allowed freely to wander about on the Acropolis whenever the full moon was shining, for as long as one wished. Those ancient stones, so brown by daylight, gleamed like mother-of-pearl. We were entranced, and on each of those three nights we spent hours inside an opalescent Parthenon, sensing the mysterious presence of Athena herself.

On our way back home we passed through Yugoslavia, our first Communist country and a complete contrast to any place we had experienced before. For one thing, one had to estimate one's fuel needs for the entire transversal and buy gas coupons for cash before crossing the border. Once inside it was almost impossible to find a service station, coupons or no coupons. The roads were indescribably rutted, so it was mostly slow going. The scenery, on the other hand, was magnificent, especially after we reached the Adriatic coast, with its picturesque harbor towns and its hundreds of islands. Before we got there, however, we had to cross a high mountain pass, so high that the temperature was below freezing in August. We breathed a sigh of relief when we saw a huge hotel at the top of the pass. But we learned to our consternation that they were already full to capacity. What can we do, where can we go? There was not another lodging for many miles around. The clerk suggested that we camp in the alpine meadow beside the hotel grounds. It was much too cold for camping, but we had no other choice. So we put on every sweater we could find and up went the tent. Ours was the only car with a West Europen license; all the others were from the East Block. This would be their vacation in the sunny South. The cold woke us up before dawn. The tent was covered with a thick layer of frost. Evangeline and Melody dashed into the car and turned on the heater. I, swathed in blankets, took down the tent with freezing fingers. Meanwhile, the other campers, hale and hearty every one, were jogging about in the lightest of workout clothes, the men's tops unzipped to the waist, the women cheerfully preparing a pre-dawn breakfast, and everyone staring at us as at the very symbol of the decadent West.

The next night we were invited to camp in the yard of a very nice house by the sea. After a pleasant supper, Evangeline went to rinse the dishes in the waters of the Adriatic. She found what seemed to be the perfect spot, a quiet pool of water where a semicircle of stones kept out the waves. Suddenly I heard a truly Wagnerian shriek. That little pool turned out to be the home of the landowner's pet octopus, who was not at all happy to share his lair with our dirty dishes.

East Germany was our second Communist country. We were keen to visit Weimar and the Wartburg Castle at Eisenach. In 1972, in Switzerland, it was almost impossible to get any accurate information about what to expect. The West German tourist office was no help at all. So we simply drove off in the general direction and hoped for the best. We were of course stopped at the border. Our car was searched and a Time magazine was confiscated. My mother was told that her passport was unsatisfactory and she would need a temporary new one. They took her away to be photographed. We were not allowed to come with her. She was gone an alarmingly long time. When I saw the photo, my heart nearly broke. Poor Mother looked absolutely terrified. At the border we had to pay a road tax plus three nights in advance at a specified hotel. We were told to go directly to Weimar, without stopping anywhere on the way, and to check in with the local police immediately on arrival.

The *Autobahn*, so well maintained in the West, was impossibly rutted, cracked, and overgrown on the far side of the border. There was practically no traffic. We did break one rule: we stopped to have a look at Erfurt on the way.

Weimar in 1972 was an experience in time travel. Except for the tourist attractions, which were immaculately maintained, the rest of the town looked frozen in 1945, high grass and rubble, shell-pocked buildings, unsmiling gray faces. The only red cheeks and happy expressions belonged to the Russian soldiers. Weimar was an up-grade from back home.

But Goethe's town house and garden house, Liszt's house, Schiller's house, and the tomb of Goethe and Schiller were utterly fascinating, vibrant with atmosphere, and supremely worth the visit.

When it was time to leave Weimar, I reported to the police station, as instructed. Assuming that the check-out would be a brief formality, I left Mother and Evangeline in our VW and went inside. Having seen few cars in the parking lot, I was unprepared for the two enormously long queues, one for residents of Weimar, one for non-residents. I had to stand in line for over two hours. At the front end of each queue there was a door. It would open just long enough for one person to slip in; then an unseen hand would slam it shut again. What were they doing in there that could possibly take so long? One poor man in the resident line seemed in a desperate hurry, he ran up to the door, knocked, and shouted that his wife was critically ill and needed permission to go to the hospital in some other city. Everyone ignored him. I thought he would have a stroke, he was so agitated. He pleaded, he begged, he cried. No one batted an eye. It was pure Kafka.

Evangeline and I returned twenty-eight years later. By the year 2000, Weimar had been transformed into a delightful town, one of the most attractive, interesting, and enjoyable in Germany.

But in 1972 we could hardly wait to breathe free air again. On the way out of East Germany we stopped to visit picturesque Wartburg Castle, rich in history and legend and especially interesting to me as the setting, along with the nearby Hörselberg and the valley between them, of *Tannhäuser*. I have always been fascinated by the compelling way in which Wagner wove together three themes associated with that beautiful region, the historical competition of the Minnesingers under Landgrave Hermann, the loving benevolence of St. Elisabeth, and the legend of Tannhäuser and the Venusberg.

Wartburg Castle

We Wagnerians had much to enjoy in Zurich. During our nineteen years there, there were two productions each of the *Holländer*, *Tannhäuser*, *Lohengrin*, *Tristan*, *Meistersinger*, and *Parsifal*. But the management used the *"Ring"* as a political carrot. They told the Swiss voters: "If you want it, you need to renovate the Opera House, enlarge the orchestra pit, and give us better stage equipment." That finally happened after we left Switzerland. But while we were still there, we had to go elsewhere for our fix, to Geneva and Strasbourg for *Das Rheingold*, to Geneva for *Siegfried*, to Munich for *Die Walküre* and *Götterdämmerung*, and—twice!—to Seattle for the whole cycle in the proper order.

Evangeline sang Isolde's "Narrative and Curse" for the leading agent in Munich. He was duly impressed and promised to find her an engagement in the role. He even tried to arrange for her to "cover" Isolde in Herbert von Karajan's Salzburg Easter Festival. That plan fell through; but he assured her that he'd find something for her. Weeks went by. We'd call him. "*Es läuft noch,*" he kept saying (literally: "It's still running"). After several months she received an offer from another agent. After much soul-searching and advice from colleagues about the "bird in the hand," she signed the offer. No engagement came of that, and she only succeeded in alienating the first agent, who had been so enthusiastic.

Evangeline, right center, as Isolde in *Autour de Tristan* at the Théâtre de la Monnaie, Brussels

But she did get to sing about half the role, with an extra "*Liebestod*" thrown in. It was at the Théâtre de la Monnaie in Brussels, in a bizarre, multi-media concoction called "*Autour de Tristan*" ("Round about Tristan"). A French movie director dreamed it up. The story of the legendary lovers, in Wagner's musical setting, would be intertwined with a modern version of their relationship, using film, and underscored by a rock band. Opera singers, a leading dancer of the Béjart Ballet, Jorge Dunn, and a young actress would play the two pairs of lovers. But, even in the big love duet, Evangeline's partner was the dancer, not the singing Tristan, whose partner was the actress. "*C'est une idée,*" as the French say of the wilder brainstorms of avant-garde directors. All went well until the rock band arrived. The moment they started to play their interpolations, there was an uproar in the pit. The opera orchestra refused to perform with them and marched out *en masse*. Consternation! Crisis! Signed contracts had to be honored! After much tense deliberation, a compromise was accepted, so that *a* performance—if not the original concept—could take place. The conductor and the orchestra would enter the pit and perform the prelude, followed by all of Wagner's music that was expected to be part of the show. Then, after the *Liebestod*, they would leave the opera house. What happened after that would be the concern of others. While the discussions were going on behind closed doors, the rock band ran through their numbers. During a break, I went up onto the stage to beg them to lower the volume on their amplifiers. My ears had suffered intense, acute, almost unbearable pain while they were playing. They looked at me and shrugged. "That's our sound, man." The decibels remained.

It was decided that the evening would be split into two parts. The first would be devoted to the legendary lovers. All the excerpts from the opera would be played in the proper order and without interruptions. After the intermission, the second half of the performance would feature the present-day lovers, the filmed sequences, and the rock band. There was still one problem: the director wanted to end the evening with the *Liebestod*. How to do that without an orchestra in the pit? I found a recording of the arrangement for orchestra alone, conducted by Hans Knappertsbusch. Evangeline listened to it over and over again in her hotel room, until she felt that she could sing with the amplified record. It's not easy to hear the beat when you're singing a high G sharp, but she was willing to risk it. So she sang the *Liebestod* twice, once with the pit orchestra, before the intermission, and once with the recording as the grand finale.

*Thaïs* in Rouen was another unique experience. The contract called for Evangeline to supply her own costumes. A kindly wardrobe mistress at the Zurich Opera helped us find some gorgeous ones, including an especially lovely accordian-pleated robe from *La belle Hélène*. The agent in Paris wrote us that Thaïs is expected to be "quite" undressed. Being Americans we took "quite" to mean "rather." He, however, like most Europeans, had been taught British English. To them "quite" means "completely, utterly, altogether." Act I ends with a playful challenge from

Evangeline as Thaïs, with José Van Dam as Athanël

Thaïs, the beautiful actress and courtesan, to Athanaël, the fanatical monk who has come to convert her. "Dare to come hither, you who defy the power of Venus," she sings, as she slips out of her robe and hits a high C. So Evangeline planned to open the spectacular robe of Helen of Troy and reveal her own very appealing curves—protected from backstage drafts by a fairly sheer body stocking with a few well-placed jewels. But that was not "undressed" enough for the stage director. He complained to the management and they threatened to sue. They refused to disappoint all those old gentlemen with binoculars in the front rows. I asked if Denise Duvol and Susanne Sarocca had actually sung the role stark naked in Paris. "Of course!" I remembered that Helen Jepson and Marjorie Lawrence had sung Thaïs at the Met in the late 1930s, and, quite recently, Leontyne Price in Chicago. Surely they had not bared their breasts. But France has its own inviolable traditions. Evangeline refused to cave in to the pressure. Fortunately, at the dress rehearsal she looked so beautiful in the shaft of golden light that all talk of a lawsuit was dropped along with her outer drapery.

Eventually, however, nudity crossed the border to Switzerland. In *Die Bernauerin* by Carl Orff a naked lady ran across the stage in the bathhouse scene. In *The Fiery Angel* by Prokofiev there were some bare-bosomed nuns. But that was nothing compared to a *Salome* we saw in St. Gallen. It was a Sunday matinee. The audience was full of little old ladies dressed in black with high laced shoes. They had presumably just come from mass in the magnificent Baroque cathedral nearby. The opening scenes unfolded more or less as usual. Then came the entrance of Herod's court. Full frontal nudity, both male and female. Evangeline, Melody, and I were sitting in the back row. "Am I seeing what I think I'm seeing?" I asked them, incredulous. Before long, everyone on stage was doing something of a lascivious nature to someone. Herodias was caressing the bare buttocks of a young man crouched between her legs. I won't mention what some other couples were up to. I thought that there would be some sort of startled reaction from the audience. I fully expected some of them to leave. But they all sat there transfixed. Needless to say, none of us heard a note of the music or a word of the text. The dance of the seven veils was of course a total anticlimax. By then we had seen so many sweating nude bodies that one more hardly made any impression at all.

You might think that ten months of opera in Zurich would be enough for anybody. But we were insatiable. We were entranced by *Daphne* and *Capriccio* in Vienna, *Intermezzo* and *Arabella* in Munich, *Elektra* and *Ariadne* in Salzburg, to mention only the operas of our beloved Strauss. What dream casts! Hilde Gueden, Fritz Wunderlich, and Paul Schöffler in *Daphne*, with James King as Apollo, looking and sounding like a young god; a radiant Elisabeth Schwarzkopf in *Capriccio* (also with Wunderlich); Lisa della Casa and Dietrich Fischer-Dieskau, both moving us to tears in *Arabella*; Astrid Varnay as Elektra—Evangeline kept the ticket stub in her purse for years as inspiration. At the Verona Arena we saw *Mefistofele* with Nicolai Ghiaurov (in those days his voice

Lisa della Casa
and Dietrich Fischer-Dieskau
in *Arabella*

was so huge we could hardly believe he wasn't being miked), *Lohengrin* (in Italian—*"Addio, cigno gentil"*), and *Aida*. There were a thousand people on stage and twenty-five thousand in the audience. The biggest ovation came in the middle of the Triumphal Scene in *Aida*. When Amonasro enters with the Ethiopian prisoners, Aida blurts out "My father!" Suspicious, they ask him "Who are you?" "Her father," he humbly replies, hoping they will not recognize him as a king and the leader of the troops. What does our Verona Amonasro do? He starts *"suo padre*" upstage, then holds the "ah" vowel for an eternity as he slowly strolls toward the audience, raising his arms higher and higher and swelling the tone to a powerful *fortissimo* with extra *vibrato* at the end for maximum effect. The audience exploded with joy. The performance came to a complete standstill while the fans shouted their heads off. And to think that the character—if not the singer—was trying to remain inconspicuous!

I recall a performance of *Aida* that was memorable for other reasons. A young tenor who had privately coached Samson and Cavaradossi with me was making his debut as the Messenger. It's a small role, but it calls for a robust voice. The nervous young man sang his extended speech well nigh perfectly. He was so relieved to have gotten everything right that when he released the final note, he took a deep breath, puffed out his cheeks, and expelled the air with great force, making his lips vibrate. It almost became a "Bronx cheer." It was a deliciously ludicrous moment and effectively ended his career at the Zurich Opera. In the same performance the Rhadames was wearing golden sandals. When he beat time with his big toe in the ensembles the shiny gold caught the light like a mirror and sent dazzling reflections careening about the stage and out into the audience.

During my nineteen years with the Zurich Opera, including four summers with the Festival of Aix-en-Provence, I was accumulating invaluable experience. I coached every opera in the standard repertoire as well as numerous rarities. During my first season as an official member of the coaching staff (before that I had "unofficially" prepared our American Hans Sachs for his debut in the role), several 20th-century works were my personal responsibility, including *Wozzeck* (*Lulu* came later), *The Love of Three Oranges*, and two pieces by Luigi Dallapiccola (*Il prigioniero* and *Volo di notte*—the composer attended our final rehearsals and praised our musical accuracy). The singers liked my way with a waltz, so I was soon inundated with Viennese operettas.

Eventually I worked my way up to *Studienleiter*, top coach. Then

I could pick and choose the operas that I particularly wanted to prepare musically myself.

Guest singers often asked me to coach them in roles they were learning for other theaters. Wilma Lipp, a famous Salzburg Queen of the Night, studied Marguerite in French with me. She was so pleased with our rapport that she tried to get me a place on the coaching staff of the Vienna State Opera (the general manager was her ex-husband). That fell through when they found out my salary in Zurich and realized they couldn't match it. Johanna Meier brushed up her Isolde with me, Helga Dernesch her Brangäne. Teresa Berganza and I worked on Schumann's *Frauenliebe und -leben*.

Some of the coaching staff of the Zurich Opera, late 1970s

Over the years, in Zurich and elsewhere, I coached the entire Wagner repertoire (including *Rienzi*), eight Strauss, eight Mozart, seven Czech (performed in German), several Baroque, and—since I was the only coach on the Zurich staff who spoke the language—numerous French, including *Pelléas*, multiple Massenet, Offenbach, Meyerbeer, Gounod, Bizet, and Ravel. Of course, I coached all the Italian operas too, but they were not my primary responsibility (except for a revival of *Butterfly*) since we always had a specialist on our staff. First it was Marcello Conati, now one of the world's leading authorities on Verdi; then came Gordon Jephtas, originally from South Africa but well known in Milan. One season I took over his operas while he went on tour with Renata Tebaldi and Franco Corelli as their accompanist. When he came back he told us a fascinating story.

During the rehearsal period in Italy he was shocked by the apparently poor condition of Miss Tebaldi's voice, scratchy and hoarse, when they were running through the arias and duets on their program. Mr. Corelli, on the other hand, didn't sing at all. He only whistled the melodies. My colleague was afraid that the tour would turn out to be a disaster. Perhaps the stars would give up and cancel. He never heard Corelli sing a single tone until the actual opening concert of their tour, which took place at the Royal Albert Hall before six thousand people. Backstage the tenor was a nervous wreck. Tebaldi, in contrast, was as calm as a clam. She started her first number rather cautiously; but her voice soon found its full bloom. Gordon was dumbfounded! Both singers sounded wonderful and the audience was deliriously happy. Clearly the famous stars at that stage of their careers needed the challenge of a public performance to bring out their best.

Most of the leading singers who were active in Europe at the time eventually appeared with the Zurich Opera. Among those not already mentioned, Anja Silja was mesmerizing as Senta, Edita Gruberova was a fabulous Zerbinetta who made every roulade expressive, Renata Scotto as Gilda gave every phrase an imaginative and individual nuance, Fiorenza Cossotto was a thrilling Eboli, Sven-Olaf Eliasson delighted us with his ideal interpretation of Lohengrin, and Reri Grist, who asked me for some coaching while we both were in Salzburg, was adorable in every one of her roles.

Reri Grist

One of the most luminous stars of that era was not a singer but a dancer. Rudolf Nureyev came to choreograph and dance in *Raymonda* by Alexander Glazunov. Evangeline and I snuck into one of his rehearsals, ducking down behind the balcony railing every time the house lights were turned on (for he had forbidden anyone unconnected with the production to attend rehearsals). We were enthralled with his artistry and intensity, even when he was merely "marking" some of the movements. It was an experience! Later Evangeline went to every performance, and I attended quite a few of them. One evening, when my rehearsal in another building was over, I watched part of the final *pas de deux* from the wings while waiting to meet Evangeline and drive her home. What a different impression I received! What had seemed utterly effortless, from out front, looked like sheer torture from six feet away. Every muscle stressed to the utmost, all the veins on face, neck, and shoulders bulging and ready to burst, fixed smiles frozen while the eyes conveyed steely concentration and more than a touch of panic! Yet my wife, in the artists' loge, noticed none of that. To her it all seemed as breathtakingly beautiful as ever.

One of the most engaging performances I experienced at the Zurich Opera featured no stars at all. We had just premiered a new production of *La bohème* with excellent singers in the cast. Luis Lima was the handsome Rodolfo, Maria Chiara the graceful Mimì. Both were thoroughly familiar with all the requirements and traditions of their roles, and delivered them with complete professionalism. Every note was in place and pleasant to hear, every move was well planned and appropriate. There was nothing to criticize at all. And yet I felt rather depressed, rather sad. I felt that I had lost something precious: I would probably never again be moved by an opera I had always loved. Perhaps I had just seen it too often, coached it too often. Then came a revelation. The Opera House gave a special performance featuring students of the International Opera Center in all the solo roles. The same production, the same orchestra, the same chorus. But what a different show. I laughed, I cried, all the old emotions returned, more movingly than ever! Those young people were inspired by the opportunity to perform a masterpiece; they poured all their energy and enthusiasm and love into those roles. They seemed to be living them. And later, in America, when I presented operas with student singers at the University of Iowa and elsewhere, I had similarly thrilling experiences. Unfortunately, at our great opera houses one sometimes gets the impression that some of the performers are set on automatic pilot. One night in Vienna, the next in London, the next in New York. The same stale repertoire, year after year. Can we really expect more of our super stars? They are all only human, after all. And the first thrill of discovery is not easy to recapture. The wonder of it, really, is that every now and then we do hear an individual performance of the highest quality, a performance that we can treasure in our memory ever after.

One day, during a coaching session, Simon Estes asked me if I would accept a teaching position at the University of Iowa. He had just received a letter from the head of the School of Music, requesting his recommendation of an all-around opera person to take over a vacant coaching position. I told Simon that I was perfectly happy where I was. I was working with many of the leading singers of the day on operas I loved. We had just done *Pelléas*, *Werther*, and *Don Qui-*

Simon Estes

chotte in French, *Capriccio*, *Ariadne*, *Arabella* and *Lulu*. I was currently responsible for a revival of *Parsifal* and soon I would be rehearsing *Tristan* with René Kollo and Hildegard Behrens, Heinz Fricke conducting. Why should I want to leave? But Simon was persistent. A week later he asked me again, this time with a glowing pep-talk about the state of Iowa, Iowa City, the University of Iowa, and the Iowa River that runs through the campus. I was still unimpressed. Then he made a fervent appeal to my conscience. I am an American. I have been soaking up European culture for nineteen years. Surely I ought to go back and share with talented young compatriots what I have learned. It was my duty. When I realized that he was not about to drop the subject, I agreed to look the place over, provided that the university would pay for my wife to fly with me, since such a drastic move would affect her life and career just as much as mine, and the decision would have to be made by the two of us together.

So the next thing I knew, we were both in Iowa City for a two-day visit in early March.

First impressions were not promising. In fact, we agreed that very first evening that we would gamely go through the motions but that Iowa City was not a second Zurich. So I met the voice faculty, the dean, and the conductor, as scheduled. I gave the expected "master class." Then I was invited to critique the staging at a rehearsal of *Dido and Aeneas*. I plunged in with both feet and started showing the student leads, respectively, how to move like a queen and a young hero, demonstrating to the Sorceress and the Witches how to revel deliciously in evil. The students came to life, the scenes took shape, the atmosphere was electrified. The professor in charge called her colleagues to come and watch. Meanwhile I realized what I had been missing for far too many years. Much as I enjoyed coaching, I had stifled my abilities as a stage director. I had been operating on only half my burners. I felt an exhilaration, a thrilling energy, and a rush of inspiration that I hadn't experienced with such force for years. That did it. Evangeline understood what I was feeling and generously agreed. I would accept the offer after all, provided that I would be the stage director as well as the coach.

I didn't learn until many years later that Simon himself had paid for my wife's round-trip flight. What a big heart, and what modesty! Apparently the university had told him that their budget could only pay the travel expenses of one person. Simon was determined that I take the position, so he dipped into his own pocket to make that possible. And no one told me.

Left: Patricia Jennings Armstrong (Sophie in Lotte Lehmann's production of *Der Rosenkavalier*), Mme. Lehmann and I (Frances Holden dimly visible behind Mme. Lehmann)

Right: Douglas Miller, Andreas Jaeckel (Grace Bumbry's husband at the time), and Evangeline, with Lotte Lehmann at the Basel Opera to see Ms. Bumbry in *Samson et Dalila*

Below: Dusolina Giannini, her husband, Alan Richter, and Evangeline

Lower right: Mme. Giannini with Melody

pper left: Evangeline as Vita Mondana in *La rappresentazione di anima e di cor*
, Salzburg Festival, 1968; upper right: as Nedda; below, left: as Marguerite; righ
ter a recital with me, her accompanist; bottom, left: the next generation on stage
Melody as the Grasshopper in *The Cunning Little Vixen*, Zurich Opera

Above: Evangeline at Castel Sant'Angelo, site of *Tosca*, Act III, and at the Wartburg, soaking up the atmosphere of *Tannhäuser*; below, left: Niece Laurel Roses with an unknown admirer in the Colosseum; right: Melody, Michael, and Alexander Talcott, my daughter, son-in-law, and grandson

Above, left: Grace Bumbry and I after a recital; right: Valerie Masterson and I at he
outdoor recital at Aix-en-Provence; below, right: I as a soldier in *Fidelio* with Lotte
Lehmann, after her very last opera production

My late friend David Blum with Birgit
Nilsson at her farm in Sweden. He wrote
a brilliant profile of Ms. Nilsson for the
New York Times.

All stage photos are from productions I directed at the University of Iowa

Above: *Madame Butterfly*, set by Ming Cho Lee; Butterfly's Entrance.

Below: *The Cunning Little Vixen*, set by Margaret Wenk,
curtain call for animals, insects, and humans

*Boris Godunov*, sets by Margaret Wenk
Above: Prologue, arrival of the pilgrims
Below: Krony Forest, revolution

*Boris Godunov*, sets by Margaret Wenk
Above: The Tsar's Study, the "Hallucination Scene"
Below: Marina's Garden

Above: *A Midsummer Night's Dream*, set by Margaret Wenk
Puck seated, center; Oberon standing, right;
Tytania and the Changeling reclining on platform, left

Below: *The Nightingale*, set by Margaret Wenk
The Nightingale performs for the Emperor

Above: *Cavalleria rusticana*, Alfio (Brian Burkhardt) and his (live) mule team
Below: *Pagliacci*, Nedda (Kerri Rosenberg Burkhardt) arrives in a donkey cart
Set designers G. Baker and W. Coberg for Tri Cities Opera

*La Bohème*, sets rented from Indiana University,
Act I, above, Act II, below

*La Bohème*, Act III, above
Act IV, below

Above: *Agrippina,* set by Margaret Wenk
Juno arrives *ex machina* for the grand finale

Below: *The Barber of Seville*, sets by Larry Kaushansky from Minnesota Opera
Everyone going crazy in a *concertato di confusione*

Above: *Faust,* Walpurgis Night ballet, choreographed by François Martinet;
below: *Così fan tutte*, sets and costumes by Margaret Wenk, the men toast their wager;
bottom: chorus and dancers celebrate la *"bella vita militar"*

Above: *The Gondoliers*, designers Miguel Romero and David Woolard for Opera Theater of St. Louis; below, left: Puck and Oberon in *A Midsummer Night's Dream* costumes by Margaret Wenk; right: Canio summons the crowd in *Pagliacci*

Above: *Manon,* top, the gambling scene, then the Cours-la-Reine ballet;
below, the Soldiers' Chorus from *Faust*

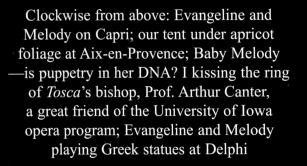

Clockwise from above: Evangeline and
Melody on Capri; our tent under apricot
foliage at Aix-en-Provence; Baby Melody
—is puppetry in her DNA? I kissing the ring
of *Tosca*'s bishop, Prof. Arthur Canter,
a great friend of the University of Iowa
opera program; Evangeline and Melody
playing Greek statues at Delphi

Destiny decreed the change in our lives. My time in Zurich ended with the glorious music of *Tristan und Isolde*. But outside the theater there were student riots. In the late spring of 1980, young people went on a rampage, and the Opera House was the focus of their rage. Demanding a home for their "alternative culture," they ripped down our posters, threw paint bombs at the well-dressed ladies who arrived for our performances, set fire to cars in our parking lot. They twice smashed the curved glass walls of our foyer.* The vandalism spread beyond the Opera House: one wild night

René Kollo coached his first Tristan with me

they broke shop windows along the whole street, throwing expensive furs and other luxury items into the river. It seemed to us like the end of an era. Time to move on.

## The Expatriates Return

In 1961, when Evangeline and I left to seek our fortunes in Europe, there had been precious few opportunities in the US to make a living in opera. When we returned to America, nineteen years later, we were astounded at the proliferation of opera companies. More or less every middle-sized city offered a season of anywhere from three to seven different productions. In the area

---

* They had already created mayhem at rock concerts provided for them at the local stadium.

in and around Iowa alone, for instance, there were professional companies in Des Moines, St. Louis, Kansas City, Omaha, Springfield, Milwaukee, and Minneapolis—not to mention Chicago, which had a long history of opera already. What an amazing change! Opera was finally catching on! I looked forward to playing whatever role I could, and my new job gave me a gratifying chance.

Before I came along, stage directors from the Theater Department had been in charge of University of Iowa opera productions. When Marilyn Somville, the new head of the School of Music, and I were told that the theater designers were too busy with their spring schedule of plays to take on our first opera, *The Cunning Little Vixen*, Dr. Somville made a swift decision. Divorce! We soon had our own enormous, well-equipped scene shop, our own costume and prop shops, and a dedicated technical team. I found a wonderful new designer, Margaret Wenk, who designed sets and cos-

tumes for all the beautiful productions that we built while I was Director of Opera Theater. She was particularly adept at creating magic out of inexpensive materials.

Hancher Auditorium, where we performed, is the show place of Eastern Iowa, frequent host to massive touring Broadway musicals, major symphony orchestras and ballet companies. It seats 2,864. The stage is slightly wider than that of the Metropolitan Opera, the lighting equipment is "state of the art." The sound system helps young singers to avoid any tempta-

Margaret Wenk at work
on an act-drop for *Faust*

tion to force their voices, without making them sound artificially amplified.

One prime asset was the university's own superb symphony orchestra, honed to a high degree of musicality and precision by Professor James Dixon. Another inestimable asset was a dance department with outstanding choreographers as well as dancers. In choosing repertoire I took full advantage of their availability. The "Walpurgis Night" ballet in *Faust,* just one of many possible examples, was the most imaginative and spectacular that I have ever seen, as choreographed by Françoise Martinet, formerly of the Joffrey Ballet. Helen of Troy emerged from a witch's cauldron; Cleopatra descended a living staircase of male dancers at her first entrance; a very nubile Salome cast off her seven veils, aided and abetted by her mother Herodias; orange and green side-lighting created dazzling optical effects during the orgiastic finale.

I took full advantage of the abundant dance talent in my selection of operas: Stravinsky's *Nightingale,* Ravel's *L'enfant et les sortilèges, The Bartered Bride,* Massenet's *Manon*—with ballet—and *Hérodiade.* I introduced extra dances into *Boris Godunov,* for instance, a "cracovienne" in the opening chorus of the Polish Act, and a peasant dance during the taunting of the boyar in Kromy Forest, besides the well-known polonaise called for in the score.

There was once another, less orthodox combination of opera and ballet. Our best singers, stationed by the proscenium arch, sang familiar arias or duets from famous operas while dancers interpreted the music in their own way, according to the fantasies of the choreographers, who freely expressed their reactions to the music, quite independent of the actual meaning of the words being sung. Evangeline sang Isolde's *"Liebestod"* gloriously in those performances, accompanied by Prof. James Dixon and the University of Iowa Symphony Orchestra.

Our daughter Melody also played a part in our productions. In *The Tales of Hoffmann,* she took the part of the Muse, who, in our version, had a long speech in the Prologue, as well as at the end. In *Madame Butterfly* she coached the cast in the authentic, artistic way to use a fan, to manage the sleeves of a kimono, to kneel gracefully and rise again without the support of one's hands, and a thousand other details that she had learned from her time in Japan, where she had had the great and unusual privilege of attending rehearsals at Kabuki and Noh theaters.

Beside Japanese, Melody had studied Chinese and starred in a Chinese opera. When the "Cultural Revolution" came, her teacher memorized all the traditional words, music, dances, swordplay. He taught her the exotic "artificial voice," a dance with two fans, and another with two swords.

Melody spent a year studying drama at the London Academy of Music and Dramatic Art ("Lamda"), and then two years at Cambridge University, where she was acclaimed for her performance of Queen

Melody

Margaret in Shakespeare's *Henry VI* in a hall that was built on the orders of the original Queen Margaret herself.

During a break between terms, Melody returned to Iowa City to perform the title role in Honegger's *Joan of Arc at the Stake* with the university's chorus and symphony orchestra. Many in the audience were moved to tears—and not just her proud parents.

Like her Dad, she had fallen in love with *Faust* at an early age. When she was fourteen, she memorized the Prologue in Heaven and the entire scene in Faust's study. I wanted a former head of Zurich's famous *Schauspielhaus* to hear her. At first he thought I was joking. "*Faust* at fourteen? *Wie süüüss!*—How sweeeeet!" But when he heard her, he agreed to give her some lessons. And, of course, she had already become a seasoned member of the children's chorus at the Zurich Opera.

At the University of Iowa, we did two main-stage productions a year, one in the spring, one in the summer. When either was particularly time-consuming to build, we sometimes rented the other. Our *Butterfly* sets had been designed by Ming Cho Lee, our sumptuous *Traviata* by Robert O'Hearn. The quality of all our productions was exceptionally high and I am proud of what we were able to present to the audiences, who came from all over the region. Besides the standard repertoire, we offered such rarities as Massenet's *Hérodiade* and Tchaikovsky's *Yolanta*, both with the superb young bass Kyle Ketelsen, who is now on his way to a fine career.

Jennifer White, Venus, and Kyle Ketelsen
in Adonis's blood-stained shirt

Incidentally, when Kyle sang the male lead in *Venus and Adonis*, the President of the University of Iowa, Hunter Rawlings III, mimed the role of Charles II (whose mistress played the part of Venus) in a prologue and epilogue. The publicity packed the house.

Every fall there were also programs of one-act operas and children's operas. Our greatest hit was *Sweet Betsy from Pike* by Mark Bucci. When I first played through the vocal score, I laughed so hard I literally fell off the piano stool. Our first performance was with orchestra. I sent a tape to the composer, who wrote back that he wept for pleasure at hearing his orchestration for the very first time. It is an opera made for touring. All you need—for the version with piano—is two clever, athletic singing-actors, a coloratura soprano and a baritone, a mezzo narrator with a gift for "camp," a small bench and a portable lectern. Most of the cast of thousands is left to the imagination of the audience. There is, for instance, a barroom brawl for the baritone and his invisible opponent. The heroine gets a coloratura death scene. We took it on tour to twenty-two different towns. Audiences went wild for it everywhere.

Another comic masterpiece was *La pizza con funghi* (= mushroom pizza) by Seymour Barab, America's most prolific composer of operas. We got a local pizza parlor to sponsor our production, so there were lots of eye-catching pictures in the papers of cast members munching pizzas and dribbling melted cheese all over themselves. Messy—but effective publicity! Our loyal support group, the "Opera Supers," marched around the mall in costume to advertise another of our projects.

One year we took a one-hour condensation of *Faust* to seven different schools, in each of which the children made their own scenery, study, street, garden, prison. In one school the children *were* the scenery, at least in the garden scene, where they played the part of the trees. All the children loved the costumes, the magical effects, the flash of light when the devil appeared, the foaming goblet, the swordplay, and the thrilling trio at the end. Of course they always giggled self-consciously during the abbreviated love scene. They had learned the "Soldiers' Chorus" and the angels' chorus at the end. Once, when their music teacher was sick, I offered to cut the Soldiers' Chorus. What a commotion! They insisted on singing it anyway and gave us the most rousing performance we had heard at any of the schools.

I soon learned that children take to opera naturally if they are actually involved in it, or exposed to it in an interesting way. I included children in as many operas as possible. After a run of *Carmen*, one little fellow's mother asked him what he wanted to be when he grew up. "Escamillo!" was the unexpected answer. Two years later he was cast as the "little changeling boy" who goes to sleep in Tytania's arms in *A Midsummer Night's Dream*. After the first rehearsal his mother asked him what he was called upon to do in the part. "Oh, it's easy: I just follow a pretty soprano around and then go to bed with her."

The children's chorus in *Carmen,* with Sven Nelson,
our would-be Escamillo, far right

Two nephews of ours, aged seven and ten, had played street urchins in *Bohème*. A month or so after the performances, I was astounded to hear them singing whole chunks of the opera by heart.

Busloads of high school students from as far away as Chicago—
four hours one way—came to see our *Carmen* and *The Bartered
Bride*, with its spectacular circus scene and acrobatic dances.

Animals played a
role as well. Our
first was Dimitri's
horse in *Boris Go-
dunov*. That created
such a sensation
that the Johnson
County Sheriff's
Posse offered to
join our *Carmen*
cast, proudly riding
four horses and a
mule in the proces-
sion into the bull-
ring. Alfio's bright-
ly-painted Sicilian
cart—an authentic
one discovered by
chance on an Iowa
farm—was drawn
by four mules. In
*The Elixir of Love*,

Barbara Buddin as Carmen with representatives
of the Johnson County Sheriff's Posse

An authentic Sicilian cart

Nemorino sang
his first aria
cradling a baby
piglet in his
arms, while
other barnyard
animals made
brief appear-
ances on Ad-
ina's farm. In
*The Bartered*

*Bride* a frolicking lamb almost stole the show.

Sometimes the wildlife came uninvited. During a performance of *The Barber of Seville* a bat flew into the theater, circling Rosina during her aria. In that same performance, a stark naked streaker dashed through the auditorium, upstaging Figaro in the middle of *"Largo al factotum."*

Albert Gammon as Basilio
in *The Barber of Seville*

Our first production was a *celebration* of wildlife. There are a few human characters in *The Cunning Little Vixen*, but they are far outnumbered by a whole family of foxes, a badger, a dog, a rooster with his harem of hens, an owl, a grasshopper, a frog, a beetle, a mosquito, and a fly. Since the Theater Department had declined to make costumes for us —and our own costume shop was just starting from scratch— we rented the animal and insect costumes from the Santa

Carol Meyer, center, as the Vixen

Fe Festival. The casting had to be done by size. Fortunately, Carol Meyer, our leading lady and a future Metropolitan Opera Papagena, could fit into the vixen's pelt. Most of the insect costumes must have been designed for midgets; so children were pressed into service early on during my administration. To help us publicize an opera that was still barely known in the U.S., we established a "Vixen Hotline." Those who dialed a certain number would get a bit of the music and a synopsis of the story over the phone. It was an idea I stole from the Seattle Opera's original *Ring* production in 1975, which, beside witty bumper-stickers, had listed a different telephone number for each of the four music dramas. I am happy to say that our first opera was a big surprise success and got us off to a very promising start.

Having fun at a rehearsal

By the time we presented *L'enfant et les sortilèges* (which we called *The Enchanted Child*) on a double bill with Stravinsky's *Nightingale* we were able to build our own, very imaginative costumes for the various fauna involved.

The best thing about my new job was that I could more or less create it as I went along, customize it for myself, so to speak. There had been opera at the University of Iowa for many years. But there was no job description, there were no rules or regulations or guidelines. The files in my office, as left by my predecessor, were full of golfing magazines. So I had a free hand in choosing repertoire, casting, planning sets and lighting, coaching, staging, and touring. I translated twenty of the operas myself. I felt like a child in a giant toy factory. And I had great help from talented theater specialists, designers, and super-efficient stage managers. I was filled with missionary zeal: I wanted everyone to love opera as I did. Not every colleague was equally thrilled with my multiple ambitions. One angry lady called me an "immature monomaniac." But most people admired the exceptionally high quality of our opera performances. My goal was to engage everyone in the audience in a moving music theater experience—especially those who had never seen an opera before and had never realized how exciting and uplifting it can be.

Yes, I was feeling fulfilled. But Evangeline had given up the life we loved in Europe for my sake. I didn't dare star her in any of my operas—there were far too many eager sopranos waiting for a role. But we did offer a semi-staged evening of excerpts from *Der Rosenkavalier* with faculty members as Octavian, Annina, and Baron Ochs and a graduate student as Sophie. And every year or two Evangeline and I gave a song recital, sometimes in the original languages, but sometimes, later, in my English translations, which were—surprisingly—very enthusiastically received by faculty and students.

Because theater presupposes vivid communication between the performers and the audience, I decided from the beginning that all complete operas we presented would be sung in English. On the other hand, every American singer who hopes to enter the world of opera professionally must be at home in Italian, German, and French. So our scenes in opera class and recitals were in the four original languages I was qualified to coach.

I want singers to *want* to be *understood*, to sing words as if they mean what they are saying. It is very frustrating to me to hear a song or an opera—in whatever language—and not be able to catch the words or the sense they are meant to communicate. During my years in academe I attended innumerable student recitals. Generally the foreign language texts could be found in the program, at least in more or less accurate translations. But then came the indispensable English group—and I was all too often in the dark. So I was constantly pestering my singers to articulate more clearly. The problem is that during rehearsals we all become quite familiar with the text. We may well have the impression that it is perfectly clear. Whereas those out front, who are hearing it for the first time, may tire of the effort to decipher the words and just tune out.

I was constantly on the lookout for good, natural-sounding translations and extensively revised most of those that I found. Sometimes none was quite satisfactory. In the case of *La traviata*, for instance, one version was witty and amusing in the party scenes and bland in the dramatic confrontations, whereas another was moving in the big moments of emotion but boring in the scenes of fun and frivolity. Obviously I had no legal right to cut and paste. So I made my own translation. When that turned out well and was taken up by other companies, I began to enjoy the puzzle-like challenge of making many more of my own. My goal was always to create the illusion that the English words were the original ones, that they had inspired the rise and fall of the phrase, its points of stress. My version of Handel's *Agrippina* was later used by Boston Lyric Opera and the University of Maryland, my *Tosca* by Anoka Opera.

In 1985, to celebrate Handel's two-hundredth birthday, we took our production of *Agrippina* to Urbino, Italy, where our distinguished musicologist Sven Hansell had connections, and Eisenstadt, Austria, the site of an annual festival directed by our conductor that summer, Don V. Moses. Our scenery was designed for travel. Poppea's bathtub was collapsible, as were all the Roman columns, the triumphal arch, and the imperial throne. Each of us was allowed one suitcase; the rest of our luggage would be scenery, costumes, props, or orchestra parts. We recruited Roman legionnaires, senators, and beggars in the towns where we performed—none of them had to sing—and managed to find a suitably vast bed for Poppea's tryst with three successive emperors in one evening. The *Haydn-Saal* of the Eszterhazy Palace in Eisenstadt was so beautiful that we decided to scrap our collapsible sets and let the room itself be the scenery. In one particularly moving aria Otho/Ottone addresses the tribunal of the gods. There they were, all of them, on the gorgeous ceiling! Juno could no longer descend from the clouds, as she had in Iowa City, but she made an effective entrance from the rear of the hall (in Urbino she had sung from the royal—or rather ducal—box). For most of our cast that tour was their first taste of Europe, an unforgettable cultural experience.

When we learned that advance ticket sales were disappointing in Urbino, we improvised a parade through the town. Professor Hansell and I were in the vanguard, he waving a banner with the name of our show and the performance dates, I beating the rhythm on a drum, followed by the orchestra playing a medley of themes from the opera. On each of our backs was taped the music for the musician immediately behind us. Then, escorted by Roman legionnaires in gilded breast-plates, came Nero, his enormously long purple train borne by several very enticing slave girls, with a ragged beggar straggling along behind them. It certainly attracted attention. Leave it to Americans to brazen out a publicity stunt like that! I don't know how many tickets we sold—but we had a lot of fun trying.

Our next big event was the Rimsky-Korsakoff version of *Boris Godunov*, our most ambitious production. It had been chosen as a showcase for Simon Estes, our much-loved opera-singing alumnus. We doubled the size of both our chorus and our budget. Malabar of Toronto supplied the gorgeous costumes for the Tsar, the boyars, and the Polish nobility. Iowa Public Television agreed to film two of our three scheduled performances.

Since Simon would not be able to join us until the week before the premiere, Kimm Julian, our Varlaam, also covered the title role and sang all the rehearsals scheduled before Simon's expected arrival. The weekend before that key date, Simon invited me to his home in New Jersey to run through the score with him, to discuss the staging, and then to fly together to Iowa City. He had an evening performance of *Parsifal* to sing at the Met. His Amfortas sounded fine to me; but he was unhappy about some of the *pianissimi* that hadn't come out exactly the way he had wanted. That night I slept in the room next to his. When I happened to wake up in the middle of the night, I was surprised to see light from his room shining through the crack under the door between us. I heard him pacing about. In the morning I went down to breakfast. Simon whispered that something alarming had happened to his voice. He would have to see his doctor. I should fly alone to Iowa City and he would join me there as soon as the doctor would give his permission.

A few hours after I had returned to my office, Simon called to say that he wouldn't be able to sing for at least two months. His participation in our production, planned for him, would have to be canceled. He asked me to arrange for a telephone interview with the local and regional news media, which I did. He made a supremely gracious statement, urging everyone to attend the performances, since—so he said—"Simon Estes isn't important; the opera is." The next day his aunt called me from Davenport, Iowa. "Beau, I thought you were Simon's friend!" Imagine my dismay when she told me that her local paper had assigned the quote to *me*! *I* was supposed to have said: "Simon Estes isn't important; the opera is." Coming from Simon, such a remark was noble; coming from *me* it was abominable! Mortified, I called the editor and set the record straight. A retraction was eventually printed in an inconspicuous spot. The harm was already done, the correction was too little and too late.

Kimm Julian—who has gone on to a successful professional career in opera (with a helpful push from *Opera News* when a critic praised his "sexy" sheriff in *Fanciulla*)—saved the show and covered himself with glory by singing and playing both Boris and Varlaam in the same performances, a stunning feat. It was possible because the two characters never appear in the same

Kimm Julian as Boris in the Coronation Scene

scenes. But it was extremely difficult and taxing, since there had to be a total change of makeup, costume, and persona after every exit. First the Coronation Scene as Boris, then the Inn Scene as Varlaam; Boris in the Tsar's Study; Varlaam in the Krony Forest, followed immediately by Boris in the moving scene of his death! Fortunately his phenomenal accomplishment was preserved on film and telecast throughout the region.

We were lucky. During my eighteen years at the University of Iowa, there was only one other major cancellation by a cast member. Again it was a guest singer who lost his voice, in this case on the day of the premiere of our *Tosca*. I was notified at five o'clock in the afternoon. Our student understudy, Philip Koffron, had sung the second orchestra dress rehearsal the day before, so that the imported star could fly to New York for an important audition. Phil had invited his friends and family to come to hear his big chance at Mario Cavaradossi in the dress rehearsal. Afterwards they went off somewhere to drink beer and talk until the wee hours. He thought his job was done. Then the phone rings a little after five. He has to get into his costume again and be ready to sing the performance. To our immense relief he rose magnificently to the occasion, outsinging and outacting our much more experienced guest. Two days later the latter had recovered his voice enough to sing the second performance. But he asked Phil to do the offstage bits in the torture scene, including the screams, to save him from as much strenuous singing as possible. Kimm Julian, already mentioned above, was our superb Scarpia, and we had two excellent Toscas, Rosemary Lack and Leslie Morgan (she went on to sing Sieglinde, Senta, Fidelio, Chrysothemis, and Turandot, among other roles, in professional companies all over the United States). Those talented young singers can all be very proud—as I am—of the thrilling recordings that were made of those performances, the enduring evidence of an outstanding achievement.

Even when every role in the opera is adequately double-cast there can be the threat of disaster. We had two ideal Roméos, for instance. Each sang a beautiful dress rehearsal. Then each caught a ghastly cold on the day of the first performance. Their colds hung on during the entire run. Before each of the three performances it was a toss-up which tenor was in worse shape. We spent anxious moments planning which high notes could be ducked if necessary. But they both had the courage to go on and the technique to sing through the cold without damage to their voices.

Michèle Crider, Simon Estes, and I

The former University of Iowa student with the most obvious subsequent success in opera is Michèle Crider, who has been singing Butterfly, Amelia in *Ballo*, the *Trovatore* Leonora, and Aida at the Met. When she joined my program she

Michèle Crider and David Rayl in Act II of *Madame Butterfly*

had never sung a complete opera role. At the end of her first year, in the summer of 1986, she performed an exquisitely moving Butterfly. During her second year she was equally convincing as Donna Anna and Violetta—three of the most demanding leading roles in the soprano repertoire in only twelve months. I predicted she'd be at the Met within ten years. My prophecy came true exactly on schedule. In the meantime, she had won a contest in Europe that led to engagements in all the major houses. In the summer of 1991 she returned to Iowa City to be our guest Leonora in *Trovatore*. By then it was already her eighth different production of that opera.

That *Don Giovanni* with Michèle, by the way, inspired a rather remarkable letter from a well-meaning member of the audience. It came in the form of an endless computer print-out, long enough for one of the folding pages in Leporello's *catalogo*. The writer liked quite a few things about our production, but he had one major beef: why didn't I do something to liven up that boring, stand-and-sing trio of the three maskers? He had plenty of suggestions: while they were singing that static piece of music, I could

Rehearsing a scene from *Don Giovanni*
with Jeffrey Hook as Leporello

have shown—behind a scrim —the guests arriving for the party, the servants moving tables and chairs into place, lighting the candles, bringing on the roast pheasant or swan, passing around refreshments, removing the drunken peasants, Don Giovanni seducing the girls, and so forth. In the days of MTV, it seems, Mozart's sublimest moment in the entire opera is insufficiently kinetic.

My next Mozartean opera, *Così fan tutte*, was memorable for a different reason. Near the end of the intermission, happy with the performance so far, I decided to treat myself to a chocolate truffle. When I bit into it I felt something sharp. I spat it out into a paper napkin and tossed it into a receptacle for cigarette butts, paper cups, and ticket stubs. Suddenly I had the horrifying sensation of an empty space in my mouth. I had just lost a front tooth! It had broken loose from the partial plate I had been wearing since my car crash twenty years before. Frantically I tried to find that crunched-up paper napkin among the trash. The bell was already ringing, I had barely time to get back to my seat in the front row. Fortunately, two kindly ushers volunteered to continue the search for my tooth while Act II was in progress. I had to remember not to smile during curtain calls. After the show, I ran out to the lobby. Thank God, they had found my tooth. But there was no way to make it stay in my mouth. So I was toothless for the big reception that folowed the opera. There I was presented to a visiting English lord, Richard Acton, who ever since has been teasing me about the quaint circumstances of our first meeting, when I kept holding a napkin in front of my mouth as we conversed.

That reception took place at the home of Iowa City's superhost, our dear friend John Fitzpatrick, whose circle consisted of artists, musicians, and others who knew their way around in the arts. His house guests included such prominent cosmopolitan visitors as Kitty Carlisle, one of his special friends, impressively stunning at what must be a rather advanced age, if one considers that she played the female lead in the Marx Brothers' immortal movie, *A Night at the Opera* back in the mid-1930s.

The next morning a dentist cemented my tooth back in place, where it has obligingly remained to this day. But if I bite into a truffle, I now do so with extra caution.

When I decided to present *Dialogues of the Carmelites* I was determined to make the convent scenes as authentic as possible. The very first Carmelite nuns I contacted—in Erie, Pennsylvania—happened to be well versed in the entire background of the opera. What an amazing piece of luck! A good friend of theirs, Dr. William Bush of Toronto, is a world expert on the martyrdom of the Carmelite nuns during the French Revolution. Mother Emmanuel and Mother Eliane answered all of my questions about convent life, telling me—and even demonstrating—all the little details of everyday routine. They passed on to me a number of historical facts that I was able to use in my production. The Carmelite martyrs, for instance, who were forbidden by the Revolution to wear  habits, went to their deaths in white robes, not in civilian dress as in the Metropolitan Opera production, because their only other clothes were all soaking wet in a washtub when the authorities suddenly came to take them to the guillotine. The nuns considered it a special grace from God that they could go singing to their martyrdom in their beloved, outlawed white habits.

In the fall of 1986 I skipped a semester to write my biography of Lotte Lehmann. Dr. Frances Holden, her heir, gave me access to all of Lehmann's vast and lively correspondence, her manuscripts,

Dr. Frances Holden in her garden,
with a bust of Lotte Lehmann in the background

her scores, her scrapbooks, all the personal possessions in the home they had shared, as well as in the Lotte Lehmann Archive at the University of California, Santa Barbara. Evangeline and I were invited to live in Lehmann's own rooms, with a magnificent view of the Pacific Ocean over flowering hibiscus, bougainvillea, orange trees, and acres of garden and greenery with not another house in sight. We had a balcony and a sundeck, a little kitchen of our own, and a work room where I set up the computer. Our bedroom closet was actually the attic, full of Lehmann's concert gowns and the leftover odds and ends of a long career. Dr. Holden herself lived downstairs, off the music room, every room a library jammed with books and scores. Outside there were picturesque terraces and patios, decorated with ceramic tiles and stained glass pictures that Lotte had made herself in a workshop adjoining the garage. There was an aviary, a kiln, a swimming pool. We lived in that paradise for almost six months. Every morning was devoted to research. Evangeline would help me by looking for interesting items in the thousands of letters placed at our disposal, as well as in the scrapbooks that fans and managers had been keeping since the first great successes in Hamburg. Afternoons were spent at the word processor. Just before sunset we would go for a long walk along the water's edge at beautiful Arroyo Burro Beach. Thanks to the special curve of the beach and the season of the year, sometimes both the rising moon and the setting sun were reflected in the waves. Then back to our rooms for more writing. In the morning I would read to Frances what I had written the day before and she would offer her opinion, make helpful comments, and dredge up useful facts and colorful impressions from her amazing memory.

She was fascinated by what I had learned about Lotte's early years in Germany from deciphering her correspondence, which was written in a form of script that virtually disappeared after World War II. Fortunately I had studied that script in high school. It was not a requirement, but I learned it for fun, like a secret code. Now that adolescent hobby provided an indispensable tool. There were boxes and boxes of letters that Lotte had written to her brother Fritz while he was working in Berlin and she was starting her career in Hamburg. The obsolete German script was not the only obstacle to reading those letters; they were written in a hastily scribbled scrawl. So I made myself a kind of Rosetta stone: I scanned the first batch of letters for similar-looking squiggles, copied them onto a sheet of paper, and sorted them into a working alphabet. Not for nothing was I once a cryptographer in the U.S. Navy. Deciphering the first letter was a laborious process, but the next was easier, and soon I could read those letters almost as quickly as I could read a newspaper And were they full of news! All of Lotte's first, vivid impressions of theater life, all the backstage gossip, all the thrills and worries and little disasters of life on the stage. There, for instance, was the great conductor Otto Klemperer chasing her around the piano in a rehearsal room or lying in ambush for her in a backstage stairwell. Lehmann always had a gift for writing and an impish sense of humor. Those letters turned out to be a treasure-trove.

My colleagues at the university had been singing the praises of their word processors, but I had never owned one. So, after writing the introductory chapter in longhand, I decided to buy a computer and learn how to use it. After the second week I was so thoroughly hooked that when the monitor broke down and I had to wait for a new one I felt totally helpless. I couldn't produce anything. My inspiration dried up without that friendly blank screen to stare at. How did Dickens ever write a novel? How did Shakespeare manage to turn out all those plays?

My teacher was remarkably patient. Once I was in danger of losing an entire day's work. I was desperate. It happened to be his wedding night, but I had the nerve—the sheer shamelessness—to call him up anyway. Fortunately chance had picked a favorable moment. He was practically purring. While his bride slept peacefully beside him he led me through all the stages needed to save my work. My telephone was in our bedroom, the computer was at the other end of the apartment. So after each step in the instructions I would have to run to the computer to try it out, then run back to the bedroom to announce a failed attempt, then back to try some new strategy. And so it went, until—finally!—the chapter was saved and my exceptionally altruistic teacher could go back to his lovely sleeping bride.

My research gave me a new respect for Lehmann's achievements. I had already known, of course, how popular she had been in Hamburg, Salzburg, and Vienna—where she was still remembered with real affection. What I hadn't realized was the extent to which she had also conquered Paris, London, Brussels, and Rome. During her heyday, many critics, composers, and conductors considered her the finest singer of her era. Richard Strauss expressed the opinion that she had the loveliest, most unspoiled voice in Europe. Puccini called her singing pure honey. The detailed reviews of her performances seemed to me to have significant historical value, not just on her account but because they gave a vivid glimpse into the operatic standards of her time. I originally included extensive excerpts in her biography (later I was forced to whittle them down rather drastically). By the time

Lehmann began the American phase of her career her voice was already well beyond its pristine prime. Here she was admired for her artistry and for her subtle interpretation of multi-faceted roles like the Marschallin, not primarily for her voice—or perhaps even in spite of her voice. Her personal charisma captivated American audiences to the point where she could give as many as eight lieder recitals in New York alone in one season.

Both Risë Stevens, who considered Lotte one of the three dearest women in her life, and Rose Bampton, who had studied many of her roles with Lehmann, gave me generously long and fascinating interviews.

The six months I spent writing the book were among the happiest of my life. The aftermath—my struggles with self-appointed editors and the publisher—was one of my most bitterly frustrating experiences.

When Capra Press offered me a contract, I had written about fifty-thousand words, half of the planned chapters, and had reached the midpoint of Lotte Lehmann's life. The publisher agreed to a hundred thousand words for the biography, since he also intended to include a lengthy discography. I didn't stop to think that the second half of Lehmann's life was far more extensively documented than the first. So I signed the contract. When the writing was finished there were a hundred and fifty thousand words, half again more than the publisher wanted. I was ordered to cut at least thirty-five pages—and that meant some brutal, painful surgery. Lots of colorful but essentially peripheral anecdotes had to go. Excerpts from reviews were so pared down that most of the details that had interested me in the first place ended in the scrap heap.

The publisher was only part of the problem. A far more serious adversary was Frances Holden herself, the same person who had chosen me to write the biography of her friend  and had greeted each chapter with so much obvious enthusiasm—each chapter, that is, until the last one. In the archives I had discovered some deeply moving correspondence between Lehmann and her revered mentor, Bruno Walter. She considered him to have been her greatest teacher, her lieder recitals with him to have been the most inspiring of her career. She respected his wisdom, humanity, and insight as much as his musicianship. Lotte, nearing the end of life, turned to him for spiritual guidance. He wrote her a wise and eloquent letter about the ways in which we can prepare to face our inevitable death. Lehmann herself had released that letter for publication in a German book about her life and art. But Frances was adamantly opposed to my including it in my biography. She resented Walter's influence over Lotte and intended to suppress all references to their spiritual bond. Another sore point was a beautiful poem by Lehmann about the afterlife that I had originally intended to use as an ending to my book. Frances told me peremptorily that she would sue me if I included it. I was forced to bow to her will. But from that day on, she turned against the book and sabotaged its success, telling everyone who would listen: "That is not the Lotte *I* knew." I was devastated by the change in her attitude to me and to my work. After I had left Santa Barbara to resume my duties at the University of Iowa, she and a friend of hers completely rewrote my last chapter, totally behind my back. Their version was all about "exclusive" country clubs and the like. Fortunately I was able to veto that monstrosity. I wrote a new final chapter that they were willing to accept. But  my original version would have been more moving.

I would like to quote here, both in the original German and in my English translation, the poem by Lotte Lehmann that Frances Holden suppressed:

> *Vergessen gibt,*
> *Ich glaube, eines Engels Hand,*
> *Denn abgewandt*
> *Sind wir von dem was einst gewesen.*
> *Genesen von vielen Menschenleben*
> *Müssen, im Aufwärtsstreben,*

*Auf's Neu' und Aberneue wir ersteh'n,*
*Bis wir verweh'n*
*In jenem Morgenrot,*
*Das golden in mein Fenster loht —*
*Im Wind — in Meereswogen —*
*Im Sternenstrahl — im Regenbogen —*
*Im Lächeln Gottes, das du leuchten siehst,*
*Wenn Abendgold im Meer zerfliesst.*

Perhaps it is an angel's hand
That grants oblivion;
For we are turned aside
From what has been before.
Though healed from many human lives,
We must be born, and ever born again,
Until we fade away
Into that golden dawn
That now is glowing through my window,
One with the wind — the waves —
The starlight — and the rainbow —
One with the smile of God,
That lights the sky
When golden sunsets melt into the sea.

The big scoop in my book was the positive confirmation that Lotte Lehmann and Arturo Toscanini did have a very torrid—if intermittent—love affair. At the time of my research, there had been much speculation, but no one seemed to know for sure. What remains of their correspondence leaves no shred of doubt. When Toscanini died, a mutual friend made it her business to retrieve and destroy all of Lotte's letters to him, before his family had a chance to discover where they were hidden. At least some of his letters to Lotte, however met a different fate. The recipient tore them into several large pieces each and tossed them into the fireplace. But she didn't have the heart to strike a match. After she had left the room, her friend Frances Holden rescued the fragments and stuffed them into a secret space in the back of a drawer in her metal filing cabinet. There they rested peacefully for many years, totally forgotten. But shortly before I started the biography, bits of them had begun to slip into the files. Frances tried to reassemble them, but they were scrawled in French and there were huge lacunae in the most interesting parts. I was determined to find the missing pieces of the jigsaw puzzle. With many contortions, thanks to my long, thin fingers, I was finally able to dislodge the last remnants. Discretion and respect for the dead prevent me from sharing with you the steamier effusions, but I shall say that the Maestro was not the least bit reticent in recalling all the details of their erotic encounters. He and Lotte, by the way, both expressed their passionately emotional natures in an addiction to multiple exclamation points—often up to seven or more! —and they both would underline key words five or six times.

Lotte Lehmann with Arturo Toscanini;
the music quoted is the opening phrase of Fidelio's aria.
The inscription: "To Lotte Lehmann, in remembrance,
Feb. 16th, 1934"

I had hoped to quote in my book some of the less intimate items, just enough to establish that there had truly been a passionate, consummated love between those two great artists. I sent copies of the relevant pages of my typescript to Walfredo Toscanini, the conductor's grandson, who was kind enough to reply that the proposed quotations seemed reasonable and tasteful enough, and were unobjectionable to him, but that final permission would have to come from his aunt, Wanda Horowitz. Later, I received a dignified letter from that lady, informing me that she could not grant my request because she could acknowledge only one woman in her father's life, and that was of course her mother. It is a matter of law that the copyright of any letter belongs to the writer and his or her heirs in perpetuity, not to the recipient.

Soon after my biography of Lehmann was published, I received an unexpected honor. The University of Iowa asked me to deliver the "Presidential Lecture" of 1988. The series had been inaugurated only a few years before, and I was the first person chosen from the arts. I based my speech on the research I had done for my book, of course. It turned out to be quite an entertaining show, with lots of slides—including one of Lotte's favorite dogs dressed up in her Act III Marschallin's costume—a variety of impressive excerpts from her recordings, and plenty of humorous anecdotes. The audience loved it. No one was struggling to stay awake. There were no glazed-over eyes. The dean and the president were generous with praise. But a few long-faced colleagues found it pathetically difficult to congratulate me afterwards. Their loss for words was positively comical. Clearly, a dozen erudite scholars felt passed over in favor of a charlatan, a performer, a man of the theater.

I sent a copy of my talk to Irene Sloan, co-founder and editor of the *Opera Quarterly*. She liked it and helped me turn it into an illustrated article, "Genius on the Opera Stage," for her magazine.

Around that time I was invited by the New York Wagner Society to participate in a panel discussion of Lotte Lehmann in celebration of her centenary. George Jellinek was the expert moderator. I had the pleasure of meeting lovely Jarmila Novotná, who happened to sit next to me for part of the program. We shared some memories of her performances at the Met and on Broadway as Helen of Troy. I gave her a copy of my book. From then on, she was a touchingly loyal correspondent until her death.

In the summer of 1988 Evangeline, Melody, and I went to Europe, partly to peddle my book, partly to do some research for a new project devoted to Rich-

Jarmila Novotná as Donna Elvira in *Don Giovanni*

ard Strauss, and partly to visit Cambridge University, where Melody had just finished the first of her two years of literary studies.

During our tour of that truly magnificent campus, by the way, I had to avail myself of the facilities. The back of the door of my stall was entirely covered with intriguing, unusually literate graffiti. My

Melody at her graduation from Cambridge

favorite: "This door is also available in paperback."

We rented a car and drove to Vienna. Two publishers there and one in Salzburg were willing to talk to me; but in the end, nothing happened. Books about opera singers, dead or alive, were not selling that year. Capra Press had a representative in Munich, but she was no help at all. I couldn't even get through the door of a German publisher. We did, however, spend a delightful afternoon with Alice Strauss, the daughter-in-law of the composer, at his villa in Garmisch. It almost turned out to be a disaster. When I called her to request the interview, she agreed on condition that her remarks would not be taped. We forgot to leave our little tape recorder in the car. It was in Evangeline's purse, and just as she was sitting down to accept a cup of tea, some lipstick or key or credit card bumped the play button and music started pouring out of her pocket book. Of course Frau Strauss assumed we were trying to put one over on her. I showed her the cassette, a pre-recorded orchestral concert. That reassured her and all was well again. She gave us a tour of the villa, the great man's library, his art collection, the desk where he had spent part of every day composing, the bed where he had died—after telling his family that he was feeling in actuality exactly what he had intuitively experienced in his imagination so many years before, as he was creating his tone poem, "Death and Transfiguration."

We were encouraged to walk around the grounds. I was deeply moved to read the inscription over a grave in the garden: "Here lies the noble young knight Guntram, slain by his own father's symphony orchestra." Strauss's first opera, his child of sorrow, had never enjoyed a success. Finally, a CD has appeared. The live concert performance is drastically cut; but I hope it may create new interest in a beautiful score.

Our next stop was Switzerland. I called ahead to ask for an interview with Elisabeth Schwarzkopf. Someone had given me a telephone number that turned out to belong to a neighbor of hers. We arrived in Zurich late at night. At 7:00 a.m. I was handed a phone and told that Frau Kammersängerin was on the line. I was still in bed and half asleep. It was quite a conversation! I explained that someone had asked me to compile a book of interviews with people who had memories of Strauss or who were leading interpreters of his work. In a deep and rather mournful voice she asked why anyone would want to write such a book in these inartistic, depressing times, "*der Untergang des Abendlandes,*" to quote her exact words (the German title of "The Decline of the West"). I tried to convince her that there were at least a few encouraging trends. She invited me to come to her house for the interview. In rushing about to get shaved and dressed and find a florist, I completely forgot to grab my tape recorder. When I arrived at her door, she greeted me with a towel wrapped around her head. After showing me into her music room, she went to make coffee and dry her hair. Then we discussed her famous, definitive interpretations of the Marschallin and the Countess in *Capriccio*, an opera especially close to her heart. I scribbled notes as fast as I could, but I am no stenographer; I cursed myself for having left my recorder behind. Well, the book deal fell through, but I enjoyed a fascinating talk with an artist I greatly admire.

Roberta Peters as Lucia

On that same trip I was busily planning the staging of *Lucia di Lammermoor*, which I was shortly to direct in Salt Lake City for Utah Opera. I had a lot of ideas that I thought were innovative, and I hoped that our star, Roberta Peters, would accept them. I realized, of course, that by then she had performed the role a zillion times already and might very possibly just want to do her well-seasoned, usual thing. As I expected, she started to take over the blocking of her opening scene with Alisa. But when she saw what I was doing with the love duet that followed, she gave me her confidence; from then on she did everything I asked her to do, and did it marvelously, with complete conviction, as well as singing exquisitely. I was delightfully surprised and very happy that she was willing to re-stage the entire "Mad Scene" according to my ideas. It was a happy time for me, and I shall always be grateful to Miss Peters for her gracious co-operation.

While planning that *Lucia*, I was simultaneously—or rather alternately—translating *Fidelio* into English for an up-coming production in Iowa. Every other year, the Cedar Rapids Symphony Orchestra and its enterprising, versatile maestro, Christian Tiemeyer, used to present an opera in what was probably a unique format. Although the instrumentalists were on the stage, in a triangular formation fanning out from the podium at the center, each production was fully staged, with scenery, costumes, furniture, props, lighting, and every bit as much action as in any normal, lively staging. There was even a large trapdoor for the grave-digging scene in *Fidelio*. The only difference was that the acting areas were pie-shaped wedges to the right and to the left of the conductor. The space between him and the audience could be used for recitatives, spoken dialogue, and any parts of the piece that did not require an eye on the baton. The singers had to remember to sing toward the audience diagonally, so that they could keep contact with the conductor. When stage right, they should face the half of the audience on their left, and vice versa, rather than singing frontally, as they are accustomed to doing in a traditional setup. All the productions have been highly successful. So far I have staged four Mozart operas and three comedies by Rossini in that format, as well as that *Fidelio*. The casts have been outstanding, gifted actors with first-class voices. We all worked hard, putting together complicated ensemble operas in little over a week. I have enormously enjoyed every one of those productions.

One of the weirdest episodes of my years in academe began when a blind soprano asked to join my opera class. We had a long talk

Julie Nesrallah in *The Italian girl in Algiers,* the Cedar Rapids Symphony production

about the problems she would ultimately have to face, the need to see the conductor, the danger of accidents, and so on. But I accepted her, as a challenging experiment. I remembered that Callas and Jan Peerce, for instance, could barely see the baton and still made great careers on stage. The phenomenon of Andrea Bocelli had not yet emerged on the horizon. So the young woman—I'll call her Janet—became a member of my opera class. I assigned scenes to her. Since she obviously could not read music, I spent many extra hours recording on tape everything she needed to learn, singing the vocal part and playing the accompaniment myself. I habitually coached all the singers, as well as directing their scenes. The rest of the class recognized that "Janet" needed extra time for every detail, but they put up with the problem. After about three semesters, she signed up for the course in opera directing as well. That was even more of a challenge. I told her that a stage director is just as responsible for what is *seen* in an opera as the conductor ultimately is for what is heard. She argued that a colleague would be her eyes and keep her informed of all the visual elements. She said that she had already staged scenes from Shakespeare and had developed her own method of directing. So I gave her the chance. She directed a number of scenes, in some of which I had to fill in for missing singers myself.

Then one day she asked me to be her faculty advisor for a pet project: she wanted to attempt a doctoral thesis combining opera stage direction with art history. I answered that I was not the man to approve her request with a good conscience, since I was personally convinced that sightedness is a prerequisite for both disciplines. I have always felt that a stage director should have a sensitive appreciation of art history, have a feeling for all the styles and epochs in art. I applauded the project, but not for *her*. She insisted that she had a vast knowledge of art history already, and began to describe some famous paintings, the overall subjects and the main colors of which she had memorized. "But can you describe what makes a painting great?" I asked her. "You may be able to tell me about the general pose of 'The Blue Boy,' as you just did; but what makes it a masterpiece?" I told her that—in my view—a stage director must see every movement, every gesture, every facial expression; he or she must be aware of every visual distraction as it occurs, must take ultimate responsibility for colors, sets, costumes, makeup, lighting effects—in short, everything that is *visual*!

Janet was disappointed, of course, but seemed to have understood my position. She was free to ask other faculty members to support her project, if they would.

Then one day the phone rang in my office. It was an editor of the student newspaper asking me to comment on twenty-seven charges that had been filed against me by one of my students. They were about to print a denunciation of me, but wanted first to hear my response. I was flabbergasted, to say the least. After I got over the initial shock, I told them my side of the story. Fortunately, they believed me and suppressed the article with its ridiculous charges. The gist of it was that I had repeatedly embarrassed a blind woman in front of my class by drawing attention to her handicap. She also accused me of having made improper sexual advances to a female student in a love scene that she was directing, claiming that I had "stroked" the lady's thigh.

When the newspaper failed to take up her cause, Janet turned to the Women's Resource and Action Center for help, as well as to the university authorities. She went so far as to report her grievances to a government department that dealt with affirmative action abuses and the denial of equal opportunity to the handicapped. A representative from that agency actually came to our campus all the way from Washington, DC, to investigate me. It was a very fair-minded, sensibly down-to-earth woman of African descent. She soon saw for herself that there was no case, there had been no abuses, and all the wild, hysterical allegations were based on nothing substantial at all.

Later I learned that Janet had left the university to take a special course in aggressive action that was being offered in Des Moines. That was the last I heard of her until two years ago, when I received a short note of apology out of the blue. How strange!

One of my self-imposed duties was to accompany my students when they were competing in the Metropolitan Opera regional auditions, which one year were held in our own theater but more usually took place in Des Moines. One very wintry day I was driving toward that city to assist at the auditions when I hit a small patch of ice, spun around, and slammed into a snowbank. Fortunately no one else was in my lane at that moment, so I didn't hit anyone and no one hit me; but the truck I had just passed gave me a lift to the next exit, where I found a service station and a tow-truck. When I arrived with the tow-truck what did I see next to my car? The four sopranos I was soon scheduled to accompany at the piano had been riding together, and their car had skidded at exactly the same spot. There they were, helplessly ensconced in snow, more or less resigned to missing their big chance to make the Met. How they cheered to see help arriving, and laughed to see *me* sitting up there beside the driver! We actually made it to our scheduled auditions—just in time and in spite of the icy roads.

The weather played a more drastic part in another of my efforts. During the summer of 1993 there was a flood of historic proportions in our part of the world. Entire streets of Iowa City were underwater. We had once thought of buying a house with a panoramic view of the Iowa River. Now its new owners had to reach it by boat. The basement of Hancher Auditorium, including the orchestra pit, was inundated and totally inaccessible. The School of Music, in a wing of that same building, was closed, as was our scene shop and our costume shop. All the scenery and costumes we had planned for *The Jacobin*, by Antonín Dvořák, were either submerged or utterly waterlogged. Wouldn't you know, it was that same summer that a Dvořák symposium had been scheduled at our campus. One hundred years before, the composer had spent the summer in Spillville, Iowa, where he had composed two of his best-known chamber works. Scholars came from all over to read their papers. Members of the composer's family came all the way from the Czech Republic to participate and to attend our production of his opera. And we had to perform it without orchestra, without scenery, and with only rudimentary lighting equipment. Our designer coordinated items of clothing that belonged to the cast in lieu of costumes. And still we had a good success, thanks to the beauty and charm of the music, and the excellence of the cast.

When I was touring with Simon Estes I learned to love "Aleko's Cavatina," a beautiful aria from Rachmaninov's first opera. It was one of Simon's specialties. So when I was casting about for a short work to pair with Tchaikovsky's gorgeous, deeply moving *Yolanta*, I thought of *Aleko*. As far as I knew, it had never been fully staged in the US and I was keen to have a premiere. But the orchestra parts were not so easy to find. After much research, I was able to locate a set, apparently the only complete one in existence. It was in the music library of the Moscow radio station. Fortunately, one of our most fervent supporters had a young friend working at the American Embassy nearby. We received permission to have the music Xeroxed and she offered to pick it up. Then—we actually learned about this first in a TV news program—the roof of the Moscow radio station collapsed, right on top of the music library. Through something like a miracle, the precious parts were undamaged. Our heroic young lady made her way through the ruins, recovered the treasure, and dispatched it to us in the diplomatic pouch! In Washington it was handed to the pilot of a private plane who flew it to us just in time for the first orchestra rehearsal.

To most of our friends and relations, Iowa was the other end of the universe. Even my own sister never undertook to visit us there, despite a standing invitation. But it was actually a little oasis of culture among the cornfields, a beehive of intellectual activity. Among the most prominent professors were Antonio Damasio and James Van Allen, both of whom have become famous in their fields, neurology and astronomy respectively, with discoveries of international importance. The poet Paul Engle had founded the Writers' Workshop and, with his wife Hualing, the International Writing Program. The university maintained an outstanding teaching hospital, a major asset. Aside from our own beautiful opera productions, world-class but untouted outside of Iowa, there were visits by major orchestras and outstanding recitals by such top singers as Leontyne Price, Thomas Hampson, and Kathleen Battle. Nevertheless, we often hankered for even greener pastures elsewhere. When the Met tour was still an annual event, we caught many of their offerings in Minneapolis.

We frequently went to Chicago for the opera. Once I had to walk out in the middle of *I puritani*. Just before the performance I had grabbed a mushroom pizza at a fast-food counter. Something must have been spoiled. I became terribly ill during the first act. But I had never seen that opera before, and I desperately wanted to hang in there till the end. The pains began to be so sharp that I had to give up. Right in the middle of June Anderson's big aria, "*Qui la voce*," of all places, I had to leave my seat and try to stagger up the aisle. I barely made it to the lobby, where I lost consciousness. The next thing I knew, I was being rushed to the hospital in an ambulance. By the next day I was well again; but I have always wondered what happens in the second half of *I puritani*. If ever, by some fluke, Miss Anderson should happen to read these pages, I sincerely extend to her my abject apologies for my unavoidable but distracting exit.

During vacations, Christmas and spring break, Evangeline and I often headed for New York. A good friend from Zurich days, Paul Mills, was a staff stage director at the Met. He often gave us tickets to dress rehearsals. We saw *Siegfried*, *Pelléas*, *Elektra*, *Les Troyens*, *Lucia*, and *Rusalka* that way. During the intermission of a *Fledermaus* performance, he took me backstage and let me watch the spectacular scene shift, one huge set with a turntable sliding magically off as another, equally enormous, silently slid into its place.

Thanks to Paul, I heard Aprile Millo sing Aida. Her ethereally lovely singing in the Tomb Scene made me feel as if I were transported to heaven. I never heard that music more exquisitely interpreted.

Paul's wife Leslie, by the way, is not only a successful teacher and a lovely soprano; she is also an expert in the field of edible weeds. One day, back in Zurich, she invited us vegetarians to a three-course dinner completely composed of weeds from the vacant lot next door. I particularly remember the delicious nettle soup and pigweed salad.

Only once in my life have I bought a ticket from a scalper. I was determined to see Luciano Pavarotti, "live." The opera was *Un ballo in maschera*, sold out of course. I waited for a while by the entrance to the box office, to see if anyone had tickets to return. No such luck. Time was running out. Someone told me that at the other end of Lincoln Center Plaza, where the taxis come and go, there would be scalpers on duty. So I bought for $115 a ticket that was marked $65. It was in the second box, close to the stage. I could practically look down Numero Uno's throat. What most intrigued me was his chewing. I don't know *what* he was chewing;

but whenever his partner in the love duet, Aprile Millo (whom I adore), was pouring her heart out in a solo moment, he would pop something into his mouth and start to chomp away. The same thing happened during his death throes; he would sing a few lines, very touchingly; then, when the ensemble took over briefly, he would do a little more chewing. Maybe he wasn't feeling well that evening. I still adore him too. Most people disdained his movie, *Yes, Giorgio*, but I believe that no one ever sang "*Nessun dorma*" or "*Cielo e mar*" more gorgeously than he did in that film.

In early 1994 I was invited by Stefan Zucker, also known as "the world's highest tenor," to appear with him on four of his late, *late* Saturday evening opera talk shows. Evangeline joined us for two of them. He had read my Lehmann book and enjoyed it, so our first three programs were devoted to her, the fourth to Dusolina Giannini. As I recall, the show started at 10:30 and ran until 2:00 a.m. The studio was at Columbia University. Though Evengeline and I were invited back for the following season, the series came to an untimely end before our scheduled reappearances. Mr. Zucker had a large, loyal following of insomniacs, and his program is greatly missed.

The morning after my first participation in that radio show, I attended a very moving dress rehearsal of *Elektra*. Then I went to the Met's Opera Shop. While I was browsing about, I happened to overhear an elegant lady right next to me ask a salesman for my biography of Lotte Lehmann. She had heard about it the night before, on the radio. What an incredible coincidence: I just happened to have a copy with me, which I immediately inscribed to her and to her husband. That was the beginning of our very warm friendship with Anne-Marie and Richard Bullen, two stalwart supporters of New York's musical life.

One day I was delighted to discover that the cat we inherited from our globe-trotting daughter was devoted to opera, most specifically to *bel canto*. I happened to be listening to an album featuring Joan Sutherland and Luciano Pavarotti in arias and duets by

Bellini and Donizetti. Kitty-Cat came into the room, curled up on my lap and purred a loud descant as long as the music lasted. Ever since that day, cat mealtimes have been announced with operatic melodies: the "Sailors' Chorus" from *The Flying Dutchman* for breakfast, "*La donna è mobile*" for luncheon, "*Una voce poco fà*" for "treat time," and the "Anvil Chorus" for supper, all with brand-new, appropriately feline-oriented English lyrics. Our other cat, Gordon, was less of a specialist; but he too would head for the food bowl the moment the first notes of any of the above pieces were sounded. Now both cats have been reclaimed by Melody; but her musical husband keeps up the tradition of announcing meals with an operatic tune, usually the "Toreador Song" or the "Ride of the Valkyries."

The next cat we happened to acquire was less responsive to opera. When we were on the way to a Wagner concert—the first lap of a trip to visit family in Ohio—the little darling peed all over me. Fortunately, I had more clothes in the trunk of the car and we didn't have to drive very far to find a men's rest room where I could wash off and change.

In 1994 I began a series of books devoted to German lieder for Leyerle Publications, starting with *Schubert's Complete Song Texts, Volumes I and II*. Bill Leyerle had been in a German class I taught at the International Opera Center in Zurich. He asked me to undertake for lieder what Nico Castel was so successfully doing for opera in an on-going series that Leyerle is publishing. This is the format: each line of the text of a song is printed in bold type; above each word the pronunciation is transcribed in the characters of the International Phonetic Alphabet; beneath each word there is a literal translation, and, below that, a paraphrase in normal English syntax. I point out variants, discrepancies, and misprints found in some editions, differences between the composer's manuscript and the various published versions, or between the original poem and its adaptation by the composer. In my commentary after each song I try to clarify the meaning of the poem, if it is not obvious at a first reading. The Schubert books were published in time for his bicentennial in 1997. Since then, the series has continued with Schumann, Brahms, Hugo Wolf, and Strauss, as well as *Selected Song Texts of Great German Lieder*, which includes 251 of the most beautiful songs by all five composers.

Between Volume I and Volume II of the Schubert, I took time off to translate the German biography of a Romanian composer, Nicolae Bretan, at the request of his daughter, Dr Judit Bretan Le Bovit. She has dedicated her energies and her resources to reviving her father's music, which had been suppressed by the Communist regime, and to rehabilitating his reputation. Thanks to her efforts, almost all of his vocal music is now available on CD. Earlier, I had presented the American premiere of his one-act

opera *Golem* at the University of Iowa.

In collaboration with Professor Gustavo Halley of the University of Missouri, Kansas City, I translated a fascinating book by the Italian tenor Giacomo

A scene from *Golem,*
Kristor Hustad, Scott McCoy, and Jennifer White

Lauri-Volpi, *Voci parallele* ("Parallel Voices"), in which he discusses most of the famous singers of the twentieth century, as well as many from the nineteenth. His strong, often controversial opinions make a stimulating read.

To find the time to work on my books, I decided to start "phased retirement" from the University of Iowa in 1995. For three more years I continued to coach and direct the spring and summer opera productions and to teach my usual courses during the spring semester.

Then our daughter Melody moved to Maine. Evangeline and I went to see her play Blanche in *A Streetcar Named Desire* at the Camden Opera House. We were overwhelmed with her scintillating performance—and with the charm of the town itself. I resigned from my job in Iowa, we put our house on the market, and bought a new home for ourselves in Camden, mid-coast Maine—in a former church, now known as "the Steeples." We own one of the four units, each quite different and all four very charming. Ours is the smaller of the two steeples, one of the stained glass windows, a bit of the choir loft, and a pew. In front of the garage there is a sign: "Thou Shalt Not Park Here." Two of our four bathrooms are rather unecclesiastically equipped with Jacuzzis. From our roof deck we can see the mountains and the islands that moved Edna St. Vincent Millay to write "*Renascence,*" and over our bed at night the stars sparkle through two sky-

"The Steeples," Evangeline at our front door

lights in the cathedral ceiling. I almost hate to close my eyes and go to sleep.

We bought the condo—through an agent—from Richard Russo, then already well known as the author of *Nobody's Fool*, which had been made into a successful movie starring Paul Newman. Mr. Russo has recently received the Pulitzer Prize for his latest novel,

The interior of the Steeples, with Wagner's bust

*Empire Falls*. As of now, I have met our predecessor twice. The first time was at the public library across the street from us, where he was giving a reading. We joined the long line waiting to greet him afterwards; when we were almost at his desk I heard him tell the man ahead of me that selling his condo in Camden had been a "tragic" mistake. So I introduced myself as the perpetrator of that tragedy. Lately I walked into a bookstore to buy *Three Junes*, the first novel of my cousin Julia Glass; while waiting for another customer to be helped, I noticed a rack with paperback copies of *Empire Falls* and bought one on a sudden impulse. When I turned around, there was Mr. Russo himself. We had a pleasant chat and I left the store. A half block away, I noticed that the glowing blurb on the back of my cousin's dust jacket was by Richard Russo, a double coincidence.

In a way, coming to live in Maine was like coming home. I have loved the rugged coast of Maine since the summer I spent on Mt. Desert Island when I was seven years old. At various times in my life I have gone back to that enchanting jewel of a place, and each time I have reveled in the unique combination of accessible mountains, pristine lakes, sea-cliffs, roaring surf, and picturesque islands. My aunt Virginia was my guide the first two times. She was game for climbing two mountains a day. The trails offered breathtaking views at every turn and an abundant supply of wild blueberries to refresh us on our way. When we were not climbing mountains (my sister-in-law from Seattle calls them "mole hills"), I would be down at the shore looking for sea urchin shells and hermit crabs, and feeding sea

I as a child, looking at the Bubble Mountains in Acadia National Park

Now as an adult at the same spot

anemones. Seven years later we were back again, this time with my sister, another Virginia. I persuaded both aunt and namesake to attempt with me the "mountain goat trail," out-of-bounds as too dangerous when I was seven. All went well until we had to cross a cliff-face on a narrow ledge, dauntingly high up. Showing off, I skipped with exhilarating nonchalance to the far end of the ledge. The two Virginias were slowly creeping—or rather sliding—along on palms and buttocks. One of them accidentally nudged a wasp's nest. My, how they jumped up and ran! There was no transition in the sudden change of tempo from *larghissimo* to *molto vivace*! Wickedly, I couldn't help laughing.

Living in the remote north-eastern tip of the United States hasn't kept me from sticking a finger into the operatic pie now and then. Since moving to Maine I have staged six operas with professional companies and given master classes at five universities, Rutgers, Indiana, Southern Maine, South-Eastern Oklahoma, and the University of Maine, Orono. We often drive to New York or Boston to see an opera. Not long ago we were moved to tears by *Fanciulla* at the Boston Academy of Music, ravished by *Die tote Stadt* at the New York City Opera, and. lifted into heaven by a glorious *Parsifal* with Domingo and Tomlinson at the Met.

Wonder of wonders, the Camden Opera House has finally earned its name by actually presenting operas, thanks to the bold vision of Karen Eisenhauer, founder of Maine Grand Opera. Janna Hymes-Bianchi is the conductor, and I have been the stage director of four productions so far, *The Magic Flute* in 2001, *Hansel and Gretel* in 2002, *La Bohème* in 2003, and *Die Fledermaus* in 2004, all with outstanding casts that would have brought credit to any opera house in the world. For the Mozart they were accompanied by members of the Bangor Symphony. Because the pit is tiny, the orchestra spilled into the boxes and parts of the auditorium. For *Hansel and Gretel*, which is much more heavily orchestrated than *The Magic Flute*, the Maine Grand Opera put together its own excellent orchestra, opened the back panels of the pit, and placed the brass section under the stage—a very practical solution.

Starting an opera company from scratch is a daunting proposition. I wonder if our founder actually had any idea what she was getting into. The availability of the Opera House, which hosts a variety of attractions, is extremely limited. The tiny pit was just one of our problems; the stage has no fly space, hardly any wing area, almost no room to store scenery. Everything has to be assembled and painted on stage, since there is no way to move in anything much larger than a harp or a kettledrum. On the day of one dress rehearsal there was no heat in the building; Pamina nearly froze in her diaphanous robe. During *Bohème* rehearsals we had to dodge drops of water from a leaking roof and avoid slipping in puddles on the floor.

We have had to count on volunteer help, some of which has been actually forthcoming. Karen's mother created stunningly effective, shimmering cloaks for the Three Ladies. But Papageno had to make his own panpipes. I loaned Colline a coat; his stovepipe hat—which has to serve as a champagne bucket—did not show up until the day of the performance.

Recruiting a chorus turned out to be much more difficult than we had anticipated. Experienced choristers were already committed to *Messiah* or "Cocoa and Carols" or the Brahms Requiem. Some singers showed up regularly for musical rehearsals, then dropped out just before staging began. The high school students who had given *Bohème*'s second act an atmosphere of lively youth, were all occupied elsewhere when we could have used them in *Fledermaus*. Some of Prince Orlofsky's guests were touchingly geriatric; his four liveried servants were grade school kids, far too young to be serving liquor.

Some crucial bits of scenery, such as Papageno's hanging tree and *Bohème*'s indolent "*caminetto*" (the all-important pot-bellied stove), arrived *after* the dress rehearsal. The dummy Witch that was supposed to fly across the stage in *Hansel and Gretel* never did get made. One of the little Gingerbread Children came down with strep throat and both Hansel and Gretel suffered a few nerve-wracking days struggling—successfully—to stave off infection. That all the elements in each of our productions came together at the last moment was practically a miracle.

Lest the dear reader get the impression that our productions were pure amateur night, on the level of a typical high school play in Podunk, let me hasten to state that each opera was thoroughly redeemed by an outstanding cast of professional singers, most of whom were recruited in Boston and New York, highly talented artists who would be acclaimed in any opera theater in America.

The audiences were enormously enthusiastic. Would that they had been enormous! There were too many empty seats, except for

*Fledermaus*; but those who came were surprised and delighted by what they saw and heard. Mr. Tom Wolf, nephew of Boris Goldovsky and head of Bay Chamber Concerts in Rockport, Maine, told us he had never seen a more enjoyable production of *The Magic Flute*, his favorite opera. Many of those who loved our first production immediately reserved seats for the second. We fully expected that word of mouth would sell out *Hansel and Gretel*. Unfortunately, cheering audiences filled only half the seats and the deficit swelled out of control. Obviously too many people thought that *Hansel and Gretel* was some kind of kid show.

Cherry Duke and Laurie Lemley
as Hansel and the Witch

After the final curtain call of the last performance of that opera, we were herded into the green room. A board member informed us that we would all be paid only 35% of our contracted salaries. The singers and the orchestra went into shock. Gretel was counting on her fee to pay the rent of her New York apartment. All of the young singers, though on the brink of highly promising careers, were living pretty close to the edge between engagements.

The future of the Maine Grand Opera looked very much in doubt, in spite of the remarkable artistic success of its first two productions.

We had almost completed the casting of our next planned production, Rossini's *Cinderella* (for which I made a new English translation, as I had also done for *Hansel and Gretel*). We were looking forward to *The Elixir of Love* a year from then. Most intriguingly, we expected to mount a real rarity, *The King's Henchman* by Deems Taylor, which had been premiered at the Metropolitan Opera in 1927. The libretto is by Edna St. Vincent Millay, who had lived and worked in Camden. Our production would have been combined with readings of her poetry and tours of the many locations around here that are associated with her or that had inspired her poems. I had played through the score and found it very appealing, especially a beautiful love scene in Act II. And the Father in *Hansel and Gretel* had given me a 78-rpm disk of Lawrence Tibbett singing two excerpts from the opera. Later, we hoped to present *A Midsummer Night's Dream* in tandem with the local theater company, we offering the opera, they the play. And of course *La Bohème* was also on the schedule. The sad part is that Camden is home to many millionaires, any one of whom could have insured the future of our company at less expense than a new sailboat.

When I recalled that my very first professional engagement in opera ended with the dissolution of the company after my second staging and without the full payment of my contracted fee, the cliché of "completing the circle" came uncomfortably to mind. That was in Seattle, at the exact opposite end of the map from Camden, Maine. Coincidence?

But Karen Eisenhauer is a very determined lady.

Everyone was eventually paid; for some—including me—it was a very long wait. Still, the company soldiered on. *Bohème*—with the world-class Mimì of Patricia Andress—won many new friends for opera and *Fledermaus* attracted the biggest audiences. A block of fifty tickets was bought by students from my new course, "Discovering Opera," which I teach at the Senior College in Belfast, Maine (the size of the class has since grown to sixty-five, and I have been asked to start the course in another community as well).

I am now looking forward to directing Maine Grand Opera's next production, *The Barber of Seville*, in 2006. It will be my third staging of that masterpiece.

Live opera is expensive. If any well-heeled angel would like to spread a love of the lyric muse over mid-coast Maine, I can recommend a worthy project.

In the summer Evangeline and I "team teach" opera and lieder at "AIMS," the American Institute of Musical Studies, in Graz, Austria. We look forward to that every year. The city itself is remarkably beautiful, with its baroque buildings, its rushing river beside the steeply towering "*Schloßberg*," and the green mountains that surround the city. The AIMS program is very well organized and offers the students—most of them from America but many from other countries as well—numerous opportunities to perform in public, in recital with piano or in concert with a superb orchestra. Every day there are interesting classes, lectures, and worthwhile musical events. Highlights for us have included the master classes of Patricia Craig and Gabriella Lechner and the wonderful lectures by Joost van Berge on great singers of the past,

The singers in our AIMS studio, after a program of scenes, summer 2005

with fascinating recordings from his vast collection.* Joost and Bodo Igesz, the well-known stage director, have been our companions on unforgettable excursions. They always know where to find the best record shops in Vienna and the coziest little restaurants on top of Styrian mountains.

It is to Joost van Berge that I owe a very special happiness. Thirty-seven years late, I finally got to hear a recording of my work with Grace Bumbry in the 1965 Holland Festival recital—a group of spirituals and the Gypsy Songs by Dvořák—as well as six exceptionally beautiful Brahms songs from our Salzburg *Liederabend* that same summer. Joost discovered that they were included in the two-CD album, *Grace Bumbry—a Portrait*, and he sent me a copy, the very last one at Tower Records. I must admit, I was thrilled to hear those lovely souvenirs of a long-ago collaboration.

More recently, another CD appeared that included some of my accompaniments. It is called "In This Life" and features some lovely singing from soprano Luba Tcheresky. I accompany her in two songs from *Dichterliebe*, as well as for *"Porgi amor"* and *"Tu che di gel."*

And now two DVD videos of Lotte Lehmann's Master Classes are available, Evangeline sings in both of them, Elsa in a scene from *Lohengrin* in the opera class and Brahms' *"O liebliche Wangen"* in the lieder class. Although my job that summer of 1961 was to assist Mme. Lehmann with her production of *Fidelio* and to stage some one-act operas, I am the accompanist for Evangeline's song, and I accompany Lotte when she demonstrates her interpretation. Memories! But let's fast-forward to the present century.

At AIMS, Evangeline and I try to arrange our teaching schedules so that we can work four days and have three days off for visits to

---

* When Joost van Berge was unable to come to Graz, Roger Pines and, more recently, Dean Southern took over the series with expertise and flair.

Venice or Salzburg or Vienna. After the final concert we stay in Europe for another couple of weeks, traveling to Italy, France, Switzerland, Germany, or the Czech Republic.

One summer we decided to go to Busseto to visit Verdi's villa and his birthplace at Le Roncole. I had made a reservation at "*I due Foscari*," the hotel owned and run by the great Verdi tenor Carlo Bergonzi. We arrived at the station rather late in the evening. The train from Bologna barely stopped. I was struggling with our luggage, about to descend to the platform, when the door closed in my face and the train started to speed away. We had no choice but to wait for the next station, get off there as fast as we could, and spend an hour with the mosquitoes on the deserted platform, until a train finally showed up to take us back to Busseto. When we arrived there, exhausted and laden with bags and suitcases, we were surprised to discover that there was absolutely no transportation to the hotel. Not a cab, not a bus. Nothing. So we had to drag our bags and our selves all the way into town, across the public square while all the local insomniacs stared at the bedraggled, overloaded American tourists, and—thanks to a kind Samaritan who gave us directions—to the darkened hotel. Signor Bergonzi was not in residence at the time. Our room was comfortable, fortunately, and free of mosquitoes. The next morning we were directed to the tourist office. There we learned that there was no possible way to get to Verdi's villa except by renting bicycles and pedaling there in the hot August sun. Busseto, it seems, had once had two taxicabs; but the drivers, apparently, were either dead or on vacation somewhere. There was no bus service and no car rental agency. Verdi fans, be forewarned and prepared! So we didn't get to see what we had come for. But we did like the town enough to spend another night there. We enjoyed the piazza, with its view of the illuminated castle and Verdi's impressive statue. We took the tour of the opera house, named after Verdi, though he had refused ever to set foot inside. He never forgot or forgave the insulting way the puritanical snobs of his hometown had treated his beloved mistress Giuseppina Strepponi, who later became his wife. Before leaving town, we attended mass at the church where

Verdi had once been the organist.

In summer 2004 we spent several days preparing a former "Aimser," Amanda Mace, for an audition at Bayreuth. She coached the role of Eva in *Die Meistersinger* with us. We were thrilled to hear, a week or two later, that she has been promised the part in the next new production at the Festspielhaus.

Two of my former students are now key people in the AIMS organization. Kerri and Brian Burkhardt fell in love during rehearsals for my *Don Giovanni* at the University of Iowa. She was Zerlina, he was Masetto. Later they were Nedda and Alfio, Adina and Belcore. She was Miss Iowa in the Miss America pageant of 1990, the same summer she played Blanche in my staging of *Dialogues of the Carmelites*. Our eleven-year-old nephew fell madly in love with her. Now she and Brian have two gorgeous little children of their own, Brandon and Karissa. Soon the second generation will be singing duets.

Brian Burkhardt and Kerri Rosenberg in *The Gondoliers*,
attended by Sven Nelson

At last we have a grandchild. And he loves opera, at the age of two and a half. His name is Alexander—which he pronounces "Alesassah." Melody met his father, Michael Talcott, a computer whiz, when they were both indulging their hobby—sailing—as students at the Chapman School of Seamanship in Florida. Michael, like Melody, is interested in absolutely everything; he plays the bagpipes—both Scottish and Irish—as well as the piano, the violin, the flute, and the guitar.

Little Alexander was sitting on my lap one day when I happened to be watching a DVD of the Met's wonderful, moving production of *La fanciulla del West*. He seemed to be fascinated and stayed attentive a long time, through an act and a half. A week or so later he watched the first two acts of *Carmen* with me, equally absorbed. Then came *Hansel and Gretel*, and now he asks for it every time he comes to our house, which is several times a week. His favorite moments are the appearance of a greenish goblin just after Hansel calls out "Who's there?" (Al-

The next generation of opera bugs, watching the Met's video of *Hansel and Gretel*

exander calls that mysterious creature "the Cuckoo," because he shows up while the cuckoo call is sounding backstage); then the pantomime of the angels, one of whom is the "Mommy Angel" because she looks like his mother; then the moment when four of the angels cover the sleeping children with a huge, billowing "sucky blanket"; and—of course—the ever-fascinating Witch, especially her broomstick ride. Though he likes to see her get pushed into the oven, he is always relieved to see her take her curtain call at the end. Each of those bits has to be repeated numerous times. The reverse button on the remote control must be nearly worn out by now.

We are grateful for those opera videos, which keep him sitting still for hours at a time. Without them, we would often be rather exhausted, following him around our three-story condo. Unwatched for even a moment, there's no telling what he might be up to. We found toy cars in the VCR slot for VHS tapes, for instance. And it's fun to throw miscellaneous objects into the garbage can. No one can ever be mad at him. His irresistible smile sees to that. And his perpetual good humor.

In October 2005 a harmonious partnership was re-established, after a forty-year intermission. I found myself accompanying Grace Bumbry again.

Except for her very first solo recital, which was accompanied by Gwendolyn Koldofsky in Santa Barbara, I had been Grace's exclusive accompanist for all the many recitals she gave in 1958 and 1959 before her departure for Europe and the start of her international career. Then, in 1964, we did some recitals in Germany. In 1965 we toured Canada and the US, then performed together in the Holland Festival and the Salzburg Festival.

Now we were finally working together again, recording Hugo Wolf's exquisite song *"Anakreons Grab,"* for the Lotte Lehmann Foundation, for a planned CD that will feature songs or arias from as many of Mme. Lehmann's surviving students as are still willing to sing for the microphone. Evangeline had recorded Schumann's *"Aus den hebräischen Gesängen"* a year ago for that project.

Grace sang most gorgeously, and it was a great joy to me to be able to make music together again, as totally in tune with each other as before.

While Evangeline and I were in New York, we attended a very moving tribute to Marian Anderson. Many former colleagues and friends took part. Alice Tully Hall was jammed. Martina Arroyo was the inimitably charming MC and organizer of the program. Grace Bumbry, Reri Grist, and Roberta Peters—to mention just those with whom I have had the pleasure of working—were among the many famous singers who shared their reminiscences of Miss Anderson, and there were some remarkable film clips that reminded us all of the phenomenal impact that Marian Anderson had on American life and culture. Besides deeply moving performances of "Deep River," "He's Got the Whole World in His Hands," and "Crucifixion" (I shall never forget hearing her sing that haunting spiritual "live" at a concert in Ocean Grove, New Jersey), Miss Anderson demonstrated her impressive mastery of German lieder. When I was in London in the 1950s I had heard her sing "*Der Doppelgänger*" with an uncanny, eerie quality of tone that no one else has ever duplicated. "*Der Tod und das Mädchen*" was another of her unique interpretations. Now we could all re-experience her deeply spiritual artistry and her mesmerizing presence.

The night before, Evangeline and I heard my former student Michèle Crider sing a beautiful Aida at the Met. In 1986 she had sung her very first complete opera role—and what a demanding one!—the lead in the University of Iowa production of *Madame Butterfly* that I directed. Her next two roles were no less challenging: Donna Anna and Violetta. Then she went to Europe and spread her wings.

What would I not have given to have a voice of decent quality myself! My mother was a lovely singer; I had to inherit my father's growl. But I can't complain. As a stage director, coach, and accompanist, I have been able to make a living in the magical world of opera and lieder. Best of all, I married a beautiful soprano whose voice is as fresh and appealing today as when I first heard her at that long ago audition.

### What does an opera coach actually *do*?

How often I have heard that question! The short answer: he or she helps the singers learn their parts. All coaches are expected to be able to point out inaccuracies in note values, pitches, intonation, and words. Most coaches guide the singer from the piano. The best have a speaking knowledge of Italian, French, and German—if not also of Russian and Czech—and a good ear for the nuances of expression in each language. They should be thoroughly familiar with the entire standard repertoire, all the various styles, and all the traditions. That's a big order. It takes a long time to acquire the knowledge, plus a lot of effort, and a fervent love of the literature and of the singing voice.

In Europe, at the smaller theaters most operas are still sung in the local language. That used to be the practice in Milan, Paris, and Vienna too; but since about 1970 the major opera houses have switched to the original languages. There are several reasons for that. Earlier, each theater—at least in the German-speaking lands—had its own "ensemble," singers engaged on a year-round basis who worked together as a team. But audiences began to demand the stars they were hearing on recordings. Soon the "*stagione*" system, imported from Italy, became the norm. "*Stagione*" means "season." Singers are individually hired for a particular opera; there will be several performances, close together, for a brief "season," with the same cast. Then that opera will be put aside, and another, with different singers in the leading roles, will be scheduled. In that way, specialists can jet from city to city, from continent to continent, doing their thing in one opera house after another; but obviously those international-name stars will not be expected to have their roles ready in several languages, not to mention in different translations of the same language. Then, starting in the 1980s, came "supertitles" (also known as "surtitles") or—as now at the Metropolitan Opera—individual screens on the back of the seat in front of you. Those running translations have made opera sung in foreign languages accessible to everyone for the first time. In the old days, we all either did our homework or spent the evening wondering what was being said so intensely. Some people just let the music wash over them and ignored the drama that was being enacted with such apparent fervor.

Before 1960, the Zurich *Stadttheater* (Civic Theater), as it was then known, performed everything in German. When Herbert Graf took over the direction, he started a new policy: since all three of the major operatic languages—Italian, French, and German— were actually "official languages" of Switzerland, why not present most of the familiar operas in their original form? It was a while, however, before *Figaros Hochzeit* became *Le nozze di Figaro.* When I joined the company there were two German coaches, one Hungarian, one Swiss, and one Italian; later we were joined by a South-African, an Argentinian, and a second American. During my last two years in Zurich I was head of the coaching staff. When agents, eager for a percentage, hoped to lure me to the major houses, they could not match my salary anywhere.

Musical rehearsals usually began two months before a premiere, a month before the first stage rehearsals. The coach, of course, had to start his or her own preparation well before that, preferably with input from the conductor as to *tempi* and how they will be indicated.

The coach needs to be familiar with all the parts, needs to sing all the cues. That is especially tricky in such complicated ensemble structures as the "Cudgel Scene" from Act II of *Die Meistersinger* or the "Flower Maidens'" sextet with chorus in *Parsifal.*

Coaching sessions, typically one hour long, are usually one-on-one, one singer and one pianist. How that hour is spent varies with the singer and the situation. Is it a totally new role, or are we brushing up an old one? Shall we go through the whole piece for a cursory overview, or start working on details from the very beginning? Is the singer receptive to suggestions, or one of those who say: "Just play the piano"? But even in the latter case the coach has the responsibility to correct mistakes, whether such incursions are welcome or not. The experienced coach develops a sense of how to approach each task most effectively and efficiently. When working with well-developed artistic egos, diplomacy and tact are also handy tools.

One singer's comment made an impression that has stayed with me. He said that he knew exactly how to sing a phrase, and with what expression, from the way I played the accompaniment. He was grateful for the lack of time-consuming explanations. Other singers, though, like to talk about the role and its interpretation. A clear concept, communicated verbally, can also save time. We try to open doors in each other's imaginations, whatever may stimulate intuition and inspiration. Some singers come already well prepared, others prefer to start from scratch. Personally, I like to be there from the very beginning; in that way many mistakes can be avoided, which are difficult to unlearn once they've been memorized, and the interpretation can develop organically, along with the learning of words and music. Some singers feel insecure when faced with a new role and need reassurance from their partner at the piano that they can cope with the imagined difficulties. The coach is there to help.

The coach does not necessarily play the piano part the way it is printed in the score. For Strauss operas, for instance, it helps the singer if I clarify the harmony of the moment by eliminating extraneous counterpoint. In atonal music, I usually play the singer's vocal line prominently over a sketch of the orchestration. Little by little, during rehearsals, I then make the singer's notes less audible, until the singer is secure enough for me to play only the accompaniment. One tries to make the piano simulate the orchestra.

After all the roles have been musically prepared in individual coaching sessions and ensemble rehearsals with the conductor, the stage rehearsals can start. That is when most singers are jolted out of complacency: when they start to think about the acting, the words and music that had seemed so securely learned tend to evaporate from their memory. That's when the prompter's work begins, and some help from the coach at the piano.

For me, the culmination of my work in preparing an opera musically was always the dress rehearsal with piano when I played through the entire score from the pit, trying to put into it all my love of the opera and all the drama inherent in its music, within the restrictions imposed by the conductor's baton.

Besides helping the singer to learn the music accurately, to pronounce the words correctly and expressively, to find the appropriate style of phrasing and presentation, the coach should *inspire* the singer to bring the combination of words and music to life and to find the inner spiritual dimensions of the role.

It is important to know what a composer actually wrote. But we should not ignore tradition. Once a work has been launched, it acquires a life of its own. New interpreters may find meanings in it that its creator had not even consciously noticed or intended. Each true artist who performs a piece may contribute a new nuance, a new insight. In that way, a work of art continues to grow, a living entity. Sometimes a tradition may originate with the composer himself, rehearsing a production after the score has been printed. He may try out a new idea and like it. Or a singer may suggest an effective change. But even those traditions that were not specifically endorsed by the creators can contribute something of value to a piece. It is part of the job of an opera coach to be familiar with all the traditions of the repertoire he or she is working on at the moment and to make them available to the singer.

Fortunately we of today have access to a century of great recordings to enrich our knowledge and understanding of the repertoire, the traditions, and the shifting styles.

Above all, a coach must have a *speaking* knowledge of the

language of the libretto or song lyric, and a good ear for it. It is definitely not enough simply to know the correct pronunciation of the words. One must have a feel for the nuances of the language, for the exact color and weight of each word, for the subtext. One must understand the vocabulary of poetry, which is not always that of every-day conversation.

Styles evolve and change. Is there a "Mozart style"? a "Brahms style"? We sense that there is. But different interpreters may perceive and transmit those "styles" differently. And fashions in interpretation are constantly changing: one decade insists upon long appoggiaturas, the next favors short ones (in the 1930s Fritz Busch, in his much-admired Mozart performances at Glyndebourne, allowed none at all). Still, fashion and style are not the same thing. Performance practice *develops* out of tradition, the research of musicologists, and individual interpretation. It is in a state of flux. During the years between the two world wars Italian singers were steeped in the "*verismo*" style; they sang early 19th-century music, the "*bel canto*" composers, in the same style as Puccini and Mascagni. Nowadays we pride ourselves on our receptivity to the sound of period instruments, on our sensitivity and versatility in dealing with differing historical styles, on our ever expanding search for authenticity—in *musical* matters, at least, if not in the visual presentation.

Style is a component of practically everything. Musical styles— "early music," Baroque, Classical, *bel canto*, Romantic, *verismo*, Late-Romantic, Impressionistic, atonal, neo-Classical, Minimalist, etc. Within those categories are further individual ones— "Handelian," "Mozartean," "Rossinian," etc. The *language* in which a piece is sung will affect the musical style! The language influences the phrasing, the breathing, the stresses, the places where *portamento* is appropriate and those where it is awkward, etc. Each language has a certain style of its own: in German, for instance (unlike French), one actually sings on certain *consonants*, such as m, n, ng, and l, prolonging them after short vowels, as in "*Wonne*" or "*kann*" (which one would not do in speech), and not just on vowels. Italian practically *demands* portamento, because of the *legato* way that the language is spoken. *Lohengrin* in Italian or *Carmen* in German or *La traviata* in French become quite different operas!

Particular care must be given to our own English language. The audience has the right to expect communication! During the rehearsal period the participants become accustomed to the words that are sung. The more often they are heard, the more readily we understand them. So we often believe that they are clear and adequately projected. But the audience has only one chance to hear them, in the moment that they are being articulated. It is very frustrating to hear an opera or a song in a language you understand and not be able to follow the words. At first one tries to catch them; then, often all too soon, one simply gives up the effort. And much is lost. Opera is theater, it is drama. It's not just a bath in beautiful melodies. Often the most engrossing moments are those that illuminate the psychology of the characters through the exact words they utter.

Clear projection of words is not just a problem in singing. Actors seem to have given up the attempt in the interests of excessive realism. Because people speak indistinctly in everyday life, we are forced to hear them mumble on the stage or on the screen. Line after line goes by, unheard. When I was young, film actors and actresses went to special speech coaches to learn the art of projecting a meaningful text. Now no one seems to bother. Again I say it: much is lost.

Here are some random examples of what a coach might say during a coaching session:

"When Violetta breaks off the phrase, the oboe takes over; try to imitate the timbre of the oboe, which will then finish the melody after she has lost her strength."

"Don't give so much emphasis to the unstressed syllables; 'MO-bi-le,' not 'mo-bi-LE.'"

"Don't let the dotted rhythm relax into triplets."

"Be careful not to aspirate the letters t, p, and k in Italian; keep that puff of air out of words like '*tutto*,' '*pace*,' '*caro*.'".

"That cadenza would be effective in something by Donizetti, but it would sound wrong in Mozart, let alone in Handel. We have to find something that fits the style."

"In French, in such words as '*tendre*,' '*ombre*,' '*encore*,' you must eliminate all trace of the n or m in the nasal vowel sounds; go directly from the nasal vowel to the d, b, or c."

"The orchestration is very thick here; you'll have to give more voice and project the consonants even more resonantly; but in this other place you can risk singing very, very softly."

"In the Queen of the Night's first aria she dazzles the prince with the flashing meteors and glittering stars of the night sky; in her second aria she shoots out sparks of anger."

"In Wolf's "*Verborgenheit*," in the phrase '*meine Wonne, meine Pein*,' make a portamento, a quick downward glide, on the *consonant*, the double n, in '*Wonne*,' and then on the diphthong ei, '*ah*-ay,' in '*meine*.' In German—or English—you can sing portamenti on the consonants m, n, ng, and l, or between vowels, when you want a graceful curve instead of angles and zigzags."

"Try an appoggiatura from below; the rising inflection is especially appropriate in a question, or when you want to express surprise or uncertainty."

"Watch that 'back ch'; it's '*Nacht*,' 'night," not '*nakt*,' 'naked'!"

"Try not to aspirate the tied notes! It's '*dell'amore*,' not 'deh-heh-

heh-heh-*hell* amore.'"

"'*Habe Dank*' needs a lovely, clear 'ah,' not 'aw' or 'uh.'"

### What does a stage director actually *do*?

Nowadays—plenty! But when I started going to the opera, in 1936, most performances at the Met did not list a stage director at all. There was a "stage manager," often a former singer, who would tell the soloists, chorus, and supernumeraries—"extras"— where to enter and exit, where to find their props onstage, and little else. That was in the days when most productions tried to reproduce as nearly as possible the staging that had been created, under the influence of the composer, for the world premiere. (That is still the rule for revivals of famous musicals.) For the Italian repertoire, for instance, singers would be sent to Italy to learn the "*scena*," the traditional staging of their roles, from an acting coach, after they had learned the musical interpretation. Then all they would need to know before performing the first act of *Tosca*, for instance, would be: on which side of the stage is the statue of the Madonna? Where is the painting of Mary Magdalene, where is the Attavanti Chapel? A Tosca might meet her Mario for the first time as she made her entrance on the night of the performance. Since both already knew the traditional moves, there was little need to rehearse. There were some individualists. No one could be sure what Feodor Chaliapin or Geraldine Farrar might do next. In Carmen, according to Giacomo Lauri-Volpi, Maria Jeritza munched on an apple while he was singing his "Flower Song" to her, then, when he kneeled at her feet, grabbed him by the hair and thrust his head between her knees. Lily Pons instructed Robert Merrill: "Never come to *me*; *I* shall come to *you*." Grace Moore had Mimì's chair nailed to the floor so that Jan Kiepura wouldn't be able to move it into an unfavorable position before her aria. But, in general, *Aida* or *La Bohème* would look pretty much the same, whether you saw it in Buenos Aires, San Francisco, London, Vienna, or Rome.

All that has changed, sometimes for the better, sometimes not—and rather drastically. The original creators wouldn't even recognize some of the current productions of their works. More of that in a moment.

When I went to Seattle in 1956 for my first engagement as a stage director, the set designer's girl friend was surprised to hear that my obligations involved more than just planning the entrances and exits. During the second half of the twentieth century, stage direction became more and more a key element in an opera production, if not the dominant one.

Opera is drama *heightened by music*. The music—as well as the words—tells the actor when and how to move, when to be still, when a gesture is called for, what inner feeling needs to be expressed.

Opera is *theater*. Theater implies *communication between performer and audience* in a mutual language each can understand.

Opera should NEVER BE BORING to a person of reasonable intelligence with an open mind. It is one of the responsibilities of the director and the performers to make sure that the audience is never bored, but always interested, involved, sometimes moved, sometimes uplifted, *but always engaged*.

Ideally there should be *a harmony between what is heard and what is seen*: the music should seem to have been composed to illustrate the action we are seeing, to express the feeling or atmosphere that is being presented on the stage at any given moment. The music—not just the music of the vocal line, but also the music coming from the orchestra pit—*belongs* to the actor: those sounds are *his or her* feelings, *his or her* reactions, *his or her* thoughts, *his or her* physical responses made audible.

Opera and spoken drama have many elements in common, but also significant differences, due to the presence of music. Music creates its own sense of time, its own non-specific but tangible atmosphere; it follows its own logic. Often, in an opera, time seems to stand still while an emotion is being explored in the music. Such moments call for a style of movement different from that which would be appropriate in the more realistic scenes of action. In actual life such feelings, such thoughts, might take up a few seconds; in an opera they may be expanded into a four-minute aria. In actual life the person might assume one expression, make one gesture or none at all; in a four-minute aria such extended stasis would become boring and untheatrical. Often we hear people making fun of the sometimes rather prolonged good-byes of characters who—according to the plot—ought to be in a hurry. Gilda and the Duke singing several pages of "addios" when she is apparently trying to rush him out of her garden before her father returns, Jeník and Mařenka in *The Bartered Bride* singing "good-bye" long after they have heard someone coming and decided to separate, Manrico stopping to sing a rousing cabaletta before running off to rescue his mother—those are examples of "unrealistic" episodes in opera which seem artificial or illogical to some people, but to me seem to be following a different kind of truth, the truth of the heart.

Then there are those differences between opera and spoken drama that are purely technical rather than aesthetic: the singers need to sing "front" to project their voices over an orchestra in a house that is usually much bigger than the theaters intended for straight drama; the singers need to see the conductor; some positions and some actions are awkward or even impossible for most singers while actually singing. Further, crying creates phlegm; agitated breathing through the mouth dries the throat: singers have to sing well no matter what, whereas actors can take certain risks with their voices.

Everything in live opera is enlarged in scale. Nuances of facial expression that would register effectively in a movie close-up will be lost in a large opera house. Body language needs to project to the back rows and top galleries. Feelings, reactions, relationships need to be made very clear, especially since sung words are usually harder to catch than spoken ones. The audience needs all the visual cues you can give to help comprehension (and thus increase interest and enjoyment). Appropriate gestures can reinforce the words.

The stage director needs to create varied and expressive *pictures,* changing visual patterns that go with changes in the *musical* patterns (that harmony between eye and ear again!!); and, as in spoken drama, all those changes and movements should be believably *motivated* from the dramatic, psychological point of view as well as the purely visual need for variety.

The stage director is *ultimately responsible for everything that the audience will* SEE, just as the conductor has a general responsibility for everything they will HEAR. That is the basic division of responsibility, though of course the two areas will and must overlap, since the way the words are projected, and the expression behind them, concern the stage director for dramatic reasons as much as they do the conductor for musical ones; and the position of soloists and chorus on the stage is as much the legitimate concern of the conductor, who needs to be sure that all can see the baton clearly when they need to, as it is of the stage director, who cares about the visual arrangement for aesthetic and dramatic reasons. The stage director in opera must be a musician, or at least must be sensitive to the language of music and the hints that it conveys. The ideal is an integrated concept shared by conductor, director, and designer.

The visual *concept* begins with the stage director. He or she needs to decide upon the style, the visual impressions he or she hopes to create, the atmosphere called for by the music and the drama at any moment. The stage director must plan the action to some extent *before* consultations with the designer, so that the technical requirements are established first—how many doors (for instance)? Do we need different levels for the chorus? What do we actually need on the stage? Then come the discussions with the designer, who must be given room for creativity and personal artistic input. Together, then, the designer and the stage director work closely, planning the look of the show, inspiring each other, doing research independently or together. The stage director makes a prop list. The stage director plans the light cues and the mood changes that the lighting designer will then realize technically. The stage director indicates for the stage manager the precise points where the curtain should be raised or lowered.

The stage director needs to notice and coordinate everything: the entrances, exits, movements, gestures, positions, and expressions of all the performers, chorus as well as soloists, the positioning of props and furniture, the integration of the lighting effects. To plan those elements in advance, the director studies the words and music very carefully and tries to form mental pictures as he or she builds up the action step by step. Sometimes those pictures do not come to mind immediately at first; then, suddenly, a later moment in the drama forms a visual image, and one can work backwards toward the troublesome blank spot and find an effective solution. Every musical "event" should have its dramatic counterpart; no musical statement should be visually meaningless. Everything *means* something (or should!).

Although the stage director ought—in my opinion—to have worked out the essential actions before the first "blocking" rehearsal, he or she must be flexible, ready to adjust a planned action to the personality and skills of the individual cast members, who may have very usable ideas to contribute themselves.

In the professional opera world time is expensive. Choruses, orchestras, and stagehands are very conscious of overtime. In the university rehearsal situations, time is also scarce and precious. We cannot afford to waste it. We need to have planned very carefully what we hope to cover at each rehearsal and which performers are needed when. We need to come with ideas. Sometimes a good new one comes spontaneously on the spot. That can be exciting and stimulating. But you can't count on instantaneous inspiration from above. You must be prepared. Too much time is lost when blocking needs to be redone because of inadequate preparation on the part of the director.

Each opera will present its own field of research, perhaps the original story or play upon which it is based, perhaps the customs of the country in which it takes place, perhaps the historical background, or authentic manners, dances, games, props, or costumes of the period, perhaps the philosophical or artistic aims of the composer. Research can be one of the most enriching aspects of our work. We need to develop a sense of the various styles, the individual style of the composer, the style of the composer's period or national school as well as the style of the period and place portrayed by the story. That sense of style is not developed overnight. Stage director and singers should constantly strive to broaden their cultural outlook and to learn all they can about history, art history, poetry, drama, and literature, since those fields all relate to and interact with opera. Study the work of great singers of the past and present; listen to records, hear the Saturday opera broadcasts, watch opera videos and DVDs; go to the theater and study the work of good actors and directors, visit art museums and study paintings and sculptures from various periods and lands. Also, needless to say, we all need to learn the three essential operatic languages: Italian, German, and French! You can't interpret what you don't understand! And our job is—above all—interpretation.

Style is not something that can easily be put into words. A sense of style is absorbed from what we have observed; it is something we accumulate, gradually, as we are exposed to life's experiences as well as to all forms of art, good as well as bad, "high" as well as "low."

Our sense of style will affect our perception of whatever we see or hear and whatever we present for others to see or hear. There can be several different styles within the same opera, a different style of movement in a lyrical aria, for instance, than in a realistic recitative.

Acting styles change. Compare Laurence Olivier and Kenneth Branagh—both outstanding Shakespearean actors but more than a generation apart—as Henry V! For a more astounding contrast listen to a recording of John Barrymore as Hamlet or Richard III in the 1920s. Each generation unconsciously absorbs to some degree the current styles, and tends to accept them as natural. When we see films from the silent era, a period well before our own time, the acting—even of the most famous actors—often seems ludicrously overdone; yet, to their contemporaries, their style was appropriate and expressive. So, today, we can not imitate the style of acting that Puccini would have experienced in the theater of his day—let alone that of Verdi's time, or Rossini's!—without running the risk of laughter from the audience. And laughter would kill the moments that we want to make most touching.

So, obviously, we need to find a way to harmonize the demands of music from the past with the expectations of modern audiences. We need to find a balance. Be true to the music; try to preserve a sense of its authentic style. But find a visual counterpart that is true to the expressive message of the music and the sense of the words and yet, at the same time, that will be appealing, moving, and entertaining to *our* contemporaries.

Realism in movies is part of the medium. Producers, set and costume designers, directors and actors all strive for authenticity of detail; yet *Marie Antoinette*, a Hollywood film of the 1930s, and *Dangerous Liaisons*, a recent hit, each gave a very different look to 18th-century France. What was it *really* like back then? We have our *ideas*, more or less well-informed guesses. But no one alive today knows for sure. So we cannot re-create the past, no matter how many old letters or diaries we decipher; we can only re-imagine it, on the basis of what we have learned in our research or from the research of others. No matter what we do, the mark of our own time will cling to it. Just look at the pictures of former opera stars, Caruso, for instance, or Patti, or Tetrazzini. Their costumes were no doubt intended to be authentic; but those costumes are totally different from anything anyone would wear today in even the most "traditional" stagings.

We *re-invent* the past; we try to *suggest* how things *might* have been, how people might have behaved. We try to stimulate the imagination of the actors and the audience. The important thing is that the performer be totally sincere and make the action his or her own through an inner conviction. That conviction will then convince the audience. We need to create *living* theater, not a mechanical reproduction of a long-dead style. Imagine that we could somehow go back in time and re-experience the premieres of *Don Giovanni* or *Tristan und Isolde* or *Aida*. That would be fascinating, wouldn't it. But if we tried to reproduce what we had seen for a modern audience we might be able to satisfy their curiosity, but we probably would not move their emotions through deep involvement in the drama. Wagner himself was deeply disappointed in the failure of his production of *The Ring*, in his own theater and under his own total supervision, to come close to the sublime visions he had imagined and which his music still powerfully conjures up for us. The great music endures. The original staging soon becomes outmoded, even if it was not inadequate to begin with. Yet how poor we would be if no effort at all were made to try to suggest the composer's vision in a way that would convey it effectively to people today.

Let us not "dumb down" to our audience. Let us assume that an intelligent person can enjoy an imaginative trip to another time and place. Let us use our imaginations! We do not need to "up-date" everything, *à la* Peter Sellars to make it "relevant." Or have we lost all interest in history?

How do we develop a sense of style? By observing great interpreters, great actors and singers. By studying great art. By reading great literature. By learning to recognize various styles and to differentiate among them.

There is no one-and-only-one right way to stage an opera! Wagner's grandson Wieland Wagner completely broke with the traditional staging that had been handed down since his grandfather's time; yet his innovations had great poetic beauty and psychological insight: *they did not go against the spirit of the music.* We want to share with the audience our love and appreciation of those great works of art that have survived the test of time, and we want to do it in a way that does not violate the spiritual integrity inherent in the piece. Our job is to bring it to vibrant life.

What about the responsibility of the individual singer? Obviously, he or she should be familiar with the whole opera, not just with his or her own role. Learning the notes and the words is the least of it. Those elements need to be re-created, to be internalized and given new life. You want to come as close as you can to the ideal image that hovered in the imagination of the poet and the composer. And

Kirsten Flagstad as Dido

that, obviously, must include your appearance! Yes, I must plead guilty of fattism. I have loved many large singers, not just for their voices, but also for artistry and acting. Kirsten Flagstad, when I first heard her in 1938, looked rather matronly, but not yet obese. In 1952 I saw her play Purcell's Dido at the tiny Mermaid Theatre in a suburb of London. Since there was no pit—the orchestra was on a balcony above the stage, the conductor was seen by the singers through a mirror, as I recall—I, in the first row, was only about three or four feet away from her at times. By then she had put on a lot of weight. But she captivated us all through the unexpected subtlety of her acting, her expressive face, and her majestic but womanly presence. A well-designed costume helped, of course. That same year I saw Maria Callas as Norma. As I have written earlier, she was statuesque, but not obese. (Nevertheless, she became an infinitely more subtle actress after her famous weight-loss.) Ebe Stignani, Adalgisa to that Callas Norma, looked more like her mother than her supposedly younger colleague; but her singing was absolutely glorious. Astrid Varnay, who was very slim—by Wagnerian standards—when I first saw her as Elsa at the Met in 1942, was far from sylph-like by 1964, when I was overwhelmed by her Isolde, Kundry, and Elektra in Zurich and Salzburg. But she knew how to create the *illusion* of seductive beauty in Act II of *Parsifal*, through some magic of movement and expression. Montserrat Caballé enchanted me as Queen Elizabeth I in *Roberto Devereux* and as Norma, thanks to the incredible beauty, expressiveness, and musicality of her singing. And she moved well, with grace and dignity.

On the other hand, many a performance has been ruined for me by singers whose looks totally contradict their function in the story. It is the obligation of a serious singer to make every effort to look the parts she or he expects to play. One owes that to the composer and to the audience. In our era, there is no excuse for obesity on the stage. No one expects an opera singer to have the body-type of a ballerina. But there are reasonable limits!

The past half-century has seen the rise of the stage director to dominance in the world of opera. Along with some remarkably brilliant and beautiful productions that fully realized the vision of poet and composer with all the resources of modern stage technology, there have been far too many artistic disasters perpetrated by arrogant and ignorant directors who attract attention and make their name by shock tactics. *Lohengrin* in a trailer camp, with Elsa's bridal dress made out of cheap curtains from her camper. The opening scene of *Un ballo in maschera* set in a men's room with open stalls, every stool occupied with a courtier reading a newspaper, his trousers around his ankles. Chrysothemis lugging around an ironing board to show her yearning for domesticity. Railroad tracks in *Parsifal*. *Don Giovanni* on a run-down street in the Bronx. Old cars and refrigerators, rapidly becoming clichés on the opera stage. What is going on?! The cancer is spreading throughout Western Europe and the British Isles from its origins in East Germany. America is—so far—a last bastion of common sense. But we are being ridiculed by a new generation of jaded European critics. They accuse us of clinging to an outmoded idea of theater. Everything must be up-dated to a drab vision of the present or the recent past. That is supposed to make the opera "relevant" and understandable to a younger, with-it audience. Movies still respect historical settings. Imagine *Braveheart* or *Gladiator* in blue jeans and T-shirts! Why must opera be detached from its period? Leading hot-shot directors of today are doing violence to the *spirit* of the operas they desecrate.

No one is asking for a return to the shabby sets and stereotyped gestures of the past. Of course the presentation of opera needs the breath of life, fresh air, new ideas, new insights, new techniques. But they should all be in the service of the piece, to bring out what is in it, not to superimpose an alien concept that contradicts the words and the music and the spiritual essence of a masterwork. I find it odd that at the very time when musicians are striving for an historically authentic sound and style, the visual side of opera should be so out of sync with the music. The ideal must surely be a harmony between what is heard and what is seen.

**A word about performing lieder:**

There are two conflicting theories about interpreting art songs. The one is based upon the definition of poetry as "the recollection of emotion in tranquillity." That school of thought maintains that the performer is basically a reader and should simply recite the poem, if possible clearly and tastefully, but with a certain emotional reserve. The other school—to which I most emphatically belong—urges the performer to re-experience the feelings that gave birth to the poem, and to communicate those feelings to the audience as vividly as possible, to give *life* to the poem—though within the conventions of the recital platform rather than those of the theater. This school is exemplified for me by Lotte Lehmann, my mentor in understanding the infinitely fascinating world of German lieder. With her voice, with her eyes, with her whole being she *lived* the song. And she brought the audience with her into its world. She did not resort to theatrical gestures; but within the accepted performance traditions of lieder, she was able to project what she felt about the song by exploiting all the expressive possibilities of body language, facial expression, and verbal nuance.

In Lehmann's day, it was customary for lieder singers to hold their hands in a clasped position. But she could do that in so many expressive ways: lightly or fervently, relaxed or tense, close to the body or reaching out. She could lean quietly against the piano; or she could surge forward vigorously. When she first attended a recital by Dietrich Fischer-Dieskau, her world-famous successor in the field of lieder, she was surprised that he kept his hands more or less lifeless at his sides. His face and voice were expressive, but his hands remained relatively inert. That perplexed her. When her students tried to adopt the new style, which has since spread everywhere, she was willing to experi-

Lehmann and Dietrich Fischer-Dieskau at her home

ment with them, always trying to keep the body expressive, even though the hands were down. She found it very difficult and very frustrating.

I find that compromise is possible. Depending upon the mood to be expressed, the hands can be at one's sides; one hand or both can touch—or grasp or rest upon—the piano lid; the hands can be clasped; one hand or both can touch the body in an expressive way. The important thing is that one's whole being be in harmony with the atmosphere and the emotions of the song, that every element be organic and artistic, and that nothing be overdone.

When I was young, song recitals were popular. Every concert series in the larger towns would feature at least one singer. But after the advent of television, those concert series gradually disappeared. And solo song recitals were the first to go. For a long time there has been a drought. But recently, thanks to special efforts made by Marilyn Horne, the Lotte Lehmann Foundation, and others, a well-organized movement to revive interest in the rich artistic heritage of the art song has started to gather momentum. Now that opera has become more popular than ever before in America, the time is ripe for audiences to discover the treasures of German lieder and French *mélodies*—not to mention the art songs of our own era and our own country.

But it is the responsibility of the singer and the accompanist to make such programs exciting and alive, to capture and fascinate the audience. It is a sin to bore them. Each song must be fully felt and fully communicated.

Every song is a vital piece of someone's life. Some special experience, some unusual situation, inspired the poet to write a poem. Ordinary, everyday events don't usually give birth to poetry. Then along came the composer, who read the poem and was inspired to create just *that* music to express the feelings it aroused in him—or her. It is our task to stimulate our imagination through a careful reading of the words and music, through letting them seep into our souls, to the point where we can attempt to re-create those original impulses out of which the song was born. In other words, we strive to give the illusion that the song is being born as we sing it. To do that, we must vividly see and feel the setting, the atmosphere, and the situation of the speaker, so that the audience can see and feel those elements too. The eyes, as Lehmann always said, are the singer's greatest tool of expression, after the voice. Study the words and music for clues: a look up, or down, or away, or askance, or into the distance, a tilt of the head. Besides the constant need to convey expression, there are practical considerations: Everyone in the audience wants to see your eyes, not just those who happen to be sitting directly in front of you. Find an appropriate motivation in the song, a change of thought or of mood, to shift your gaze to the right or to the left or up toward the balcony.

Study the accompaniment for clues. Every modulation, every change in tempo or dynamics calls for its visual component. A sudden forte or sforzato chord obviously must mean something dramatically; use it! Involve as many senses as possible in imagining a scene: smell, taste, touch, as well as hearing and seeing. How we breathe before a line determines the emotion we can give to that line, as if anger, fear, love, admiration, doubt, mistrust, jealousy were all elements floating around in the air, and all we had to do was just to breathe them in. Breath is the vital energizer of life.

But above all: make sure that the words are coming across to the very back of the hall. The poem inspired the song. If the words are not clearly understood, the listener will tune out. The great songs, like the great operas, are a beautiful mating of word and tone. To each its due!

The songs of Schubert, Schumann, Brahms, Wolf, Strauss, Debussy, Fauré, and Duparc have meant as much to me as the great operas that have filled my life with their eternal fascination.

## Opera Then and Now—Seventy Years of Shifting Styles

This opera bug, at eighty, can look back at many changes in the way that opera has been presented over the years.

The most striking development is the ascendancy of the stage director. Back in the 1930s very few Metropolitan Opera programs even mentioned such a functionary. The stage manager (Désiré Defrère for the Italian and French repertoire, Leopold Sachse for the German) was in charge of the blocking, which was basically fixed by tradition. It was he—always a male in those days—who gave the supers their instructions, supervised entrances and exits, and coached neophytes in the histrionic rudiments of their roles. An early exception was Herbert Graf, fresh from the triumph of Toscanini's Salzburg *Meistersinger*, which Graf had staged. He made his Met debut in 1936 with *Samson et Dalila*, and the critics duly noted a new look, not altogether favorably.

Still, he set new standards at the Met for integrated productions, especially with his highly successful staging in 1940 of *Le nozze di Figaro*, with Ezio Pinza, Bidú Sayão, Elisabeth Rethberg, and

*Le nozze di Figaro*, Act II, in Herbert Graf's production at the Met

Risë Stevens, a production that inspired in the habitués of the old Met a sudden appreciation of the operas of Mozart, which had previously played to half-empty houses.

In 1961 and 1962 at the Zurich Opera, where I was working at the time as a coach and assistant stage director, I had numerous opportunities to observe Dr. Graf in rehearsal (and again in 1968 at Salzburg, when he directed José Van Dam, Suzanne Sarocca, and my wife, Evangeline Noël, among others, in a spectacularly lavish production of *La rappresentazione di anima e di corpo* in the quasi-outdoor *"Felsenreitschule."* At that point in his career he

The final scene of *La rappresentazione di anima e di corpo* at Salzburg, 1968

seemed to take surprisingly little interest in *Personenregie*, in the acting, interacting, and reacting of the principal singers, in the psychological motivation of the individual characters. During his first seasons in Zurich, he left much of that in the hands of Lotfi Mansouri, [*] whom he had brought over from America to assist

---

[*] Lotfi Mansouri did opera an enormous service in introducing "surtitles" (or "supertitles") for the first time

him, and to whom he assigned all the operas that he was disinclined to direct himself. Graf's specialty was the management of crowds, the movement of the chorus, and the grand overall design. He was in his element at the Verona Arena. There I thoroughly enjoyed his productions of *Aida*—a thousand people on stage!—and *Lohengrin*. And he took pride in his innovations, such as the use of the revolving stage in Act III of *Der Rosenkavalier*, when the audience could follow Baron Ochs's flight from the inn, pursued by the crowd, and the final trio and duet were sung in the moonlit garden, with the lights of Vienna twinkling in the distance. In *Der Fledermaus* we saw the upstairs as well as the downstairs of the Eisenstein home, and could watch Adele as she snitched her mistress's ballgown. In Act II Prince Orlovsky's liveried servants served champagne to the audience during the New Year's Eve performance.

*Die Fledermaus*, Act I set, Herbert Graf production, Zurich Opera

But back to the good old days, or bad old days, according to your perspective!

I started to attend operas at the Met in the spring of 1936, when I was ten years old. My first opera was *Rigoletto* with John Charles Thomas in the title role and Bruna Castagna, who had only recently made her debut, as Maddalena. I found the experience entrancing. To me the opening scene, bathed in pink and blue light, was the essence of glamour.[*] I was thrilled by the exciting storm in the last act, with its exceedingly realistic lightning, scudding clouds, and the moaning thirds of the offstage chorus as the wind. On Saturday matinee broadcasts I heard Lucrezia Bori sing Mignon and later Magda in *La rondine*. And I had started a scrapbook in December 1935 with every newspaper photo and review that I could find. I well remember reading about the new productions of *La traviata* (on opening night) and *Die Walküre* (Marjorie Lawrence's debut as Brünnhilde).

The following season I saw *Carmen* with Rosa Ponselle (whom I met backstage afterwards) and Ezio Pinza. Fascinating! Marvelous! Then came *Traviata* with Eidé Norena and Lawrence Tibbett. I sketched all the sets in my diary. Everything seemed perfect. But, of course, I had nothing with which to compare those early impressions. At some point during my first Ring Cycle disillusionment began to creep into my consciousness. The water effects and the swimming Rhine Maidens were impressive enough; but red steam was hardly magic fire; the Valkyries' Rock from the new production of *Die Walküre* was striking; but in *Götterdämmerung* the curtain rose on a depressingly decrepit version of that crag, vintage World War One or earlier.

The old Met had no storage space for scenery. It was stacked up on the sidewalk behind the opera house, on Seventh Avenue, exposed to wind, rain, sleet, and snow, waiting to be hauled to a distant warehouse. No wonder those flats showed signs of premature aging after only a few performances, let alone over decades of use. Weather was not the only culprit: assistant conductors were constantly poking holes in the set, so that they could see the conductor

---

* There is a photograph of the set on page 16.

when they had to relay his beat to offstage soloists, instumental-
ists, or choruses. There were no convenient closed-circuit TV
monitors back then. Since assistant conductors came in all shapes
and sizes, each one had to poke his own hole at just the right
height. Many a princely palace began to look as if it were made of
Swiss cheese. Painted drops, moreover, after being repeatedly
rolled up and unrolled, soon showed cracks. The sky was full of
wrinkles. Solid walls trembled at a touch, or shivered in a backstage draft. I recall that the rigging of Enzo's ship in Act II of *La
Gioconda* was a particularly unseaworthy mess. Some of the
productions had once been satisfying to the eye: I have seen
beautiful, imaginative designs, and impressive photos of sets when
they were new. But by the 30s and 40s, far too many of the older
settings, as photographed for the pages of *Opera News*, looked
decidedly tattered and moth-eaten.

Soloists were responsible for their own costumes, wigs, and
jewelry. What the leading lady would be wearing—how she
would "dress the role"—was of paramount interest to many in the
audience. The range of styles was sometimes startling. Adrian, a
famous designer of that era, veiled the ample figure of Helen
Traubel in sleekly modern, vaguely classical draperies that con-
trasted oddly with the traditional garb of her Wagnerian colleagues on stage. Marjorie Lawrence stylized her Tosca with the
latest look from Paris. One of the designers of the *Folies Bergères*
created her Salome costume, a sort of latticed bathing suit. Lily
Pons and Lucrezia Bori showed up in the same shocking pink in a
scene from *Mignon*. Rosa Ponselle created a sensation when she
first stepped on stage in the fourth act of *Carmen*: she was wearing
a feminine version of a bullfighter's costume, but in slinky black
with a train.[*] Ezio Pinza as Mephistophélès was criticized for
dressing the devil in green instead of in red. Most soloists,
however, ordered costumes so standardized by tradition that they
could be worn in any opera house in the world and would still fit
right in. Successful singers had to travel with multiple trunkloads

---

[*] Ponselle as Carmen can be seen on page 18, Lawrence as Salome on page 28.

Ezio Pinza as Mephistopheles in *Faust*

of costumes, accessories, wigs, and shoes.

By the time I saw my first *Traviata*, the crinolines of the Second Empire had become traditional for the ladies in the cast; but before World War I it was possible to see a mixture of three centuries: Violetta in the latest Worth creation from Paris, Alfredo in the style of Louis XIV (the period of the premiere production of the opera), and the elder Germont in mid - nineteenth - century dress (the period of the premiere of the original play).

Staging of the standard repertoire was essentially the same everywhere. An effort was

Lily Pons, in *Lakmé*, the first to bare her belly button at the Met

made to duplicate the original production as faithfully as possible, much as touring productions of Broadway musicals are still expected to do. Staging instructions could be rented from the publishers along with the scores and orchestra parts. The blocking was so interchangeable that leading singers rarely needed to rehearse. In fact, there was often a clause in their contracts that there would be no rehearsals. That was the case when Lauritz Melchior made his debut at the Met as Tannhäuser, and remained the rule well into the 1930s. He had to sing some of his most strenuous new roles without a single rehearsal. It was not at all rare that one met one's partner for the first time on stage during the performance. That still happens, of course, even in our more enlightened times, when a guest singer has to "jump in" at the last moment to save the show.

During her heyday, Adelina Patti used to send her maid to rehearsals, to inform the other cast members where Madame would be standing or sitting at any given moment.

At the Met, integrated productions were rare until the advent of Rudolf Bing in 1950, after which they became the rule, not the exception.

Before then, acting styles varied widely, depending upon the talent of the individual performer. They say that Feodor Chaliapin, Mary Garden, Olive Fremstad, and Geraldine Farrar were mesmerizing on stage. They were before my time, of course. Some of the finest acting that I saw in opera came from Lotte Lehmann as the Marschallin, Astrid Varnay as Isolde, Kundry, and Elektra, Risë Stevens as Octavian, Dalila, and Carmen, Ezio Pinza and Cesare Siepi as Don Giovanni and Figaro, Boris Christoff as Boris Godunov, Dietrich Fischer-Dieskau as Mandryka, Hans Hotter as Wotan, and Anja Silja as Senta, to name some examples that quickly come to mind. I saw Maria Callas as Turandot in 1948 and as Norma in 1952, before she was molded by the likes of Visconti into one of opera's great actresses. Her Norma at Covent Garden did not impress me histrionically: she lumbered when she walked, and her gestures were mostly semaphoric.

How did singers prepare for an operatic career during the inter-war years? Well, the following case is probably typical. I knew Ina Souez during the 1950s in California. She had made her name at Glyndebourne twenty years earlier, singing Fiordiligi and Donna Anna to great acclaim. She told me that one of the fraternal organizations in Denver had raised money to send her to Italy to study. There she went first to a vocal coach and learned four or five roles musically. He then sent her to a stage manager who taught her the standard moves for each role. That was it. Then came auditions. Some stage experience in the provinces—Mimì at age twenty. Since she had an outstanding voice, she soon found herself singing Micaëla and Liù at Covent Garden.

The accepted style of acting in opera in those days derived from the need to project emotional states and dramatic tensions over the orchestra pit and out into a vast space to reach the back rows and the top galleries. Some outstandingly great singing actors were able to work very effectively within those conventions. In these days of cinematic realism, something may have been lost, after all. Facial expressions cannot be read much beyond the tenth row, if that far.

The 50s brought about far-reaching changes. Wagner's grandsons revolutionized the way his music dramas were staged. Gone were winged helmets, braids, and "*Wagner'sche Schritte*," the Wagner-ian stride. Banished were Siegfried's bear and Brünnhilde's horse. Masterful lighting effects took the place of scenery on an unclut-tered stage. There were striking images. The look of "New Bayreuth" soon spread all over Europe, wherever Wagner's op-eras were performed. It lasted well into the 60s.

Meanwhile, in America, stage directors were summoned from the "legitimate" theater to create integrated productions and try to make actors out of opera singers.

"New Bayreuth" style, *Die Walküre*, Act III, above,
just before Wotan's angry entrance;
*Götterdämmerung*, Prologue, the Three Norns, below

It had been tried before, of course, but not on such a consistent scale. During preparations for the world premiere of *Der Rosenkavalier* in Dresden, for instance, Strauss and his brilliant librettist Hugo von Hofmannsthal were conscious that their new opera seemed to call for a new style of acting, a style that thoroughly eluded the gentleman who had been asigned by the theatre to the task of staging the opera. They sent out an SOS to their good friend, the famous theatrical wizard Max Reinhardt. Not wanting to hurt the feelings of the nominal director, Reinhardt never set foot on the stage. But when a singer was finished with a scene, there would be a brief whispered conversation in the darkened auditorium. Then, when the singer was again needed on stage, there would be a noticeable transformation: all of a sudden the character had come to multifaceted life, fully fleshed, as if by magic! Not every opera house, however, had a Reinhardt available. Tradition and routine continued to be the norm almost everywhere for a long time to come.

"Instant opera" has a long history, and not just in the hinterlands. When I was working as a coach at the company now known as New York City Opera, a young American soprano made her debut as Musetta after a brief rehearsal with Alcindoro and none at all with her Marcello. When my wife Evangeline sang Nedda for the "New York Summer Opera" at Randall's Island, the stage director spent an hour with the cast on Act I, then announced that he had to leave for some rehearsals in Florida, leaving the singers entirely to their own devices for the tricky "*commedia*" that forms the second half of the opera. I worked out the moves for my wife and her Arlecchino. My first professional job in opera was as stage director of *La traviata* for the Northwest Grand Opera, the predecessor of Seattle Opera. Our leading lady, Dorothy Kirsten, arrived the day *after* the dress rehearsal. At least we had our own scenery and could rehearse the chorus and minor roles adequately. When Jeanette MacDonald sang Marguerite in a production of *Faust*, the stage director had no clue what the sets would look like, where the entrances and furniture might be, until the rented drops arrived, just before the first performance.

During my nineteen years in Zurich I saw many truly beautiful productions. That was before beauty became synonymous with "*Kitsch*" in the minds of a new generation of stage directors. I had the good fortune to work with Jean-Pierre Ponnelle, Otto Schenk, Günther Rennert, Göran Järvefelt, and Lotfi Mansouri, all of whom brought masterpieces of opera to stunning life with imagination and flair, without violating the spirit of the words or the music. Yet there were already a number of young stage directors—most of them from the spoken theater or films and insensitive to the language of music—who delighted in contradicting whatever the music was expressing at a given moment. I used to cringe every time I heard one of them say: "*gegen die Musik*"—"against the music," acting *against* the music instead of *with* it, in deliberate violation of the spirit of Wagner's ideal: "acts of music made visible."

Around the time I left Europe, in 1980, a new wave was starting to sweep away all vestiges of "*Werktreue*" (faithfulness to the work). The more freakish the "concept," the uglier the sets and costumes, the sooner the perpetrators were launched into careers. Booing, rather than applause, became the measure of success. It guaranteed notoriety, and notoriety guaranteed engagements. Soon the booers were shamed into silence, stigmatized as hopelessly Philistine fuddy-duddies who failed to appreciate such subtle insights as staging the opening chorus of *Ballo in maschera* in a men's toilet.

We in America have so far been spared more than an occasional whiff of "eurotrash." For that reason, we are often ridiculed abroad as unthinking, immature consumers of "culinary" entertainment.

In spite of all the changes in the way opera has been presented during my lifetime, certain aspects of the art have not changed and never will. The ideal will always be an indissoluble union of word and tone, a harmony between what is seen and what is heard, and the integrity of the composer's creation—all the greatest artists understand that, whatever they may be called upon to do in an eccentric staging.

## Now—Just for Fun

When I was standing night watch on my various ships in the Navy, I used to entertain myself during the long, monotonous hours by making up songs in my head, romantic ballads or satirical ditties, according to my mood. Some of them found their way into a musical play that I staged when we went into drydock at Portsmouth, Virginia.

A big news item in those days was the squabble between Helen Traubel, the leading Wagnerian soprano of the Met, and Rudolf Bing, the General Manager, over whether a Metropolitan Opera star was compromising the dignity of the institution by singing in night clubs and in comedy shows on the radio.

Madam Traubel's Revolt

The overture started…the golden curtains parted…
But Madam Traubel wasn't on the scene!
The prompter tore his hair…but still the stage was bare…
While backstage the director turned a sickly shade of green.
His star refused to go on! How could he put the show on?
She said she wouldn't sing a single note—QUOTE:

SORRY, NO BRÜNNHILDE TONIGHT, MR. BING.
I hate to put you in the bight.
But I'm tired of singing Wagner while the patrons doze;
I wanna sing the type of thing he didn't compose:
One high-dee-ho earns more dough than ten ho-yo-to-hos.
SORRY, NO BRÜNNHILDE TONIGHT.

You can mark Valhalla for rent, Mr. Bing;
Your valkyrie has taken flight.
I'm tired of singing love songs to a ten-ton truck;
My big romantic moments always find me stuck
With a little shrimp or a blimp. I wanna change my luck.
SORRY, NO BRÜNNHILDE TONIGHT.

SORRY, NO BRÜNNHILDE TONIGHT, MR. BING.
And furthermore: go fly a kite!
Durante has an act he wants to do with me.
I've signed a juicy contract with the Chez Paree.
I'm cuttin' loose! A real chanteuse is what I long to be.
SORRY, NO BRÜNNHILDE TONIGHT.

I'd tell you where to stuff all that culture of yours
If I were not so darn polite.
I'm tired of being Mrs. Astor's caviar—
I know I'd be a knockout as a nightclub star!
If I'm your way again some day, you can book me in the bar.
SORRY, NO BRÜNNHILDE TONIGHT.

SORRY, NO BRÜNNHILDE TONIGHT, MR. BING.
I hope the Met makes out all right,
But they want me in Las Vegas and I'm heading West.
The wings upon this helmet wouldn't feather my nest.
I've lugged those spears for years and years;
Now I deserve a rest!
SORRY, NO BRÜNNHILDE TONIGHT.

Your policies are high-hat, you cater to snobs;
The common man is my delight!
They tell me I'm the biggest thing to hit TV
And honky-tonks seem nice and democratic to me.
Those drunks won't know if I go a little bit off-key.
Sorry, Mr. Bing, I quit, Mr. Bing! Git, Mr. Bing!
NO BRÜNNHILDE TONIGHT!

Helen Traubel in Valkyrie costume, clowning with Jimmy Durante

# Index

**Photo Credits** (page numbers in parentheses)

Nadine Conner (2), Ina Souez (48): De Bellis, NY; William Wildermann (2): J. Abresch, NY; Evangeline Noël (5, 61): Bruno of Hollywood, NYC; Scenes from *Faust* and *Götterdämmerung* (13 and 14): The Victrola Book of the Opera, 1917; *Rigoletto* Act I (16), Lily Pons (204): Elcar Studios; Hilda Burke (17), Rosa Ponselle (18), Eleanor Steber (22), Cesare Siepi (85), Martina Arroyo (94), Roberta Peters (152): The Metropolitan Opera Archives; Risë Stevens (27), Jarmila Novotná (150): Constance Hope Associates, NYC; Flagstad and Melchior (28): The Metropolitan Opera Guild; Marjorie Lawrence (28): Edgar Vincent Associates; Marguerite D'Alvarez (43): Carl van Vechten; Kathleen Ferrier (45): London Records; Maria Callas (45): George Burr; Astrid Varnay (47): Liselotte Strelow; Elisabeth Schwarzkopf (49): H. Rosenthal, London; Lotte Lehmann (56): Lotte Meitner-Graf, London; Lotte Lehmann, Grace Bumbry, B. Glass (59), Lotte Lehmann and Hilde Gueden (95), Lotte Lehmann and Arturo Toscanini (148): Lotte Lehmann Archive, Santa Barbara; *Fidelio* Chorus (63): Hal Boucher, Santa Barbara; James McCracken and Sandra Warfield (65): Eugene Cook; Evangeline Noël as Musetta (75): Photo Canera-Nell, Genève; as the Marschallin (76), Lisa della Casa and Marga Schiml (80): Hertha Ramme, Zürich; Teresa Berganza and José Carreras (83), Ruggero Raimondi (84): Susan Schimert-Ramme, Zürich; Grace Bumbry and B. Glass (100): Carolyn Mason Jones, San Francisco; Evangeline Noël, José Van Dam, and Herbert Graf (102): Foto A. Madner, Salzburg; Costanza Cuccaro (106): Krapich Photo, Berlin; Wartburg Castle (111): Wartburg Stiftung Eisenach; *Autour de Tristan* (112): R. Kayaert, Bruxelles; Scene from *Thaïs* (114): Ellebé, Rouen; Lisa della Casa and Dietrich Fischer-Dieskau (116): Heinz Köster, Berlin; Zurich Coaching Staff (118): Christian Altorfer, Zürich; Reri Grist (119): Fayer, Wien; René Kollo (123): Ariola-Eurodisc/s Toepfer; Jennifer White, Kyle Ketelsen, and B. Glass (127), University of Iowa rehearsal photos (132 and 140): Patrick Nefzger; Barbara Buddin with a horse for *Carmen* (130): Dennis Full / Full Photographics; Carol Meyer as the Vixen (131): Max Haynes / The Daily Iowan; Michèle Crider, Simon Estes, and B. Glass (138): Michael Williams – A/E; Frances Holden and B. Glass (142): Judy Sutcliffe; Cambridge graduation (150): Spicer Hallfield; Kirsten Flagstad (193): Mermaid Theatre, London; *Le nozze di Figaro* Act II set (199): the Metropolitan Opera Ass'n; *La rappresentazione di anima e di corpo* final scene (200): Photo Ellinger, Salzburg; *Fledermaus* Act I (201): W.E. Baur, Zürich; Ezio Pinza (204): A. Genardy, Verona '29; "New Bayreuth" (207): Festspiele Bayreuth / Lauterwasser.

# MATHEMAGIC

## Raymond Blum
*Illustrated by Jeff Sinclair*

 Sterling Publishing Co., Inc.   New York

# DEDICATION

This book is dedicated to my wife Gerri and my daughter Katie, for all the magic that they bring into my life.

**Library of Congress Cataloging-in-Publication Data**

Blum, Raymond.
    Mathemagic / Raymond Blum ; illustrated by Jeff Sinclair.
        p.      cm.
    Includes index.
    Summary: Dozens of number tricks from easy to expert.
    ISBN 0-8069-8354-X (trade)
    1. Mathematical recreations—Juvenile literature.
    [1. Mathematical recreations.]   I. Sinclair, Jeff, ill.   II. Title.
    QA95.B52   1991
    793.7'4—dc20                91-22523
                                     CIP
                                     AC

10  9  8  7  6  5  4  3

First paperback edition published in 1992 by
Sterling Publishing Company, Inc.
387 Park Avenue South, New York, N.Y. 10016
© 1991 by Raymond Blum
Illustrations © 1991 by Jeff Sinclair
Distributed in Canada by Sterling Publishing
% Canadian Manda Group, P.O. Box 920, Station U
Toronto, Ontario, Canada M8Z 5P9
Distributed in Great Britain and Europe by Cassell PLC
Villiers House, 41/47 Strand, London WC2N 5JE, England
Distributed in Australia by Capricorn Link Ltd.
P.O. Box 665, Lane Cove, NSW 2066
*Manufactured in the United States of America*
*All rights reserved*

Sterling   ISBN 0-8069-8354-X   Trade
                     0-8069-8355-8   Paper

# CONTENTS

# TO KIDS—BEFORE YOU BEGIN

You don't have to be a top student to perform these tricks, but after performing them for family and friends, you will look like a genius!

Here is what you need to know so that you will have the most fun with this book:

1. The tricks in each chapter are organized from the easiest to the hardest. Choose those tricks that are right for you.

2. Before you try working any trick, read the directions several times so that you thoroughly understand it.

3. Practice a trick by yourself first. When you have worked it through successfully two or three times, you are ready to perform it for your friends.

4. Don't worry if you make a mistake. You can always blame evil spirits for causing things to go wrong. Make up a magic spell that will drive them away, and then try the trick again or move on to a different trick.

5. Perform each trick slowly. If you take your time, you won't make careless errors and the trick will practically work itself.

6. Magicians never reveal their secrets. When someone asks you how a trick works, just say, "It's magic!"

7. Never repeat a trick for the same person. If people see a trick for the second time, they sometimes figure out how it's done.

Now you're ready to surprise and dazzle your family and friends. Good luck and, above all else, have fun!

# INTRODUCTION—A NOTE TO PARENTS AND TEACHERS

Everyone loves magic! It's fun to watch and even more fun to perform for others. Here are dozens of number tricks for children of all abilities, ages nine and up. There are easy tricks for younger children and beginners, and there are more challenging tricks—including an "Extra For Experts" chapter for older children and teachers. With a little practice, children will be able to astound and entertain their family and friends or their entire class.

Number magic is easy to learn and perform because the tricks practically work themselves. There is no sleight of hand, and special magic skills are not required. No expensive magic equipment is needed and all supplies can easily be found in the home or purchased for minimal cost. Tricks have clear, uncomplicated, step-by-step instructions so that they are easy for children to read and understand.

Number magic adds variety and excitement to any math class and helps make learning fun. Teachers at any level will be able to perform these tricks for their students. All the tricks have been classroom tested and kids love them.

# 1. CALCULATOR CAPERS

BEWITCHED
GIVE ME 5!
TALKING CALCULATOR
SECRET CODE
FAMILY SECRETS
POCKET MONEY
HAUNTED CALCULATOR
SUBTRACTION SORCERY

# BEWITCHED

Someone has placed an evil spell on your calculator. No matter which number your friend enters, it is ghoulishly transformed into the unlucky number 13!

## Materials

A calculator

## Presentation

Have a friend:

|  | **Example** |
|---|---|
| 1. Enter in the calculator any number that is easy to remember —address, age, phone number, etc. (This number must be less than 8 digits.) | **77** |
| 2. Double that number. | $77 \times 2 = 154$ |
| 3. Add 15 to that answer. | $154 + 15 = 169$ |
| 4. Triple that result. | $169 \times 3 = 507$ |
| 5. Add 33 to that total. | $507 + 33 = 540$ |
| 6. Divide that answer by 6. | $540 \div 6 = 90$ |
| 7. Subtract her original number. | $90 - 77 = 13$ |

This is a trick that can be repeated several times with the same friend. The final answer always ends up "unlucky"!

# GIVE ME 5!

With your X-ray vision, you are able to see through the back of a calculator and reveal the number that appears in the display!

## Materials

A calculator

## Presentation

Have a friend:

|  |  |
|---|---|
| 1. Enter any number that is easy to remember in the calculator without letting you see it. (This number must be less than 8 digits.) | **Example** **365** |
| 2. Multiply that number by 3. | $365 \times 3 = 1{,}095$ |
| 3. Add 15 to that result. | $1{,}095 + 15 = 1{,}110$ |
| 4. Multiply that answer by 2. | $1{,}110 \times 2 = 2{,}220$ |
| 5. Divide that result by 6. | $2{,}220 \div 6 = 370$ |
| 6. Subtract his original number from that total. | $370 - 365 = 5$ |

Finally, tell him to hold the *back* of the calculator towards you. Pretend that you have the power to see through solid objects, and then announce the total that appears in the display. No matter which number your friend chooses, the final total will always be 5!

## Variations

When repeating this trick, change Step 3 and the final total will be a different number.

Step 3

| Add | 3 | 6 | 9 | 12 | 15 | 18 | 21 | 24 | 27 | 30→ |
|---|---|---|---|---|---|---|---|---|---|---|
| **Final Total** | 1 | 2 | 3 | 4 | 5 | 6 | 7 | 8 | 9 | 10→ |

# TALKING CALCULATOR

Your friend secretly selects two numbers, works a few math problems, and hands you the calculator. When you hold the calculator up to your ear, it whispers the two numbers that she chose!

## Materials
A calculator                    Paper and pencil

## Presentation
Have a friend write down a 1-digit number and a 2-digit number on a piece of paper without showing you.

Then hand her the calculator and ask her to:

|  | Example<br>6 & 82 |
|---|---|
| 1. Enter her 1-digit number. | 6 |
| 2. Multiply that number by 5. | $6 \times 5 = 30$ |
| 3. Add 5 to that answer. | $30 + 5 = 35$ |
| 4. Multiply that result by 10. | $35 \times 10 = 350$ |

12

| 5. Add 20 to that total. | $350 + 20 = 370$ |
| 6. Multiply that result by 2. | $370 \times 2 = 740$ |
| 7. Subtract 8 from that answer. | $740 - 8 = 732$ |
| 8. Add her 2-digit number to that result. | $732 + 82 = 814$ |

Finally, ask her to hand you the calculator with the final total. Say that you are going to activate the calculator's talking mode by entering a special code. Subtract 132, push =, and your friend's two numbers will appear in the display.

$$\begin{array}{r} 814 \\ - 132 \\ \hline 6\underline{82} \end{array}$$

Sneak a peek at the two numbers as you put the calculator up to your ear. Pretend that the calculator is whispering to you, and then announce your friend's two numbers!

## An Exception
When you subtract 132 and get only two digits, your friend chose 0 for the 1-digit number.

$$\begin{array}{rr} \textbf{Example} & 159 \\ \textbf{0 \& 27} & - 132 \\ \hline & 27 = \underline{0}\,\underline{27} \end{array}$$

# SECRET CODE

Your friend thinks of an important date in his life, and then works a few problems on a calculator. When he is finished, you enter a magical secret code and his date suddenly appears in the display!

## Materials

A calculator                    Paper and pencil

## Preparation

Write this month chart on a piece of paper.

| | | | |
|---|---|---|---|
| 1-Jan. | 4-April | 7-July | 10-Oct. |
| 2-Feb. | 5-May | 8-Aug. | 11-Nov. |
| 3-March | 6-June | 9-Sept. | 12-Dec. |

## Presentation

Ask a friend to think of any important date in his life—his birthday, for instance, or a favorite holiday.

Hand him the calculator and tell him to:

| | **Example** |
|---|---|
| 1. Enter the number of the month from the month chart without letting you see it. (September = 9) | **Sept. 10** **9** |
| 2. Multiply that number by 5. | $9 \times 5 = 45$ |
| 3. Add 6 to that total. | $45 + 6 = 51$ |
| 4. Multiply that answer by 4. | $51 \times 4 = 204$ |
| 5. Add 9 to that total. | $204 + 9 = 213$ |
| 6. Multiply that answer by 5. | $213 \times 5 = 1,065$ |
| 7. Add the number of the day. (Sept. <u>10</u>) | $1,065 + 10 = 1,075$ |
| 8. Add 700 to that total. | $1,075 + 700 = 1,775$ |

Finally, tell your friend to hand you the calculator with the final total. Just enter the secret code (minus 865 equals) and the important date that he thought of will magically appear! The first digit is the number of the month, and the last two digits are the number of the day.

$$\begin{array}{r} 1775 \\ -\ 865 \\ \hline \underline{9}\,\underline{10} \\ \uparrow\ \ \uparrow \end{array}$$

**Sept. 10**

## An Exception

When you subtract 865 and get four digits, the first two digits are the number of the month.

**Examples**   $1031 = \underline{10}\,\underline{31} = $ Oct. 31
$1205 = \underline{12}\,\underline{05} = $ Dec. 5

# FAMILY SECRETS

After a friend works a few problems on a calculator, you are able to divulge how many brothers, sisters, and grandparents she has!

## Materials
A calculator

**Example**
**4 brothers**
**3 sisters**
**2 grandparents**

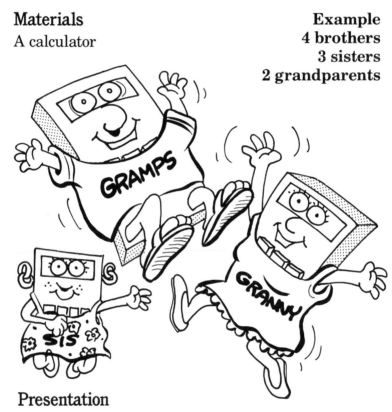

## Presentation
Have a friend:

1. Enter her number of brothers in the calculator.      4

2. Multiply that number by 2.      $4 \times 2 = 8$

3. Add 3 to that total.      $8 + 3 = 11$

| 4. Multiply that answer by 5. | $11 \times 5 = 55$ |
|---|---|
| 5. Add her number of sisters to that total. | $55 + 3 = 58$ |
| 6. Multiply that answer by 10. | $58 \times 10 = 580$ |
| 7. Add her number of grandparents to that total. | $580 + 2 = 582$ |
| 8. Add 125 to that answer. | $582 + 125 = 707$ |

Finally, tell her to hand you the calculator with the final total. Just subtract 275 and her number of brothers, sisters, and grandparents magically appear!

$$
\begin{array}{r}
707 \\
-275 \\
\hline
\textbf{brothers} \rightarrow \quad 432 \quad \leftarrow \textbf{grandparents} \\
\uparrow \\
\textbf{sisters}
\end{array}
$$

## Exceptions

When you subtract 275 and get only two digits, your friend has no brothers.

**Example: 12 = 0̲1̲2̲ so number of brothers = 0.**

When you subtract 275 and get only one digit, your friend has no brothers and no sisters.

**Example: 2 = 0̲0̲2̲ so number of brothers = 0 and number of sisters = 0.**

# POCKET MONEY

After your friend works a few problems on a calculator, you are able to reveal his favorite number and how much loose change he has in his pocket!

## Materials
A calculator

## Presentation
Have a friend:

**Example**
**Favorite Number-25**
**Loose Change-47¢**

1. Enter his favorite number in the calculator. (This number must be five digits or less.)

**25**

2. Multiply that number by 2.

**25 × 2 = 50**

3. Add 5 to that answer.

**50 + 5 = 55**

4. Multiply that result by 50.

**55 × 50 = 2750**

5. Add the loose change in his pocket. (This amount must be less than $1.00)

**2750 + 47 = 2797**

6. Multiply that total by 4.

**2797 × 4 = 11188**

7. Subtract 1000 from that answer.

**11188 − 1000 = 10188**

Then, tell him to hand you the calculator with the final total. Just divide that total by 400 and your friend's favorite number and his loose change will magically appear!

18

$$10188 \div 400 = \underline{25}.\underline{47}$$

Favorite    Loose
number    change

## Exceptions

If you divide by 400 and there is only one number after the decimal point, add on a 0 to get the loose change.

**Example: $311040 \div 400 = 777.6 = \underline{777}.\underline{60}$**
**Loose change = 60¢**

If you divide by 400 and there are no numbers after the decimal point, your friend has no loose change.

**Example: $2800 \div 400 = 7. = \underline{7}.\underline{00}$**
**Loose change = 0¢**

## HAUNTED CALCULATOR

A supernatural power is summoned and asked for the year that your friend was born. Suddenly and mysteriously, the year appears in the calculator's display!

## Materials

A calculator            Paper and pencil

| Presentation | Example |
|---|---|
| Have a friend: | **Born in 1980** |

1. Write down any 4-digit number on a piece of paper without letting you see it. Tell him that all four digits must be different. **2796**

2. Rearrange the four digits in any order and write this new number below the first number. **9267**

3. Subtract the two numbers on a calculator. Tell him to enter the larger number first.

$$\begin{array}{r} 9267 \\ -\,2796 \\ \hline 6471 \end{array}$$

4. Add the digits of his answer together.      $6471 \rightarrow 6 + 4 + 7 + 1 = 18$
*If his answer has more than one digit, tell him to add those digits together until there is only one digit.*      $18 \rightarrow 1 + 8 = 9$

5. Add 25 to that digit.      $9 + 25 = 34$

6. Add the last two digits of the year that he was born to that answer.      $34 + 80 = 114$

Finally, ask him to hand you the calculator with the final total. Say that you are going to ask the number spirits for assistance by entering a secret code in the calculator. Pretend to do some supernatural hocus pocus as you add 1866 to his total. When you push the equal sign, the year that he was born magically appears in the calculator's display!

$$114 + 1866 = 1980 \text{!!!}$$

## An Exception
For birthdays in the 2000's, add 1966.

## SUBTRACTION SORCERY

You ask a friend to work a subtraction problem on a calculator. After she tells you just one digit of the answer, you are able to divulge the entire answer!

### Materials
A calculator                    Paper and pencil

### Presentation                                **Example**
Ask a friend to:
   1. Write any 3-digit number on a piece of
paper without letting you see it. Tell her
that all three digits must be different.     **427**

   2. Reverse this number and write it below
the first number.     **724**

   3. Subtract the two numbers on a     **724**
calculator. Tell her to enter the larger     **− 427**
number first.     **297**

Finally, ask her to tell you either the first digit or the last digit of the total. You are now able to divulge the entire answer!

21

## How to Do It

Here are all the possible answers when you subtract two 3-digit numbers as described.

**99** **198** **297** **396** **495** **594** **693** **792** **891**
(099)

Notice that the middle digit is always 9 and that the sum of the first digit and the last digit is 9. So just subtract what your friend tells you from 9 to get the missing digit.

## Example

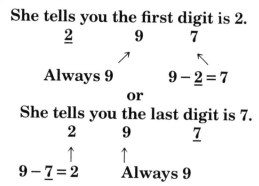

**She tells you the first digit is 2.**

**2**      **9**      **7**

Always 9      9 − 2 = 7

**or**

**She tells you the last digit is 7.**

2      9      7

9 − 7 = 2      Always 9

## An Exception

If your friend tells you that the first digit or last digit is 9, her answer will be 99.

# 2. CARD CONJURING

SWITCHEROO
ELEVEN IN A ROW
CRYSTAL BALL
INVISIBLE DECK
ABRACADABRA
FOUR ACE BAFFLER
MYSTERIOUS FORCE
POCKET PUZZLER

# SWITCHEROO

A deck of cards is divided into two piles. Your friend secretly takes a card from each pile and places it in the opposite pile. Even though each pile is thoroughly shuffled, you are able to find your friend's two cards!

## Materials

A deck of playing cards without Jokers

## Preparation

Put all the even cards in one pile (2, 4, 6, 8, 10, Queen) and all the odd cards in another pile (Ace, 3, 5, 7, 9, Jack, King). Shuffle each pile so that it is well mixed.

## Presentation

1. Have your friend shuffle each pile separately without looking at the cards. Spread both piles face down on the table.

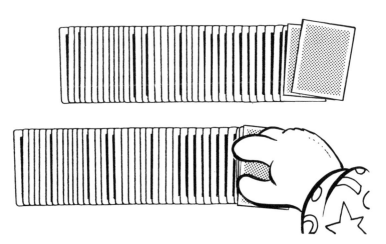

2. Tell her to choose one card from the group at the top, look at it, and place it in the group on the bottom. Then have her choose a different card from the group at the bottom, look at it, and place it in the group on the top.

3. Have her shuffle each pile, put one pile on top of the other, and hand you the deck of cards. Within seconds, you are able to reveal her two cards!

## How to Do It

The odd card that is chosen will be surrounded by even cards, and the even card that is chosen will be surrounded by odd cards.

**Example: The** ♡4 **and** 〈K〉 **are chosen.**

<u>odd cards</u> ♡4 <u>odd cards</u>   <u>even cards</u> 〈K〉 <u>even cards</u>

26

# ELEVEN IN A ROW

Eleven cards are placed face down in a straight row on a table. After you leave the room, your friend moves some of the cards. When you return, you are able to tell how many cards were moved even though the row looks exactly the way it did when you left the room!

## Materials

A deck of playing cards

## Preparation

Take the following eleven cards out of the deck: Any Joker and any cards from Ace through 10. Place them face down on a table in order in a straight row.

| J oker | A | 2 | 3 | 4 | 5 | 6 | 7 | 8 | 9 | 10 |

Left       *(All cards should be face down)*       Right

## Presentation

1. Tell your friend that when you leave the room, he should move some cards from the left end of the row to the right end of the row, *one card at a time*. He may move any number of cards from 0 to 10.

2. Before you leave the room, move some of the cards yourself to show him how they should be moved. You are really doing this to get your *Key #*.

**Example**
**You move 3 cards.**
**(This is your *Key #*—remember it!)**

Left [J oker] [A] [2] [3] [4] [5] [6] [7] [8] [9] [10] [J oker] [A] [2] Right

3. Leave the room and have your friend move some of the cards.

**Example**
**He moves 5 cards.**

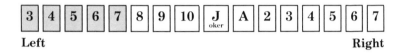

4. When you return, perform some hocus pocus and pretend that the cards are speaking to you. Tell your friend that the cards will reveal the number of cards that he moved. Remember your *Key #* and count over that many cards from the *right end* of the row. Turn this card over and the number on that card will tell you how many cards your friend moved! (The Joker = 0 and Ace = 1.)

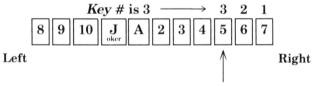

**Turn this card over. It is a 5 so your friend moved 5 cards.**

## A Variation
Use a different *Key #* each time you perform the trick.

# CRYSTAL BALL

Your calculator becomes your magical crystal ball when it mystically reveals a 2-digit number that is concealed inside a deck of cards!

## Materials
A deck of playing cards     A calculator

## Preparation
Remove all the 10s and face cards from a deck of cards so that your deck has only Aces through 9s.

## Presentation
Ask your friend to shuffle the deck, remove two cards without looking at them, and place them face down on the table. The rest of the deck can be set aside.

Tell him to secretly look at either card and memorize its number (Ace = 1). Its suit is not important. You look at the other card, and then both cards are returned face down on the table. Put your card one inch to the right of your friend's card. Explain that the two cards represent a 2-digit number and that the calculator will be your crystal ball that will reveal that number.

**Example**
**Friend's Card—9**
**Your Card—3**

Hand your friend the calculator and have him:

1. Enter the number of his card. **9**

2. Multiply that number by 2. **9 × 2 = 18**

3. Add 2 to that result. **18 + 2 = 20**

4. Multiply that answer by 5. **20 × 5 = 100**

5. Subtract the Magic Number.
*The Magic Number is*
    *10 minus your card number.*
        **(10 − 3 = 7)** **100 − 7 = 93**

Finally, have your friend turn over the two cards on the table. The 2-digit number that is formed by the two cards will match the number that appears in the crystal ball!

## INVISIBLE DECK

After your friend picks a card from your "invisible deck" and works a few problems on a calculator, you are able to announce the name of her invisible card!

## Materials

A calculator                    Paper and pencil

## Preparation

Write these charts on a piece of paper.

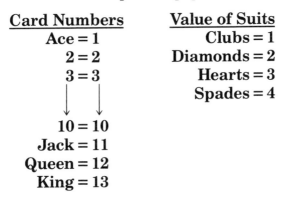

| Card Numbers | Value of Suits |
|:---:|:---:|
| Ace = 1 | Clubs = 1 |
| 2 = 2 | Diamonds = 2 |
| 3 = 3 | Hearts = 3 |
| ↓     ↓ | Spades = 4 |
| 10 = 10 | |
| Jack = 11 | |
| Queen = 12 | |
| King = 13 | |

## Presentation

Pretend to have an invisible deck in your hands. Shuffle it thoroughly, and then ask a friend to pick a card from your "deck." Tell her to write the name of her card on a piece of paper.

### Example: 7 of Hearts

Hand her the calculator and ask her to:

1. Enter the card's number.                    **7**

2. Add the number that is one
more than this number.
$(7 + 1 = 8)$                    **$7 + 8 = 15$**

3. Multiply that result by 5.                    **$15 \times 5 = 75$**

4. Add the value of the suit to that
answer. (Hearts = 3)                    **$75 + 3 = 78$**

5. Add 637 to that result.                    **$78 + 637 = 715$**

Then, tell your friend to hand you the calculator with the final total. Just subtract 642 and her card will magically appear!

$$\begin{array}{r} 7\,1\,5 \\ -\,6\,4\,2 \\ \hline 7\,\underline{3} \end{array}$$

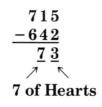

**7 of Hearts**

## An Exception

When you subtract 642 and get three digits, the first two digits are the card's number.

**Example: $\underline{1}\,2\,\underline{4}$**

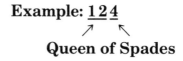

**Queen of Spades**

## A Variation

Perform the trick with two or more friends at the same time. Before you announce their cards, pretend to +, −, ×, and ÷ their totals so that they will think that their answers are somehow related to each other.

# ABRACADABRA

Your friend mentally chooses a card from a pile of 21 cards. When the magic word "ABRACADABRA" is spelled out, your friend's chosen card suddenly appears!

## Materials

A deck of playing cards

## Presentation

1. Shuffle the deck, count out 21 cards, and set the rest of the deck aside.

2. Deal out three piles of seven cards each, face down on the table. Deal the cards from left to right, one pile at a time, as if you were dealing to three players in a card game. There is no need for you ever to see the faces of any of the cards.

3. Ask your friend to choose one of the piles. Take the pile that he chose in your hand, fan out the cards to-

wards him, and ask him to mentally select any card.

4. Put the pile that he chose between the other two piles so that you again have a pack of 21 cards in your hand.

5. Once more, deal out three piles of seven cards each, face down on the table. Taking up one pile at a time, fan out the cards towards your friend and ask him which pile has his chosen card. Again, put the pile that has his chosen card between the other two piles so that you have a pack of 21 cards in your hand.

6. Repeat Step 5 one more time.

7. Tell your friend that you are going to say the magic word "ABRACADABRA" and his chosen card will magically appear. Slowly spell "ABRACADABRA," turning over one card for each letter. The last card that you turn over will be your friend's chosen card!!

## FOUR ACE BAFFLER

Three cards are randomly removed from the deck and they are all Aces! Then the "number spirits" are summoned and the fourth Ace mysteriously appears!

## Materials
A deck of playing cards

## Preparation
Put an 8 card in the eighth position down from the top of the deck and put the four Aces in the ninth, tenth, eleventh and twelfth positions.

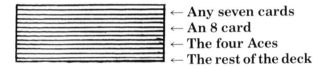

← **Any seven cards**
← **An 8 card**
← **The four Aces**
← **The rest of the deck**

## Presentation

1. Ask a friend for a number *between* 10 and 20. (*Caution:* 10 will work, but 20 will not.)

**Example**
**13**

2. Deal that number of cards into a small pile one card at a time. Place the rest of the deck next to the small pile.

← **13 cards**

3. Ask your friend to add the digits of that number.

$13 \rightarrow 1 + 3 = 4$

4. Return that many cards to the top of the big pile one card at a time.

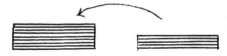

**Return four cards**

35

5. The top card of the small pile will be an Ace! Turn this card face up and show your friend.

6. Set the Ace aside and put the small pile on top of the big pile.

7. Repeat the six steps with two *different* numbers between 10 and 20 to remove two more Aces.

Finally, pretend to do some supernatural hocus pocus as you ask the "number spirits" for a sign to help you find the last Ace. Pretend that they tell you to turn over the top card. It will be an 8. Count down eight more cards and the eighth card will be the fourth Ace!

# MYSTERIOUS FORCE

You secretly predict which card will be chosen from the deck, and then the "number spirits" mysteriously force your friend to choose that card!

## Materials

A deck of playing cards, complete with 52 cards plus two Jokers

Paper and pencil
A calculator, if needed

## Presentation

1. Have your friend shuffle the cards as many times as she wants.

2. When she hands you the cards, say that you forgot to take out the Jokers. Turn the cards over, remove the Jokers, and sneak a peek at the bottom card. This is the "predicted card."

3. Secretly write the name of the "predicted card" on a piece of paper, fold it several times, and put it aside until later.

4. Tell your friend that a supernatural mathematical power will force her to choose your predicted card.

5. Deal out twelve cards face down from the top of the deck and spread them out on the table. Ask your friend to turn any four of these cards face up.

6. Put the other eight cards on the *bottom* of the deck.

### Example

7. Hand your friend the deck and tell her to deal cards face down below each of these cards. She should start with the number on the face up card (All face cards = 10 and Aces = 1), and then keep dealing cards until she gets to 10. For example, if the face-up card is a 6, she would deal four more cards to get to 10.

**37**

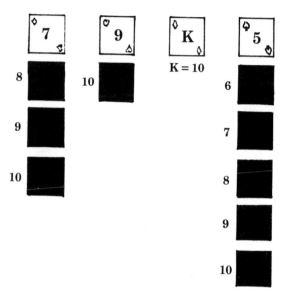

8. Tell her to keep the four face up cards on the table and put all the face down cards on the *bottom* of the deck.

9. Ask her to find the sum of the four cards:

**(10)**

$$7 + 9 + K + 5 = 31$$

10. Have her count down that many cards in the deck and turn the last card face up. (Turn card #31 face up.) This is her chosen card. Finally, unfold your prediction and show your friend that it matches her chosen card!

## A Variation

If your deck of cards has no Jokers, sneak a peak at the bottom card after your friend hands you the deck.

38

# POCKET PUZZLER

Your friend removes four cards from the deck and secretly puts one of them in her pocket. After performing some number magic on a calculator, you are able to reveal the card that is hidden in your friend's pocket!

## Materials
A deck of playing cards     A calculator
Paper and pencil

## Presentation

1. Ask your friend to write any 4-digit number on a piece of paper without letting you see it. Tell her that all four digits must be different.

**Example**
**8756**

2. Tell her to add the four digits together and write the sum below the first number. $(8 + 7 + 5 + 6 = 26)$

**− 26**

3. Have her subtract the two numbers, using a calculator.

**8730**

4. Hand her the deck of cards and ask her to secretly remove four cards that have the same numbers as the four digits. (Ace = 1 and 0 = King) Also, tell her that each card must be of a different suit.

**Example**
**8 = 8 of Hearts**
**7 = 7 of Clubs**
**3 = 3 of Diamonds**
**0 = King of Spades**

5. Tell her to put one of the cards *that is not a King* in her pocket, and then hand you the other three cards.

**Example: She puts the 3 of Diamonds in her pocket and hands you the 8 of Hearts, the 7 of Clubs, and the King of Spades.**

6. Mentally add the values of these three cards.

$$8 + 7 + 0 = 15$$

*If your answer has more than one digit, add the digits together until there is only one digit.*

$$15 \rightarrow 1 + 5 = 6$$

7. Mentally subtract this number from 9, and the value of the card that is in your friend's pocket will magically appear.

$$9 - 6 = 3$$

The card that is in your friend's pocket is a 3 and since the only suit that is missing is Diamonds, your friend's card is:

**The 3 of Diamonds!**

## An Exception

When you mentally subtract from 9 and get 0, your friend's card is a 9—not a King.

# 3. MEMORY MAGIC

WHAT'S ON YOUR MIND?
WHAT'S THE DIFFERENCE?
BRAIN WAVES
MISSING DIGIT
THE HUMAN CALCULATOR
MEMORY WIZARD
EXTRASENSORY PERCEPTION
MIND READING

# WHAT'S ON YOUR MIND?

Your friend randomly selects a 2-digit number. You are able to read his mind and reveal the number that he is thinking of!

## Materials

10 scraps of paper          A shoe box

## Presentation

1. Ask your friend to name any 2-digit number.

2. Write that number on a scrap of paper, fold it several times, and drop it into a shoe box. Make sure that no one sees what you are writing.

3. Repeat Steps 1 and 2 several times until your friend has named about ten different numbers.

4. Have your friend reach into the shoe box and open up one of the scraps of paper without letting you see it.

5. Rip up the remaining scraps of paper so that their powerful mathematical vibrations will not interfere with your mindreading.

6. Ask your friend to concentrate on the number that he is holding. Pretend that you are reading his mind, and then reveal that number!

## How to Do It

Write the first number that your friend names on *every* scrap of paper. If every scrap of paper has the same number, it will be very easy to tell him what's on his mind!

43

# WHAT'S THE DIFFERENCE?

Your friend will be amazed when you correctly predict the answer to a subtraction problem. Then, when she works a different problem, you are able to read her mind and reveal that answer, too!

## Materials
A calculator                    Paper and pencil

## Preparation
Secretly write a prediction (198) on a piece of paper, fold it several times, and put it aside until later.

## Presentation

1. Ask your friend to write down any three-digit number whose digits are in decreasing order.

**Example**

**765**

2. Then tell her to reverse this number and write it below the first number.

**− 567**

3. Finally, have her subtract the two numbers on a calculator.

**198**

*The answer will always be 198!*

When your prediction is opened, it matches her answer!

4. Next, tell your friend to follow the same directions with any four-digit number whose digits are in decreasing order. Tell her not to show you the answer.

$$\begin{array}{r} 3210 \\ -\ 0123 \\ \hline 3087 \end{array}$$

*The answer will always be 3087!*

Ask your friend to concentrate on the entire answer. Pretend that you are reading her mind as you reveal that the answer is 3087!

## A Variation

A humorous variation on the three-digit trick is to open your prediction upside down.

Your friend will think that you have made a mistake until you turn the answer over and it reads:

# BRAIN WAVES

This is a trick that you and your friend can perform together. After you leave the room, your friend asks someone to choose a number. When you return, not a single word is spoken yet you are able to reveal the chosen number!

## Materials
None

## Preparation
Practice with your friend before performing the trick for others.

## Presentation
1. You leave the room and your friend asks someone to choose any number from 1 to 10.

2. When you return, tell your friend to concentrate on the chosen number. By laying your hands on your friend's head, you are able to hear his thoughts and reveal the chosen number!

## How to Do It
When you put your hands on your friend's head, place your fingertips on his temples. If your friend keeps his mouth closed and slightly tightens his jaw, you will be able to feel movement under your fingertips. So if the chosen number is seven, your friend tightens his jaw seven times. With a little practice, no one will be able to see your friend's jaw move and you should have no trouble receiving his "brain waves"!

# MISSING DIGIT

Your friend works a subtraction problem and tells you all the digits of her answer except for one. Within seconds, you are able to reveal the missing digit!

## Materials

A calculator                    Paper and pencil

## Presentation

1. Have your friend write down any 4-digit number without letting you see it.

**Example**
**2759**

2. Tell her to add the four digits together and write the sum below the first number. $(2 + 7 + 5 + 9 = 23)$

$-\quad$ **23**

3. Ask her to subtract the two numbers.

**2736**

4. Tell her to circle any digit in her answer that is *not 0*.

2⑦36

5. Ask her to slowly read off the remaining digits in any order. After a few seconds, you are able to reveal the circled number!

## How to Do It

Mentally add the digits that your friend reads to you.

$$2 + 3 + 6 = 11$$

*If your answer has more than one digit, add those digits together until there is only one digit.*

$$11 \rightarrow 1 + 1 = 2$$

Mentally subtract that number from 9 and the missing digit will magically appear!

$$9 - 2 = (7)$$

## An Exception

When you add the remaining digits together and end up with 9, your friend circled a 9.

**Example:**   8962
              − 25
              8(9)37    $8 + 3 + 7 = 18$   $18 \rightarrow 1 + 8 = (9)$

## A Variation

This trick will work for any number of digits. Ask your friend to choose the 8-digit serial number from any dollar bill.

# THE HUMAN CALCULATOR

You can amaze your friends by adding five 3-digit numbers in just a few seconds!

## Materials
Paper and pencil                    A calculator

## Presentation

1. Ask a friend to write a 3-digit number on a piece of paper. The digits must be different and may not form a pattern.

2. Ask him to write a second number below his first number.

3. Ask him to write one more number. This third number is your *Key #*. ——————→

4. You write a three-digit number so that the sum of the first and the fourth numbers = 999.

5. You write a three-digit number so that the sum of the second and the fifth numbers = 999.

6. Give your friend the piece of paper and ask him to add the five numbers using the calculator without letting you see the Final Total.

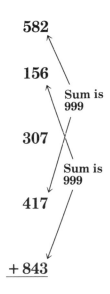

**582**

**156**

Sum is
999

**307**

Sum is
999

**417**

**+ 843**

**(2,305)**

When he returns the paper to you, pretend that you are adding the five numbers in your head, and then write down the Final Total in one or two seconds!

## How to Do It

When your friend hands you the paper, all you have to do is look at the *Key #*, because the Final Total is:

$$2000 + (Key\ \# - 2)$$

**Example: <u>Key #</u> is 307.**  $307 - 2 = 305$

**The Final Total:**  $\begin{array}{r} 2{,}000 \\ +305 \\ \hline 2{,}305 \end{array}$

## An Exception

Your friend writes a 9 for the first digit of the first number or the second number.

# Example

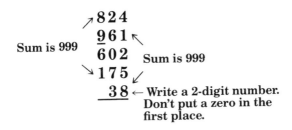

Sum is 999

$$824$$
$$961$$
$$602$$
$$175$$
$$\underline{\phantom{0}38}$$

Sum is 999

← Write a 2-digit number. Don't put a zero in the first place.

## Variations

Using seven three-digit numbers, follow the same procedure and the Final Total is:

**3000**
**+ (Key # − 3)**

Using nine three-digit numbers, follow the same procedure and the Final Total is:

**4000**
**+ (Key # − 4)**

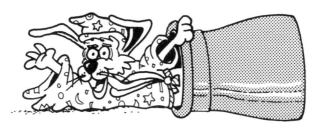

# MEMORY WIZARD

Your friends are amazed that you are able to memorize a 26-digit number!

## Materials
Paper and pencil

## Preparation
Write this on a piece of paper:

$$35,831,459,437,077,415,617,853,819$$

Put this on a second piece of paper:

——, ——, ——, ——, ——, ——, ——, ——, ——

## Presentation
Hand your friend the piece of paper that has the 26-digit number written on it. Tell her that you have memorized the number and that you would like her to test you. Show her that there are no numbers written on the second piece of paper, and then write down all 26 digits!

## How to Do It
You don't have to memorize the entire number. Just remember the first two digits, and then add to get the remaining 24 digits.

1. Write down the first two digits.    **35**

2. To get the next digit, mentally add those 2 digits together.

$$3 + 5 = \underline{8} \qquad\qquad 35,\underline{8}$$

3. Mentally add the last two digits to get the next one. If this sum is 10

or greater, write down only the
number that is in the ones place.

$$5 + 8 = 1\underline{3} \qquad 35,8\underline{3}$$

4. Continue adding the last two
digits to get the next one until you
have written down all 26 digits.

| | |
|---|---|
| $8 + 3 = 1\underline{1}$ | 35,831 |
| $3 + 1 = \phantom{0}\underline{4}$ | 35,831,4 |
| $1 + 4 = \phantom{0}\underline{5}$ | 35,831,45 |
| $4 + 5 = \phantom{0}\underline{9}$ | 35,831,459 |
| $5 + 9 = 1\underline{4}$ | 35,831,459,4 |

and so on until you get:

**35,831,459,437,077,415,617,853,819!!**

## A Variation
Prepare a number that is longer than 26 digits and you
will really impress your friends!

15,617,853,819,099,875,279,651,673,033,695

# EXTRASENSORY PERCEPTION

You prepare a deck of 30 index cards, each with a different number written on it. When the blank side of a card is shown to your friend, he is able to tell you whether the number on the other side is odd or even!

## Materials

30 blank index cards          pencil

## Preparation

Write a different number from 1 to 30 on each card.

## Presentation

Have your friend sit across the table from you. Tell him that you have reason to believe that he has psychic powers and that you have developed a test to prove it. Shuffle the cards thoroughly and then put one even card and one odd card face up on the table.

Fan out the rest of the index cards in your hand. Be careful that your friend doesn't see any of the numbers. Then hold up one card at a time—*blank side* facing your friend—and ask him if the number on the other side is odd or even. (Pretend that you are choosing cards randomly from different parts of your hand but actually choose all 14 even numbers first!)

If your friend says "Even," put the card *face down* on the left pile. If he says odd, put the card *face down* on the right pile.

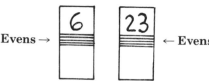

Evens →          ← Evens

When all fourteen even cards are down, turn one even card over and put it face up on the right pile. Take one of the odd cards from your hand (they will all be odd) and put it face up on the left pile.

Hold up the remaining cards one at a time as before. This time, if your friend says odd, put the card face down on the left pile. If he says even, put the card face down on the right pile.

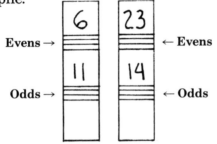

At this point, the left side is correct and the right side is incorrect. Gather up the cards on the left side and hand them to your friend so that he can see how well he did.

As he is looking at those cards, gather up the cards on the right side and secretly move the face-up odd card (23 in the example) to the top of the pile. This move will make the right side correct.

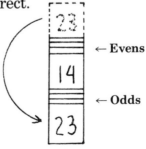

Finally, show your friend that the right side is correct too. He won't believe that he got them all right! He will think that he has E.S.P.!

## A Variation

Use playing cards instead of index cards.

# MIND READING

You can amaze your friends with your mindreading powers. Here, you reveal their deepest mathematical thoughts, and then you look into the future and predict which card will be chosen from the deck!

## Materials

A deck of playing cards          Paper and pencil

## Preparation

Put your favorite card at the bottom of the deck. Example: 10 of Hearts

Number a blank piece of paper from 1 to 3.

## Presentation

1. Show your friend that there are no answers written on the piece of paper. Then tell her to think of any math

word—"Fraction," for example. Pretend that you are reading her mind and write your favorite card (10 of Hearts) *after #3* on the paper. Don't let your friend see what you are writing and she will think that you are writing her math word after #1. Ask her which math word she thought of. When she tells you, smile as you look at the paper and say, "Great."

2. Tell your friend to think of any 3-digit number (907, for example). Pretend that you are reading her mind and then write her math word (Fraction) *after #1* on the paper. Ask her which 3-digit number she thought of. When she tells you, repeat her 3-digit number and say, "Terrific."

3. Tell your friend that you are going to predict which card will be chosen from the deck. Pretend to be deep in thought as you write her 3-digit number (907) *after #2* on the paper.

```
1. Fraction

2. 907

3. 10 of ♡
```

4. Ask your friend to cut the deck into two equal piles. Tell her that you are going to count to see how well she did. Ask her to count the cards from the top half of the deck while you count the cards from the bottom half. If you count your pile one card at a time, your favorite card will come to the top. Take your pile and put it on top of her pile to complete the cut. Your favorite card is now at the top of the deck.

5. Finally, unfold the paper and show your friend that the math word and the three-digit number are correct. Read your prediction and then have her turn over the top card of the deck. It matches your prediction!

# 4. FUNNY STUFF

HOW TO BECOME AN INSTANT MILLIONAIRE

MATH WITH MUSCLE

INSTANT CASH

HAND CALCULATOR

?!? THE 3½ OF CLUBS ?!?

THE NAME OF THE CARD IS . . .

4½ CENTS

2 HALVES = 1 HOLE

?? $7 \times 13 = 28$??

# HOW TO BECOME AN INSTANT MILLIONAIRE

This is a trick that you can play on your mom or dad. It shows you how to turn a penny into millions of dollars!

## Materials
2 sheets of paper          Pen

## Preparation
Copy the "contract form" and the bill onto the two sheets of paper.

## Presentation
Tell your parents that you are going to do the dishes every night for the next 30 days. (Trust me—please read on.) Say that they don't even have to give you your regular allowance anymore. Tell them that you only want 1¢ for doing the dishes the first night, 2¢ for the second night, 4¢ for the third night, double that to 8¢ for the fourth night, and so on. If they agree, have them sign a contract like the one shown here.

---

## CONTRACT

I, _____, agree to pay _____
    Parent's Name                         Your Name

1¢ for doing the dishes the first night, 2¢ for the second night, 4¢ for the third night, double that to 8¢ for the fourth night, and so on for the next 30 days.

_____
Parent's Signature

---

After they sign this contract, present them with their bill. It will be quite a shock, so have them sit down first!

# THE BILL

| DAY | PAY |
|:---:|:---:|
| 1 | $.01 |
| 2 | $.02 |
| 3 | $.04 |
| 4 | $.08 |
| 5 | $.16 |
| 6 | $.32 |
| 7 | $.64 |
| 8 | $1.28 |
| 9 | $2.56 |
| 10 | $5.12 |
| 11 | $10.24 |
| 12 | $20.48 |
| 13 | $40.96 |
| 14 | $81.92 |
| 15 | $163.84 |
| 16 | $327.68 |
| 17 | $655.36 |
| 18 | $1,310.72 |
| 19 | $2,621.44 |
| 20 | $5,242.88 |
| 21 | $10,485.76 |
| 22 | $20,971.52 |
| 23 | $41,943.04 |
| 24 | $83,886.08 |
| 25 | $167,772.16 |
| 26 | $335,544.32 |
| 27 | $671,088.64 |
| 28 | $1,342,177.28 |
| 29 | $2,684,354.56 |
| 30 | $5,368,709.12 |
| **GRAND TOTAL** | **$10,737,418.23!!!** |

# MATH WITH MUSCLE

This number trick will show you how to do hundreds of situps in just a few seconds!

## Materials
A watch or clock

## Presentation
Tell your friends that you are going to do between "two and three hundred situps" in less than one minute. Be careful that you don't say, "between two hundred and three hundred situps"! Have a friend time you and when he says, "Go," just sit down and do five situps. After all, 5 is between 2 and 300!

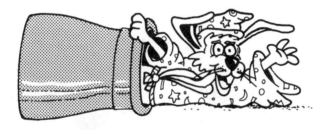

# IN$TANT CA$H

This is a great math joke that shows you how to turn a small investment into thousands of dollars of profit—magically—in just a few days!

## Presentation
Tell your parents that you have a great idea for how they can invest their money. Explain that if they do exactly as you say, they will make over $8,000 in less than a week! (That should get their attention.)

Here's your financial advice:

First, they should build a medium-size animal pen in the backyard. Tell them that you will help and that it won't cost very much money.

Second, they should go to a local pig farmer and buy five female pigs (five sows). They should have them delivered to your backyard and put in the animal pen.

Finally, they should go to a wildlife farm and buy five male deer (five bucks). They should have them delivered to your home and put in the pen with the pigs.

That's it! If your parents have followed your financial advice, they now have five pigs and five deer in their backyard pen and they just made over $8,000!

Your parents will probably think that you've lost your mind! They won't understand—until you explain to them—that in just a few days they have turned a small investment into 10 sows and bucks (10 thousand bucks)!

# HAND CALCULATOR

Your friends are amazed when you magically transform your hands into a calculator and multiply on your fingers!

## Materials
Pen

## Preparation
Draw these calculator keys on your palms with a ballpoint pen.

## Presentation
Tell your friend that she can multiply *by 9* on your hands just as she would on a regular calculator. After she enters the numbers and pushes $\boxminus$ , just bend over the finger that is multiplied by 9. The fingers that are standing up tell her the answer!

**Example: 9 × 4 = 36**

**Bend over finger #4**

**Example: $9 \times 8 = 72$**

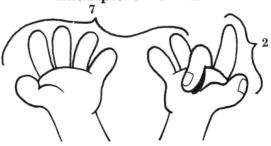

7

2

**Bend over finger #8**

## An Exception

**Example: $9 \times 10 = 90$**

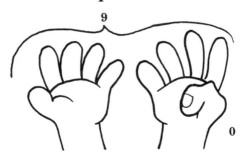

9

0

**Bend over finger #10**

**$\underline{9}$ fingers on the left and $\underline{0}$ fingers
on the right = $\underline{9}\,\underline{0}$.**

# ?!? THE 3½ OF CLUBS?!?

A card that is sealed in an envelope has exactly half the value of a randomly selected card. The trick works even if the selected card is odd!

## Materials
A deck of playing cards
 with a Joker
A calculator
An envelope
Tape

## Preparation

Photocopy the 3½ of Clubs on this page and then tape or laminate it over one of the Jokers.

Seal the 3½ of Clubs inside an envelope.

Put the 7 of Clubs in the fifth position down from the top of the deck.

## Presentation

Tell your friend that he will randomly select a card from the deck and that the card in the envelope will have exactly half the value of his selected card.

**Example: If he selects the 10 of Hearts, the 5 of Hearts will be in the envelope.**

**Example
(555) 246-4468**

Hand your friend the calculator and have him:

| | |
|---|---:|
| 1. Enter his phone number. | **2464468** |
| 2. Multiply that number by 10. | **24644680** |
| 3. Subtract his phone number from that answer. | **22180212** |
| 4. Divide that total by his phone number. | **9** |
| 5. Subtract the number of digits in his phone number (7 digits) from that answer. | **2** |
| 6. Add the number of digits in his area code (3 digits) to that answer. | **5** |

Announce once more that the card in the envelope will have exactly half the value of the randomly selected card. Ask your friend for his total (it will always be 5), count down that many cards in the deck, and turn over the fifth card—the 7 of Clubs.

Your friend will think that you have made a mistake, because an odd number can't be divided in half evenly. Will he be surprised when he opens the envelope!

*½ of the 7 of Clubs is the 3½ of Clubs!*

## A Variation

There is a way of shuffling the cards so that the 7 of Clubs remains in the fifth position down from the top. Divide the deck into two piles and riffle the ends together allowing the two piles to interweave. Let the top seven to ten cards fall last and the 7 of Clubs will remain in the fifth position no matter how many times you shuffle. Practice this many times before you try it with a friend.

# THE NAME OF THE CARD IS . . .

You secretly predict which card will be chosen. Then you ask a friend to randomly select a number and count down that many cards in the deck. At first this card doesn't match your prediction, but after a few comical adjustments, the name of the card mysteriously appears!

## Materials

A deck of playing cards     A calculator
Paper and pencil

## Preparation

Put the 10 of Hearts in the eighteenth position down from the top of the deck.

## Presentation

Announce that you are going to predict which card will be chosen from the deck. On a piece of paper, write:

**THE NAME**
**OF**
**THE CARD IS**

Fold the paper so that your friend doesn't see what you've written and put it aside until later.

Ask your friend to:

| | |
|---|---|
| 1. Enter a 3-digit number into the calculator. (The first digit must be larger than the last digit.) | **Example** **845** |
| 2. Reverse this number and subtract it from the first number. | **−548** **297** |

3. Add the digits in the answer.

$$2 + 9 + 7 = 18$$

*The digits will always add up to 18!*

Tell him to count down that many cards in the deck. It will be the *10 of Hearts*. Finally, ask him to open the piece of paper and read your prediction. He'll read, "THE NAME OF THE CARD IS". Say that you were in such a hurry that you forgot to finish your prediction. Then make these adjustments and his card will mysteriously appear!

—cross off the H in THE
—cross off the AME in NAME
—cross off the T in THE
—cross off the CD in CARD
—change the I in IS to a T by crossing the top

THE NAME          TEN

OF               OF

THE CARDS      HEARTS

# 4½ CENTS

You tell your friend that the number of pennies hidden in your hand is exactly half the number that he will randomly choose. Hold it! What happens if he chooses an odd number?

## Materials
5 pennies                           A calculator
Paper and pencil

## Preparation
You will need help to prepare for this trick. Have an adult bend a penny back and forth with two pairs of pliers until it breaks in half.

Hide 4½ pennies in your hand.

## Presentation
Tell your friend that the number of pennies hidden in your hand is exactly half the number that he will choose at random.

1. Ask him to write down any number that has 8 digits or less. Tell him that all the digits must be different.

**Example**
**19,573**

2. Have him rearrange the digits in any order and write this new number below the first number.

**93,175**

3. Ask him to subtract the two numbers using a calculator. Tell him to enter the larger number first.

$$\begin{array}{r} 93,175 \\ -\ 19,573 \\ \hline 73,602 \end{array}$$

4. Tell him to add the digits of his answer together.

$$73,602 \rightarrow 7 + 3 + 6 + 0 + 2 = 18$$

*If his answer has more than one digit, tell him to add those digits until there is only one digit.*

$$18 \rightarrow 1 + 8 = 9$$

*The final answer will always be 9!*

Your friend will think that you have made a mistake because ½ of 9 is 4½. How can you have 4½¢? Open your hand and show him!

# 2 HALVES = 1 HOLE

You show your friend how to cut a large band of paper into 2 separate loops. This is very easy to do, but when your friend tries, she ends up with something entirely different!

## Materials
A pair of scissors          A newspaper
Cellophane tape

## Preparation
Cut out four-inch-wide strips of newspaper. Tape them together to make two seven-foot strips.

Take one of the seven-foot strips of paper and tape the ends together to make one large band.

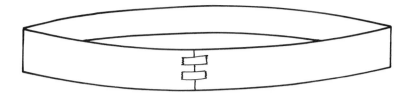

Do the same with the second seven-foot strip, but give one end of the strip a half twist before taping the ends together.

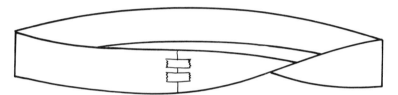

## Presentation

Show your friend how easy it is to cut a band of paper into two separate loops. Use the band that does not have the half twist. Carefully cut straight down the middle until you get back to where you started and you will end up with two separate pieces.

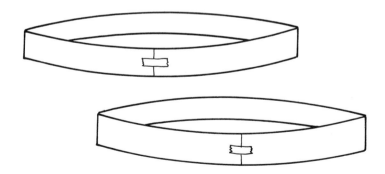

Give your friend the pair of scissors and the band with the half twist. She won't notice the half twist if you lay the band in a small pile on a table in front of her. Tell her to carefully cut straight down the middle until she ends up with two separate loops. It looked so easy when you did it, but she won't be as lucky. It's impossible to cut this band into two separate pieces. A band with a half twist actually has only one side, so it stays in one piece when cut in half. She'll end up with a giant 14-foot loop!

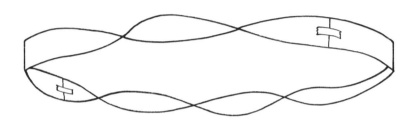

## Variations

Here are some other tricks that you can try by yourself. Use shorter strips of paper that are about three inches by 28 inches.

1. Give one end of a strip of paper *two* half twists (1 full twist) before taping the ends together. Cut straight down the middle of the band until you get back to where you started. If you cut carefully, you will end up with 2 loops!

2. Give one end of a strip of paper a half twist before taping the ends together. Instead of cutting down the middle as before, cut one inch in from the right edge of the band. Keep cutting until you go around the band *twice* and get back to where you started. You will end up with two loops again, but the result will surprise you!

3. Experiment with more twists and different cuts and see what happens. What do you think would happen if you cut your friend's 14-foot loop straight down the middle? Try it and see!

# ??7 × 13 = 28??

Your friends are thoroughly confused when you "prove" to them that $7 \times 13 = 28$!

## Materials
Paper and pencil

## Presentation
Only a number magician could prove that $7 \times 13 = 28$. Here are three different ways to prove it. If you talk fast enough, you will be able to fool your friends.

## FIRST WAY—MULTIPLICATION

7 times 3 equals 21 and
7 times 1 equals 7.
21 + 7 = 28

So: $7 \times 13 = 28$!!

$$
\begin{array}{r}
13 \\
\times\ 7 \\
\hline
21 \\
+\ 7 \\
\hline
28
\end{array}
$$

## SECOND WAY—DIVISION

7 does not divide into 2, but it does divide into 8 one time. Put down the 1 and subtract 7. That leaves 21. 7 divides into 21 three times.

You multiply to check division.

$$
\begin{array}{r}
13 \\
7\overline{)28} \\
7 \\
\hline
21 \\
\underline{21}
\end{array}
$$

If $\quad 2\overline{)8}^{\,4} \quad$ then $\quad 2 \times 4 = 8$

So, if $\quad 7\overline{)28}^{\,13} \quad$ then $\quad 7 \times 13 = 28$!!

## THIRD WAY—ADDITION

Multiplication is repeated addition so $7 \times 13$ is seven thirteens added together.

Add up the column of 3's and get 21. Then add down the column of 1's and get 7 more (21 + 7 = 28).

So: $7 \times 13 = 28$!!

| | | |
|---|---|---|
| *(22)* | 13 | *(21)* |
| *(23)* | 13 | *(18)* |
| *(24)* | 13 | *(15)* |
| *(25)* | 13 | *(12)* |
| *(26)* | 13 | *( 9)* |
| *(27)* | 13 | *( 6)* |
| *(28)* | + 13 | *( 3)* |
| | 28 | |

# 5. ODDS AND ENDS

HOCUS POCUS

MAGICAL LINKING PAPER CLIPS

SUM FUN

BELIEVE IT OR NOT

TIME WILL TELL

KNOT THAT FINGER

SECRET WORD

# HOCUS POCUS

You ask your friend to choose any domino when your back is turned. When the magic words "Hocus Pocus" are entered in a calculator, the number of dots on each part of the domino suddenly appear!

## Materials
A set of dominoes
A calculator

## Presentation
You spread a set of dominoes out on a table, and then ask your friend to secretly choose one.

**Example**

Hand him the calculator and tell him to:

1. Enter one of the domino's numbers. (Blank = 0)

$$\underline{3}$$

2. Multiply that number by 5.

$$3 \times 5 = 15$$

3. Add 7 to that answer.

$$15 + 7 = 22$$

4. Double that total.

$$22 \times 2 = 44$$

5. Add the domino's other number to that result.

$$44 + \underline{6} = 50$$

Finally, tell your friend to hand you the calculator with his answer. Enter the magic words "Hocus Pocus" by pushing

As you push the buttons, say "Ho-Cus-Po-Cus," and the number of dots on both parts of the domino will magically appear!

$$50 - 14 = \underline{3}\,\underline{6}$$

**(If your friend had entered the 6 first, your final total would have been $\underline{6}\,\underline{3}$.)**

## Exceptions
When your friend chooses a domino with one blank and enters the 0 first, your final total has only one digit.

**Example: The final total is 5.**
**$5 = \underline{0}\,5$ so the domino has a blank and a 5.**

When your friend chooses a domino with two blanks, your final total will be 0 because $0 = \underline{0}\underline{0}$.

# MAGICAL LINKING PAPER CLIPS

Two paper clips are magically joined together without anyone touching them. And, when a rubber band is added, all three become linked together by some mysterious mathematical force!

## Materials
4 paper clips
A 3-inch (7.5 cm)
  rubber band

A strip of paper—
  $3 \times 11$ inches
  (7.5cm $\times$ 27.5 cm)

80

## Presentation

Curve a strip of paper into an S-shape. Then attach two paper clips so that it looks like this:

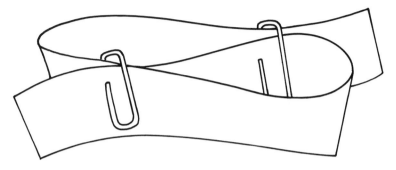

Slowly pull the ends of the paper apart in the direction of the arrows. When the two paper clips are almost touching, pull harder and they will magically join together!

Next, loop a rubber band around the strip of paper before attaching two more paper clips so that it looks like this:

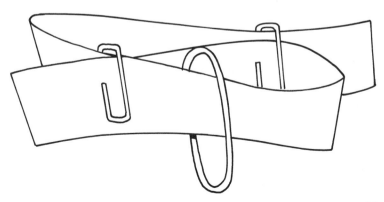

When you pull the ends of the strip of paper apart, the paper clips will be linked together and hanging from the rubber band, which is still attached to the strip of paper!

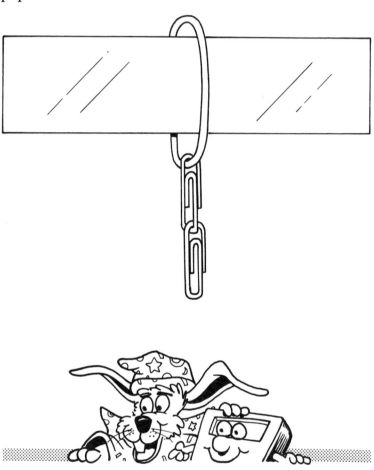

## Variations

Attach two paper clips on each side of the strip of paper and you end up with four paper clips joined together. Try other variations and see what happens.

Instead of a strip of paper, use a dollar bill.

# SUM FUN

Numbers are written on both sides of some index cards. When your back is turned, your friend mixes them up and turns some of them over. You are able to announce the sum of all the numbers that are showing without ever looking at them!

## Materials

5 index cards or pieces    A calculator
of paper

## Preparation

Write a "1" on one side of an index card and a "2" on the other side. In the same way, write a "3" and "4" on a second index card, a "5" and "6" on a third, a "7" and "8" on a fourth, and a "9" and "10" on a fifth.

## Presentation

Hand your friend the five index cards. Tell her to mix them up, turn some over, and lay them out on the table when your back is turned.

**Example**

Have her find the sum of the five numbers using a calculator.

$$1 + 8 + 4 + 5 + 10 = 28$$

Ask her how many of those numbers are odd (1, 3, 5, 7, 9).

### "There are two odd numbers."

Mentally subtract this number from the "Magic Total," which is 30, and you will get the sum of all 5 numbers!

$$30 - 2 = 28$$

**Magic Total**    **two odd numbers**    **The Sum**

## Variations

Change the number of index cards and subtract from a different Magic Total.

| Index cards | Numbers | Magic Total |
|---|---|---|
| 6 | 11 & 12 | 42 |
| 7 | 13 & 14 | 56 |
| 8 | 15 & 16 | 72 |
| 9 | 17 & 18 | 90 |
| 10 | 19 & 20 | 110 |

# BELIEVE IT OR NOT

When your back is turned, your friend chooses a magazine at random and concentrates on one of the pages. Unbelievably, you are able to read his mind and describe what appears on that page!

## Materials

10 magazines or books          A calculator

## Preparation

Put 10 magazines in a row on the table.
Study page 27 in the fourth magazine.

## Presentation

Hand your friend the calculator and have him:

**Example:**

1. Enter any number between 1 and 100.                           **50**

2. Add 28.                              $50 + 28 = 78$

3. Multiply by 6.                       $78 \times 6 = 468$

4. Subtract 3.                          $468 - 3 = 465$

5. Divide by 3.                         $465 \div 3 = 155$

6. Subtract 3 more than his original number ($50 + 3 = 53$).     $155 - 53 = 102$

7. Add 8.                               $102 + 8 = 110$

8. Subtract 1 less than his original number ($50 - 1 = 49$).     $110 - 49 = 61$

9. Multiply by 7.                       $61 \times 7 = 427$

*The final total will always be 427!*

With your back turned, tell your friend to look at the first digit of his final total, count over that many magazines, and remove it from the row. Then tell him to look at the last two digits of his final total and turn to that page number in the magazine.

$$\underline{4} \quad \underline{2 \quad 7}$$

magazine   page

Finally, ask him to concentrate on that page for about 30 seconds. You should have no problem "reading his mind" and describing what appears on that page, since you studied it before the trick started!

# TIME WILL TELL

Your friend mentally selects any hour on the face of a clock. After performing some number magic, the clock reveals the hour that he is thinking of!

## Materials
A clock or a picture of    A pencil
  a clock drawn on
  a piece of paper

## Presentation
Ask your friend to think of any hour on the clock without telling you. Explain that you are going to point randomly to different numbers on the clock while he silently counts up to 20. Tell him to start with the hour that he is thinking of and add one every time you point to a number.

**Example: He's thinking of 8:00 so he counts
9 when you point to the first number,
10 when you point to the second number,
etc.**

When he gets to 20, he should say, "Stop!", and your pencil will be pointing to the hour that he is thinking of!

## How to Do It

As your friend is counting up to 20, you are counting, too. The first seven numbers that you point to can be any numbers on the clock. However, the eighth number must be 12. Then go backwards around the clock until your friend tells you to stop.

**Example: Your friend is thinking of 8:00.**

| He counts: | 9 | 10 | 11 | 12 | 13 | 14 | 15 | 16 | 17 | 18 | 19 | 20 Stop! |
|---|---|---|---|---|---|---|---|---|---|---|---|---|
| You count: | 1 | 2 | 3 | 4 | 5 | 6 | 7 | 8 | 9 | 10 | 11 | 12 |
| You point to: | any number | | | | | | | 12 | 11 | 10 | 9 | 8:00 |

---

# KNOT THAT FINGER

---

This is a trick that you can do for a group of your friends or relatives. While you are out of the room, a string is tied around someone's finger and everyone hides their hands. When you return, you work some number magic and within seconds, you can tell who has the string! You are also able to reveal the hand and the finger that the string is tied on!

## Materials

A calculator                          Paper and pencil
A piece of string

## Presentation

Pick one of your friends to be your assistant, and then number the rest of your friends starting with #1. While you leave the room or turn your back, have your assistant tie a string on someone's finger. Also, tell her to write down that person's number and the hand and finger that has the string. Tell everyone to hide their hands.

**Example**
**Friend #7**
**Left Hand  Fourth Finger**

Hand your assistant the calculator and have her:

1. Enter the number of the
person who has the string.                          **7**

2. Multiply that number by 2.            $7 \times 2 = 14$

3. Add 3 to that result.                  $14 + 3 = 17$

4. Multiply that answer by 5.            $17 \times 5 = 85$

5. Add 8 if the string is on the
right hand.
   Add 9 if the string is on the
left hand.                                $85 + 9 = 94$

6. Multiply that total by 10.          $94 \times 10 = 940$

7. Subtract 46 from that result.      $940 - 46 = 894$

8. Add the number of the finger
(The thumb is 1.).                      $894 + 4 = 898$

9. Add 600 to that total.          $898 + 600 = 1498$

89

Finally, ask your assistant to hand you the calculator with the final total. Just subtract 774 and you will be able to find that string!

$$
\begin{array}{r}
1498 \\
-\ 774 \\
\hline
7\underline{2}4
\end{array}
$$

Number →      ← Number
of        ↑       of
Person     Hand    Finger
          1 = right
          2 = left

## An Exception

When you subtract 774 and get four digits, the first two digits are the number of the person.

$$
\begin{array}{r}
\textbf{Example:}\ \ 2687 \\
-\ 774 \\
\hline
1913
\end{array}
$$

Person #19 → $1\underline{9}1\underline{3}$ ← Third Finger
             ↑
        Right Hand

---

# SECRET WORD

---

A friend looks through a book and secretly selects a word on any page. After performing some number magic, you are able to find her selected word from the thousands of words in the book!

## Materials

A book with at least 100 pages

A calculator

Paper and pencil

## Presentation

Ask your friend to turn to any page in the book and write down its page number without letting you see it.

**Example**
**Page 47**

Tell her to choose *any of the first 9 lines* on that page and write down its number.

**Line 8**

Have her choose a word on that line *from among the first 9 words* and write down its number and the word.

**Word 3**
MAGIC

Hand her the calculator and ask her to:

1. Enter the page number.

**47**

2. Multiply that number by 2.

$47 \times 2 = 94$

3. Multiply that answer by 5.

$94 \times 5 = 470$

4. Add 20 to that total.

$470 + 20 = 490$

5. Add the line number to that answer (*line 8*).

$490 + 8 = 498$

6. Add 5 to that answer.

$498 + 5 = 503$

7. Multiply that total by 10.

$503 \times 10 = 5030$

8. Add the word number to that answer (*word 3*).

$5030 + 3 = 5033$

Then, tell her to hand you the calculator with the final total.

Just subtract 250 and the page number, the line number, and the word number will magically appear!

$$
\begin{array}{cccc}
5 & 0 & 3 & 3 \\
- & 2 & 5 & 0 \\
\hline
4 & 7 & 8 & 3 \\
\text{page} & & \text{line} & \text{word}
\end{array}
$$

Turn to that page in the book, count down that many lines and over that many words, and you'll find your friend's word—MAGIC!

## Exceptions

When your friend chooses a 1-digit page number, your final answer has three digits.

**Example:** $\underline{7}$ $\underline{3}$ $\underline{2}$
page  line  word

When your friend chooses a 3-digit page number, your final answer has five digits.

**Example:** $\underline{1\ 6\ 3}$ $\underline{9}$ $\underline{5}$
page  line  word

# 6. DICE, COINS, AND CALENDARS

DOT'S ALL, FOLKS!

X-RAY VISION

PENNIES FOR YOUR THOUGHTS

WHICH HAND?

THIS MAKES CENTS

WHAT'S THE DATE?

CALENDAR CONTEST

CALENDAR CONJURING

# DOTS ALL, FOLKS!

Your friend rolls three dice when your back is turned. After performing some number magic, you are able to disclose the three top numbers on the dice!

## Materials
3 dice ("Monopoly," "Yahtzee," and many other games have dice.)          A calculator

## Presentation
While your back is turned, have a friend:

| | **Example**<br>**3, 1, 5** |
|---|---|
| 1. Role three dice. | |
| 2. Multiply the top number on the first die by 2, using a calculator. | $\underline{3} \times 2 = 6$ |
| 3. Add 5 to that answer. | $6 + 5 = 11$ |
| 4. Multiply that result by 5. | $11 \times 5 = 55$ |
| 5. Add the top number on the second die to that total. | $55 + \underline{1} = 56$ |
| 6. Multiply that result by 10. | $56 \times 10 = 560$ |
| 7. Add the top number on the third die to that answer. | $560 + \underline{5} = 565$ |
| 8. Subtract 3 from that result. | $565 - 3 = 562$ |

Then, tell your friend to hand you the calculator with the final total. Subtract 247 and the number appears!

$$\begin{array}{r} 562 \\ -247 \\ \hline \text{1st die} \rightarrow \underline{3}\,\underline{1}\,\underline{5} \leftarrow \text{3rd die} \end{array}$$

↑<br>**2nd die**

# X-RAY VISION

You throw 6 dice on the table. Before your friend can add the top numbers, you are able to add those numbers *plus* the bottom numbers that no one can see!

## Materials
6 dice

## Preparation
Memorize these multiples of 7:

| | |
|---|---|
| 1 × 7 = 7 | 6 × 7 = 42 |
| 2 × 7 = 14 | 7 × 7 = 49 |
| 3 × 7 = 21 | 8 × 7 = 56 |
| 4 × 7 = 28 | 9 × 7 = 63 |
| 5 × 7 = 35 | 10 × 7 = 70 |

## Presentation

1. Tell your friend that you are going to have a contest to see who can add faster. Say that you are going to throw six dice on the table and that she should add the top numbers. Explain that you will add those numbers *plus* the hidden bottom numbers before she gets her answer.

2. Throw six dice on the table, wait two or three seconds as you pretend to add the top numbers, and then say "42!"

3. Check to see if you're correct by slowly adding the top numbers. Then carefully flip over the dice and add the bottom numbers. The total will be 42! Your friend will think that you have X-ray vision!

## How to Do It

On any die, the top number plus the bottom number equals seven. So, if six dice are thrown, the total of all the tops and bottoms is:

**6 × 7 = 42**
**dice    total**

## Variations

When you repeat the trick use a different number of dice, so that you get a different total. The total will equal the number of dice × 7.

**Example: 8 dice**        **8 × 7 = 56**
                        **dice    total**

---

## PENNIES FOR YOUR THOUGHTS

You secretly make a prediction before you begin. Then a friend randomly chooses five numbers and adds them together. Your prediction is unfolded and it matches his answer!

## Materials

A calculator                5 pennies
Paper and pencil

## Preparation

Write this grid on a piece of paper. Make it large so that you can use pennies to cover the numbers.

| | | | | |
|---|---|---|---|---|
| 6 | 24 | 12 | 18 | 5 |
| 1 | 19 | 7 | 13 | 0 |
| 15 | 33 | 21 | 27 | 14 |
| 4 | 22 | 10 | 16 | 3 |
| 11 | 29 | 17 | 23 | 10 |

## Presentation

1. Tell your friend that you are going to make a prediction. Then secretly write this on a piece of paper:

*The sum of the 5 numbers that you choose will be 72*

Fold your prediction several times and put it aside until later.

2. Hand your friend five pennies and ask him to place a penny on any number in the grid. Then tell him to cross off all other numbers in that same row and column.

**Example: He puts a penny on 7.**

| | | | | |
|---|---|---|---|---|
| 6 | 24 | ~~12~~ | 18 | 5 |
| ~~1~~ | ~~19~~ | (7) | ~~13~~ | ~~0~~ |
| 15 | 33 | ~~21~~ | 27 | 14 |
| 4 | 22 | ~~10~~ | 16 | 3 |
| 11 | 29 | ~~17~~ | 23 | 10 |

3. Ask him to place a second penny on any other number that isn't already covered or crossed off. Then tell him to cross off all other numbers in that same row and column.

**Example: He puts a penny on 16.**

| 6 | 24 | 1̶2̶ | 1̶8̶ | 5 |
|---|---|---|---|---|
| 9̶ | 1̶9̶ | ⑦ | 1̶3̶ | 9̶ |
| 15 | 33 | 2̶1̶ | 2̶7̶ | 14 |
| 4̶ | 2̶2̶ | 1̶0̶ | ⑯ | 3̶ |
| 11 | 29 | 1̶7̶ | 2̶3̶ | 10 |

4. Tell him to follow these same directions for the third and fourth pennies and to put the fifth penny on the last number that is not covered or crossed out.

**Example: He puts the third penny on 11, the fourth penny on 33, and the fifth penny on 5.**

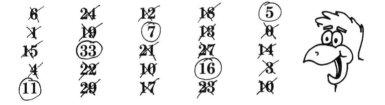

5. Have your friend find the sum of the five numbers that he covered with the pennies and announce the total.

$$7 + 16 + 11 + 33 + 5 = 72$$

**(The total will always be 72, so don't repeat this trick with the same person.)**

Finally, unfold your prediction and show your friend that it matches his total!

## Variations
Don't make a prediction ahead of time. After your friend

adds up the five numbers, have him concentrate on the total and pretend to read his mind.

---

# WHICH HAND?

Your friend hides a dime in one hand and a penny in the other. After performing some hocus pocus, you are able to figure out which coin is in which hand!

## Materials
A dime and a penny

## Presentation
Ask your friend to put a dime in one hand and a penny in the other without letting you see. Tell her to multiply the value of the coin in her left hand by 2, 4, 6, or 8, and then multiply the value of the coin in her right hand by 3, 5, 7, or 9. Have her add these two amounts together and tell you her final total.

If her final total is *odd*, the penny is in her *right* hand.
If her final total is *even*, the penny is in her *left* hand.

### Examples

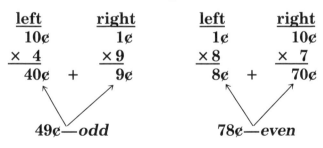

So the penny is
in her *right* hand.

So the penny is
in her *left* hand.

# THIS MAKES CENTS

When your back is turned, your friend arranges some pennies on the table. She removes some of the coins, and you are able to reveal the number of coins that remain!

## Materials
20 to 30 pennies

## Presentation
Turn your back and ask a friend to choose an odd number of pennies. Tell her to arrange them in two rows on the table so that the top row has one more coin than the bottom row.

**Example: She chooses 25 coins.**

| 1 | 2 | 3 | 4 | 5 | 6 | 7 | 8 | 9 | 10 | 11 | 12 | 13 |
|---|---|---|---|---|---|---|---|---|----|----|----|----|
| 1 | 2 | 3 | 4 | 5 | 6 | 7 | 8 | 9 | 10 | 11 | 12 | |

Next, ask her to name a number that is greater than 0 but less than the number of coins in the top row. Tell her to remove that number of coins from the top row.

**Example: She says "5" (This is the *Key #*— remember it), so she removes five coins from the top row.**

| 1 | 2 | 3 | 4 | 5 | 6 | 7 | 8 | X | X | X | X | X |
|---|---|---|---|---|---|---|---|---|---|----|----|----|
| 1 | 2 | 3 | 4 | 5 | 6 | 7 | 8 | 9 | 10 | 11 | 12 | |

Then have her count the number of coins remaining in the top row and remove that number of coins from the bottom row.

**(There are 8 coins remaining in the top row so she removes 8 coins from the bottom row.)**
**Example:**

| 1 | 2 | 3 | 4 | 5 | 6 | 7 | 8 | X | X | X | X | X |
|---|---|---|---|---|---|---|---|---|---|---|---|---|
| 1 | 2 | 3 | 4 | X | X | X | X | X | X | X | | |

Finally, tell her to remove all the coins remaining in the top row. Ask her to count the number of coins remaining in the bottom row and concentrate on that number.

**Example: X X X X X X X X X X X X X**
**1  2  3  ④ X  X  X  X  X  X  X  X**

Just subtract 1 from the *Key #* and you will be able to "read her mind" and reveal the number that she is concentrating on!

*Key #* minus 1 = Remaining coins
in the bottom row

**Example: 5 − 1 = ④**

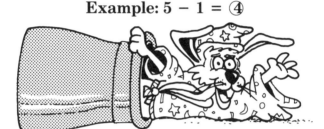

# WHAT'S THE DATE?

Your friend circles three dates on a calendar, adds them together, and announces the total. Within seconds, you are able to reveal the three dates!

## Materials
A calendar                          A calculator

## Presentation
Hand your friend the calendar and let him choose any month. Ask him to choose any three consecutive dates in a row or in a column without letting you see. Finally, tell him to add the three dates and hand you the calculator with the final total.

## Examples

| APRIL | | | | | | |
|---|---|---|---|---|---|---|
| S | M | T | W | T | F | S |
| | | | | 1 | 2 | 3 | 4 |
| 5 | 6 | 7 | 8 | 9 | 10 | 11 |
| 12 | 13 | 14 | 15 | (16) | (17) | (18) |
| 19 | 20 | 21 | 22 | 23 | 24 | 25 |
| 26 | 27 | 28 | 29 | 30 | | |

| JUNE | | | | | | |
|---|---|---|---|---|---|---|
| S | M | T | W | T | F | S |
| | | 1 | 2 | 3 | 4 | 5 | 6 |
| (7) | 8 | 9 | 10 | 11 | 12 | 13 |
| (14) | 15 | 16 | 17 | 18 | 19 | 20 |
| (21) | 22 | 23 | 24 | 25 | 26 | 27 |
| 28 | 29 | 30 | | | | |

$$16 + 17 + 18 = 51 \qquad 7 + 14 + 21 = 42$$

Ask him if the three dates that he circled are in the same week.

*If he says YES:*

Divide the final total by 3 to get the middle date. Then mentally add and subtract 1 to get the other two dates.

$$51 \div 3 = 17$$
$$17 + 1 = 18$$
$$17 - 1 = 16$$

**The three dates are 16, 17, & 18!**

*If he says NO:*

Divide the final total by 3 to get the middle date. Then mentally add and subtract 7 to get the other two dates.

$$42 \div 3 = 14$$
$$14 + 7 = 21$$
$$14 - 7 = 7$$

**The three dates are 7, 14, & 21!**

# CALENDAR CONTEST

Your friend chooses nine dates from any month on a calendar. Then you have a contest to see who can add the numbers faster. It's no contest. You win easily every time!

103

## Materials

A calendar           Paper and pencil
A calculator

## Presentation

Tell your friend that you would like to have an adding contest. Tell him that he can use a calculator and that you will use only paper and pencil. He can even choose the numbers. Who could turn down an offer like that?

Hand him the calendar and let him choose any month. Then tell him to draw a box around any group of nine numbers that form a $3 \times 3$ square.

### Example

| FEBRUARY | | | | | | |
|---|---|---|---|---|---|---|
| s | m | t | w | t | f | s |
| | 1 | 2 | 3 | 4 | 5 | 6 |
| 7 | 8 | 9 | 10 | 11 | 12 | 13 |
| 14 | 15 | 16 | 17 | 18 | 19 | 20 |
| 21 | 22 | 23 | 24 | 25 | 26 | 27 |
| 28 | 29 | | | | | |

Whoever finds the sum of all nine numbers first is the winner. Hand him the calculator and start the contest. You will have the answer within seconds!

## How to Do It

There is a trick for quickly finding the sum of all nine numbers. Just look at the smallest number, add 8, and multiply your result by 9. It works every time!

$$
\begin{array}{r}
3 \\
+\ 8 \\
\hline
11 \\
\times\ 9 \\
\hline
99
\end{array}
$$

104

# CALENDAR CONJURING

You secretly make a prediction before any numbers are chosen. Then a friend chooses four dates from a calendar and adds them together. When your prediction is opened, it matches her answer!

## Materials

A calculator          Paper and pencil

A calendar

## Presentation

Hand your friend the calendar and let her choose any month. Then tell her to draw a box around any group of sixteen numbers that form a 4 × 4 square.

**Example**

**NOVEMBER**

| S | M | T | W | T | F | S |
|---|---|---|---|---|---|---|
| 1 | 2 | 3 | 4 | 5 | 6 | 7 |
| 8 | 9 | 10 | 11 | 12 | 13 | 14 |
| 15 | 16 | 17 | 18 | 19 | 20 | 21 |
| 22 | 23 | 24 | 25 | 26 | 27 | 28 |
| 29 | 30 | | | | | |

As your friend is drawing the box, look at the two dates in either pair of opposite corners (3 and 27 or 6 and 24). Mentally add either pair together and multiply that sum by 2.

**3 + 27 = 30 and 30 × 2 = 60**

The final answer is your prediction. Tell your friend that you have looked into the future and have seen the sum of the four dates that she will randomly choose. Secretly write your prediction on a piece of paper, fold it several times, and put it aside until later.

Ask your friend to circle any date on the calendar. Then tell her to cross off all other dates in that same row and column.

**NOVEMBER**

| S | M | T | W | T | F | S |
|---|---|---|---|---|---|---|
| 1 | 2 | 3 | 4 | 5 | 6 | 7 |
| 8 | 9 | 10 | (11) | 12 | 13 | 14 |
| 15 | 16 | 17 | 18 | 19 | 20 | 21 |
| 22 | 23 | 24 | 25 | 26 | 27 | 28 |
| 29 | 30 | | | | | |

**Example: She circles 11.**

Ask her to circle any other date that isn't already circled or crossed off. Then tell her to cross off all other dates in that same row and column.

**NOVEMBER**

| S | M | T | W | T | F | S |
|---|---|---|---|---|---|---|
| 1 | 2 | 3 | 4 | 5 | 6 | 7 |
| 8 | 9 | 10 | (11) | 12 | 13 | 14 |
| 15 | 16 | 17 | 18 | 19 | 20 | 21 |
| 22 | 23 | 24 | 25 | (26) | 27 | 28 |
| 29 | 30 | | | | | |

**Example: She circles 26.**

Tell her to follow the same directions for a third date. The fourth date will be the last number that is not circled or crossed out.

**NOVEMBER**

| S | M | T | W | T | F | S |
|---|---|---|---|---|---|---|
| 1 | 2 | 3 | 4 | 5 | (6) | 7 |
| 8 | 9 | 10 | (11) | 12 | 13 | 14 |
| 15 | 16 | (17) | 18 | 19 | 20 | 21 |
| 22 | 23 | 24 | 25 | (26) | 27 | 28 |
| 29 | 30 | | | | | |

**Example: She circles 17 so the fourth date is 6.**

Have your friend find the sum of the four dates that she circled.

**11 + 26 + 17 + 6 = 60**

Finally, unfold the paper and show that your prediction matches her final answer!

**106**

# 7. EXTRA FOR EXPERTS

# YOUNG GENIUS

Your friends will think that you are ready for college when you add five large numbers in your head in just a few seconds!

## Materials
Paper and pencil             A calculator

## Preparation
Write this chart on a piece of paper.

| A | B | C | D | E |
|---|---|---|---|---|
| 366 | 345 | 186 | 872 | 756 |
| 69 | 840 | 582 | 971 | 558 |
| 168 | 246 | 87 | 575 | 657 |
| 762 | 147 | 285 | 377 | 954 |
| 960 | 543 | 483 | 179 | 855 |
| 564 | 48 | 780 | 674 | 459 |

## Presentation

While your back is turned, have a friend choose *one number* from each of the five columns and write them on a piece of paper. Tell her to add the five numbers using a calculator and write the answer underneath.

**Example**
```
    762
    246
    483
    674
 +  756
 ------
  2,921
```

Finally, ask her to read off slowly the five numbers in any order so that you can add them in your head. You will have the answer in seconds!

## How to Do It

As your friend reads the five numbers, just mentally add the *five last digits*.

$$2 + 6 + 3 + 4 + 6 = \underline{21}$$

Mentally subtract this sum from 50.

$$50 - 21 = \underline{29}$$

Put the second number in front of the first number to get the sum of all five numbers!

$$\underline{2, 9} \ \underline{21}!$$

# PHOTOGRAPHIC MEMORY

Your friends are really impressed when you show them that you have memorized fifty different 6-digit and 7-digit numbers!

## Materials

50 index cards

Paper and pencil

## Preparation

Copy these numbers onto index cards—one to each card. The card number appears in italics.

| | | | | | |
|---|---|---|---|---|---|
| *1* | 5,055,055 | *11* | 5,167,303 | *21* | 5,279,651 |
| *2* | 6,066,280 | *12* | 6,178,538 | *22* | 6,280,886 |
| *3* | 7,077,415 | *13* | 7,189,763 | *23* | 7,291,011 |
| *4* | 8,088,640 | *14* | 8,190,998 | *24* | 8,202,246 |
| *5* | 9,099,875 | *15* | 9,101,123 | *25* | 9,213,471 |
| *6* | 112,358 | *16* | 224,606 | *26* | 336,954 |
| *7* | 1,123,583 | *17* | 1,235,831 | *27* | 1,347,189 |
| *8* | 2,134,718 | *18* | 2,246,066 | *28* | 2,358,314 |
| *9* | 3,145,943 | *19* | 3,257,291 | *29* | 3,369,549 |
| *10* | 4,156,178 | *20* | 4,268,426 | *30* | 4,370,774 |

| | | | |
|---|---|---|---|
| *31* | 5,381,909 | *41* | 5,493,257 |
| *32* | 6,392,134 | *42* | 6,404,482 |
| *33* | 7,303,369 | *43* | 7,415,617 |
| *34* | 8,314,594 | *44* | 8,426,842 |
| *35* | 9,325,729 | *45* | 9,437,077 |
| *36* | 448,202 | *46* | 550,550 |
| *37* | 1,459,437 | *47* | 1,561,785 |
| *38* | 2,460,662 | *48* | 2,572,910 |
| *39* | 3,471,897 | *49* | 3,583,145 |
| *40* | 4,482,022 | *50* | 4,594,370 |

## Example

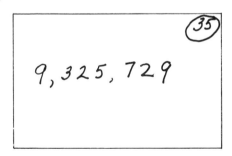

## Presentation

Shuffle the deck of index cards so that they are not in order, and then hand them to your friend. Tell her that there is a different number written on each card and that you have memorized all fifty numbers. Ask her to choose any card. When she tells you the card number, you are able to tell her which 6-digit or 7-digit number is on that card!

## How to Do It

1. When your friend tells you the card number, mentally add 4 and then reverse your answer. The result is the first two digits.

### Example: Card #35
### 35 + 4 = 39 and 39 reversed is 93.

The first two digits are 93.

2. To get the next digit, mentally add the first two digits together. If this sum is less than 10, write it down. If it is 10 or greater, only write down the number that is in the ones place.

$$9 + 3 = 1\underline{2} \qquad\qquad 93\underline{2}$$

3. Continue adding the last two digits to get the next one until you have written down all seven digits.

$$3 + 2 = \underline{5} \qquad 932\underline{5}$$
$$2 + 5 = \underline{7} \qquad 9325\underline{7}$$
$$5 + 7 = 1\underline{2} \qquad 93257\underline{2}$$
$$7 + 2 = \underline{9} \qquad 932572\underline{9}$$

**Answer: 9,325,729**

## Exceptions

If your friend picks a card number that ends in 6, the number on that card has only six digits.

### Example: Card #36
### 36 + 4 = 40 and 40 reversed is 04
### The number is 0,448,202

*(Don't say "Zero")*——↑

If your friend picks a card number from 1 to 5, mentally put a zero in the tens place before reversing your answer.

**Example: Card #3**
**3 + 4 = 7 and *0*7 reversed is 70**
**The number is 7,077,415**

## A Variation

You can work the trick backwards. Tell your friend to give you the 6-digit or 7-digit number, and then you tell her the card number! When she tells you the number, reverse the first two digits and then subtract 4 to get the card number.

**Example: The number is 1,235,831**
**12 reversed is 21 and 21 − 4 = 17**
**The card number is 17.**

## An Exception to This Variation

If your friend gives you a 6-digit number, mentally put the zero back in front, and then work the trick backwards.

**Example: The number is 336,954**
**(0,336,954)**

**03 reversed is 30 and 30 − 4 = 26**
**The card number is 26.**

# BRAIN POWER

Your friends will think that you are an amazing number magician when you find the sum of ten numbers in just a few seconds!

## Materials

A calculator                    Paper and pencil

## Preparation

Write the numbers 1–10 on a piece of paper, one under the other.

## Presentation

1. Tell your friend to write any 1-digit number on the first line and a different 1-digit number on the second line.

2. Ask him to add these two numbers together and write their sum on the third line.

$$5 + 9 = 14$$

3. Have him add line 2 and line 3 and write that sum on the fourth line.

$$9 + 14 = 23$$

4. Tell him to continue adding in this manner until there is a list of ten numbers. Make sure that he is adding correctly. Each number in the list (except the first two) must be the sum of the two numbers above it.

**Example
5 and 9**

1. 5
2. 9
3. 14
4. 23
5. 37
6. 60
7. 97
8. 157
9. 254
10. 411

When your friend writes down the last number, quickly

**114**

look at his list and pretend that you are adding all ten numbers in your head. Secretly write your answer on a piece of paper, fold it several times, and put it aside. Ask your friend to slowly add all ten numbers, using a calculator.

**(Example: 1,067)**

He will be amazed when you unfold the paper and your answer matches his final total!

## How to Do It

When ten numbers are added in this manner,
*The Final Total = the seventh number × 11!*
So when you look at your friend's list, just look at the seventh number. Multiply that number by 11 on your piece of paper to get the final total.

Here is a quick way to multiply by 11:
Multiply the seventh number by 10. (97 × 10)  970
Add the seventh number to that answer.   +   97
                                          1,067

Cross off your work so that your friend does not discover your secret. Make it look as if you have underlined your answer.

## A Variation

Start with two 2-digit numbers and your friends will really be amazed!

115

# MYSTERY POWDER

You and your friend write down five 4-digit numbers and add them using a calculator. When your secret mystery powder is rubbed over a piece of plastic, the correct answer magically appears!

## Materials

A calculator
Paper and pencil
Glue stick
Ground cinnamon

Any piece of white
plastic, such as the
white lid from a
plastic container

## Preparation

Put a small amount of cinnamon or any dark spice into a small container. This is the mystery powder.

Write a number in the 20,000's on a piece of white plastic with a glue stick.

### Example: 23,156

This is the Final Total. The number should be invisible yet remain sticky.

116

Figure out your *Key #*. First add 2 to the Final Total, and then cross off the first digit of your answer.

$$\begin{array}{r} \mathbf{23{,}156} \\ \underline{+\qquad 2} \\ \mathbf{23{,}158} \\ \textit{\textbf{Key \#}} \end{array}$$

## Presentation

1. Ask a friend to write a 4-digit number on a piece of paper. The digits must be different and not form a pattern.

2. You write the *Key #*. ⟶

3. Tell your friend to write a different 4-digit number below your number.

4. You write a 4-digit number so that the sum of the first and fourth numbers = 9,999.

5. You write a 4-digit number so that the sum of the third and fifth numbers = 9,999.

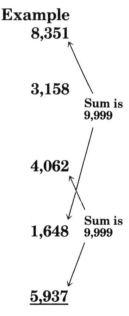

**Example**
**8,351**

**3,158**

Sum is
9,999

**4,062**

Sum is
1,648   9,999

**5,937**

Give your friend the piece of paper and ask him to add the five numbers using a calculator.

**(23,156)**

Sprinkle your mystery powder over the piece of white plastic, and then perform some hocus pocus as you rub it around. Blow off the excess powder and—like magic—the Final Total mysteriously appears!

## An Exception

Your friend writes a 9 for the first digit of the first number or the third number.

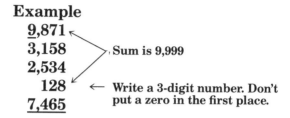

**Example**
**9,871**
**3,158**
**2,534**
   **128** ← Write a 3-digit number. Don't put a zero in the first place.
**7,465**

> Sum is 9,999

---

# HAS ANYONE SEEN A GHOST?

---

This is a trick that you can do for a group of your friends or relatives. A prediction is put inside a shoe box and three random numbers are added using a calculator. When the shoe box is opened, your incorrect prediction has been mysteriously replaced by the correct answer!

## Materials

A calculator
Shoe box
Marker
An index card
Pencil

A small spiral notebook that looks the same no matter which side is up

## Preparation

1. Write any 4-digit number on an index card with a marker, then cross it off. This is your prediction. Write a different 4-digit number (between 1000 and 2000) below the first number. Make it look like this number was written by a ghost. Put the card face down on the table.

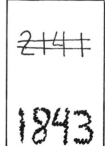

2. Open the notebook to the middle and write down three 3-digit numbers. Make it look as if each 3-digit number was written by a different person. The sum of these numbers should equal the ghostly number on the piece of paper. Turn the notebook over and put it on the table with the blank side up.

526
847
470

## Performance

Give the calculator to a friend who is in the back of the room and tell him that you will need his help later.

Show your friends that there is nothing inside the shoe box, and then put your prediction and the marker inside. Put the top on the shoe box and give it to your friend to hold.

Ask another friend to come up to the table and write a 3-digit number on the blank page in the notebook. Repeat this with two other friends. Don't let anyone turn over the notebook.

When the third number is written down, pick up the notebook and take it to your friend with the calculator.

As you are walking over to your friend, *secretly turn over the notebook*. Show him the top page (*your* three numbers) and ask him to add the three numbers using the calculator. Close the notebook so that no one sees the other side. Tell your friend to announce the answer.

When your friend says the answer, look disappointed and admit that your prediction in the shoe box is incorrect. Make up a story about a ghost who is a friend of yours and explain that he will assist you with the trick. Ask your invisible friend to enter the shoe box, pick up the marker, cross off your prediction, and write the correct answer underneath. Repeat the answer one more time and then ask your friend to remove the piece of paper from the shoe box. To everyone's surprise, your ghostly assistant has saved the day by writing the correct answer below your prediction!

## THE HUMAN COMPUTER

You can astound your friends by adding five 6-digit numbers in just a few seconds!

**Materials**

A calculator                    Paper and pencil

## Presentation

1. Ask a friend to write a 6-digit number on a piece of paper. The digits must be different and not form a pattern.

2. Tell her to write a second 6-digit number below her first number.

3. Ask her to write one more number. This third number is your *Key #*. ⟶

4. You write a 6-digit number so that the sum of the first and the fourth numbers = 999,999.

5. You write a 6-digit number so that the sum of the second and fifth numbers = 999,999.

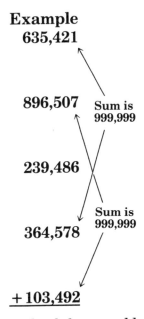

**Example**
**635,421**

**896,507**  Sum is 999,999

**239,486**

**364,578**  Sum is 999,999

**+ 103,492**

Give your friend the piece of paper and ask her to add the five numbers using a calculator without letting you see the Final Total—

**(2,239,484).**

When she hands you the paper, pretend that you are adding the five numbers in your head and quickly write down the Final Total!

## How to Do It

When your friend hands you the paper, just look at the *Key #*, because the Final Total = 2,——————

(*Key #* minus 2).

121

**Example:**
*Key #* is 239,486
(*Key #* minus 2) = 239,484

**The Final Total = 2,239,484**

## An Exception

Your friend writes a 9 for the first digit of the first number or the second number.

**Example**

9̲56,231
623,178     Sum is 999,999
279,651
 43,768 ← Write a 5-digit number. Don't
376,821     put a zero in the first place.

## Variations

**Seven 6-digit numbers:**
    The Final Total = 3,_____
                          (*Key #* minus 3)

**Nine 6-digit numbers:**
    The Final Total = 4,_____
                          (*Key #* minus 4)

# PSYCHIC PREDICTION

You are able to predict the sum of five 5-digit numbers before the trick begins! Also, when the digits of this sum are translated into letters, they spell your friend's name!

## Materials
Paper and pencil          A calculator

## Preparation
Write this chart on a piece of paper.

| 0 | 1 | 2 | 3 | 4 | 5 | 6 | 7 | 8 | 9 |
|---|---|---|---|---|---|---|---|---|---|
| A | B | C | D | E | F | G | H | I | J |
| K | L | M | N | O | P | Q | R | S | T |
| U | V | W | X | Y | Z | . | , | ! | ? |

Pick a friend who has three to six letters for a first or last name. (See *Variations* for more ideas.) The first letter must be a letter in the 2-column—C, M, or W.

### Example: Cosby

Use the chart to translate your friend's name into a 6-digit number. This number is the Predicted Sum.

**Cosby!**
**248,148**

Figure out your *Key #*. Just add 2 to the Predicted Sum, and then cross off the first digit of your answer.

$$248,148$$
$$+\quad\ 2$$

## Presentation

$$\cancel{2}48,150$$

Announce that you will write down the answer to a math problem before any numbers are given. Write the Predicted Sum on another piece of paper, fold it several times, and put it aside until later.

1. Ask your friend to write a 5-digit number on a piece of paper. The digits must be different and not form a pattern.

**Example**
**38,607**

2. You write down the *Key #*. → 

**48,150** Sum is 99,999

3. Ask him to write another 5-digit number.

**76,231**

4. You write a 5-digit number so that the sum of the first and the fourth numbers = 99,999.

**61,392** Sum is 99,999

5. You write a 5-digit number so that the sum of the third and the fifth numbers = 99,999.

**+ 23,768**

6. Ask him to add the five numbers on a calculator.

**248,148**

Finally, unfold your prediction and show your friend that it matches his answer! Then use the chart to translate his answer into letters and his name will magically appear!

**248,148**
**COSBY!**

## Variations for Choosing a Name

**MR.C.!**   **MS.G.!**   **MRBLUM**   **MSROTH**   **MRS.J.**

## Other Variations

You could make words appear.

Example: MONDAY, MATH!!, MAGIC!, COLD!!, WEIGHT, etc.

Use your imagination! You could also rearrange the chart so that different letters appear in the 2-column. Then you could make many more names or words appear!

## An Exception

Your friend writes a 9 for the first digit of the first number or the third number.

```
        Example
        9̲2,761  ⟵
        48,150      Sum is 99,999
        49,135  ⟋
         7,238  ⟵  Write a 4-digit number. Don't
      + 50,864      put a zero in the first place.
        248,148
        COSBY!
```

# INDEX

# ABOUT THE AUTHOR

Raymond Blum has been a middle-level math teacher for over 20 years. On weekends and in the summer, he entertains professionally with his daughter, Katie. Their stage show is called, "Raynbow and The Amazing Kaytee's Juggling & Magic Show." He has been a speaker at state and national math conferences where he shares his "Razzle Dazzle Number Magic" with other classroom teachers. Ray is currently teaching seventh grade at Schenk Middle School in Madison, Wisconsin.